DISCARD

Bermuda

Ned Friary, Glenda Bendure

Contents

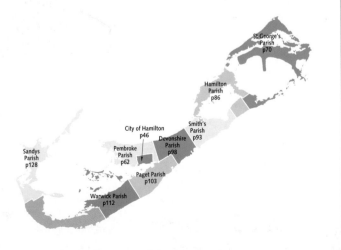

Destination Bermuda

'You go to heaven if you want – I'd rather stay here in Bermuda.' So gushed Mark Twain in the 19th century, and Bermuda's promise of sun and sea still lures vacationers to its shores. These days celebs like Michael Douglas and Catherine Zeta-Jones call Bermuda home, and millionaire executives pop over for a little R&R.

The island makes for a delightful getaway vacation. If you're looking for peace and quiet, Bermuda has pampering resorts to soothe your soul. Romantics will find atmospheric inns with four-poster beds and candlelight dining. Or perhaps you want to really let loose. Jump on a motor scooter and let the wind whip through your hair. Go out on the town and dance the night away.

The island is surrounded by a fantastic coral reef that harbors colorful fish and has ensnared scores of shipwrecks, all of which makes for memorable diving and snorkeling. The crystal-clear waters also provide perfect conditions for everything from swimming to kayaking and yachting. The offerings on land are splendid as well. You can play a round at a world-class golf course, hike peaceful trails and sunbathe on glorious pink-sand beaches. Or stroll the crooked streets of the colonial settlement of St George, Britain's oldest surviving town in the New World, which is so well preserved it's been made a World Heritage site.

Bermuda boasts a balmy climate that's comfortable all year round and friendly people who readily strike up conversations with strangers. And there's plenty of distinctive local color as well, from a landscape of tidy pastel houses to dapper businessmen dressed in Bermuda shorts.

NED FRIARY

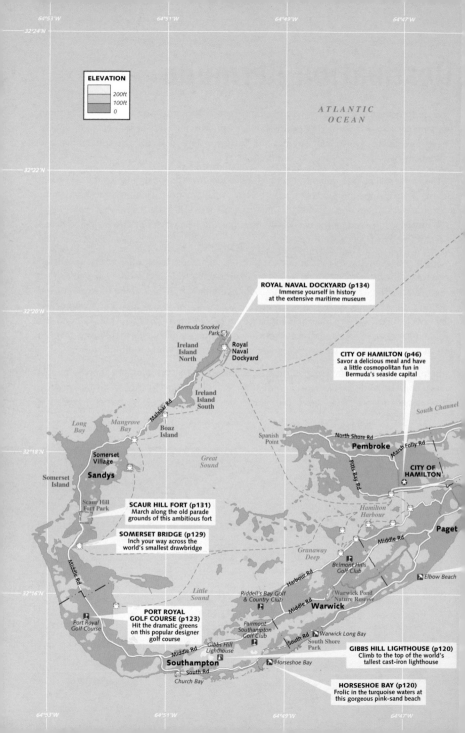

ELEVATION

200ft
100ft
0

ATLANTIC
OCEAN

ROYAL NAVAL DOCKYARD (p134)
Immerse yourself in history
at the extensive maritime museum

CITY OF HAMILTON (p46)
Savor a delicious meal and have
a little cosmopolitan fun in
Bermuda's seaside capital

Bermuda Snorkel Park

Ireland Island North

Royal Naval Dockyard

Ireland Island South

South Channel

Mahkar Rd

Boaz Island

Spanish Point

North Shore Rd

Pembroke

Marsh Folly Rd

Long Bay

Mangrove Bay

Somerset Village

Great Sound

Pitts Bay Rd

★ **CITY OF HAMILTON**

Sandys

Somerset Island

Hamilton Harbour

Scaur Hill Fort Park

SCAUR HILL FORT (p131)
March along the old parade
grounds of this ambitious fort

SOMERSET BRIDGE (p129)
Inch your way across the
world's smallest drawbridge

Granaway Deep

Paget

Middle Rd

Belmont Hills Golf Club

Elbow Beach

Middle Rd

Little Sound

PORT ROYAL GOLF COURSE (p123)
Hit the dramatic greens
on this popular designer
golf course

Port Royal Golf Course

Riddell's Bay Golf & Country Club

Warwick Pond Nature Reserve

Warwick

Middle Rd

Fairmont Southampton Golf Club

Warwick Long Bay

South Shore Park

South Rd

GIBBS HILL LIGHTHOUSE (p120)
Climb to the top of the world's
tallest cast-iron lighthouse

Gibbs Hill Lighthouse

Middle Rd

Southampton

South Rd

Church Bay

Horseshoe Bay

HORSESHOE BAY (p120)
Frolic in the turquoise waters at
this gorgeous pink-sand beach

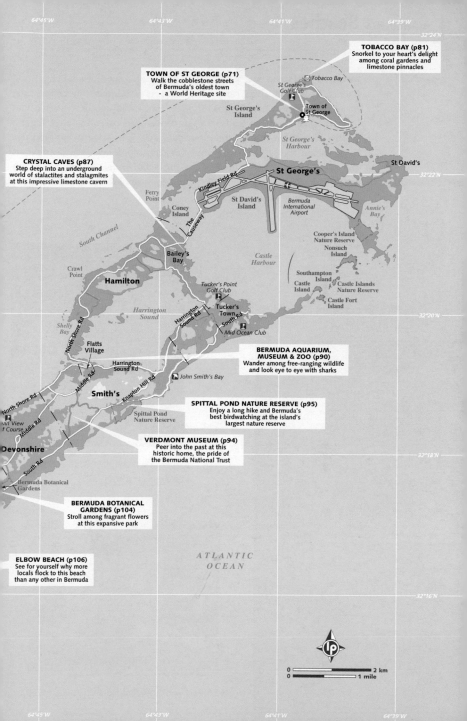

TOBACCO BAY (p81)
Snorkel to your heart's delight among coral gardens and limestone pinnacles

TOWN OF ST GEORGE (p71)
Walk the cobblestone streets of Bermuda's oldest town – a World Heritage site

CRYSTAL CAVES (p87)
Step deep into an underground world of stalactites and stalagmites at this impressive limestone cavern

BERMUDA AQUARIUM, MUSEUM & ZOO (p90)
Wander among free-ranging wildlife and look eye to eye with sharks

SPITTAL POND NATURE RESERVE (p95)
Enjoy a long hike and Bermuda's best birdwatching at the island's largest nature reserve

VERDMONT MUSEUM (p94)
Peer into the past at this historic home, the pride of the Bermuda National Trust

BERMUDA BOTANICAL GARDENS (p104)
Stroll among fragrant flowers at this expansive park

ELBOW BEACH (p106)
See for yourself why more locals flock to this beach than any other in Bermuda

Tobacco Bay
St George's Golf Club
St George's Island
Town of St George
St George's Harbour
St George's
St David's
Kindley Field Rd
St David's Island
Bermuda International Airport
Annie's Bay
Ferry Point
Coney Island
The Causeway
Bailey's Bay
Castle Harbour
Cooper's Island Nature Reserve
Nonsuch Island
Crawl Point
Hamilton
Tucker's Point Golf Club
Tucker's Town
South Rd
Mid Ocean Club
Southampton Island
Castle Island
Castle Islands Nature Reserve
Castle Fort Island
Harrington Sound
Harrington Sound Rd
Shelly Bay
North Shore Rd
Flatts Village
Harrington Sound Rd
John Smith's Bay
Middle Rd
Smith's
Knapton Hill Rd
North Shore Rd
Spittal Pond Nature Reserve
Middle Rd
Devonshire
South Rd
Bermuda Botanical Gardens

ATLANTIC OCEAN

South Channel

0   2 km
0   1 mile

Bermuda's pink-sand beaches with their glistening turquoise waters are world famous. **Elbow Beach** (p106) caresses beachgoers with some of the softest sand imaginable. **Warwick Long Bay** (p113) offers a splendid unbroken stretch that lures beachcombers and leads to a run of secluded coves and bays. A great way to enjoy the morning with someone special is by taking a **horseback ride** (p115) along the south shore's lovely beaches. Ideal swimming conditions can be enjoyed all year round in the protected waters of **John Smith's Bay** (p96), while **Tobacco Bay** (p81) stands out for stunning scenery both above and below the surface of the water.

Throw in a fishing line at Astwood Park beach (p115)

GREG JOHNSTON

Slow down the pace at historical St George's Harbour (p71)

GREG JOHNSTON

LEE FOSTER

Spread your towel at Horseshoe Bay (p120)

Bermuda is so steeped in history that the entire northeast end of the island has been declared a World Heritage site. Step back into a colonial setting at the **Verdmont Museum** (p94), a former plantation house. Two grand standouts among Bermuda's numerous colonial forts are **Fort Hamilton** (p52), towering above the City of Hamilton, and **Scaur Hill Fort** (p131), which stretches clear across the island in Sandys near the amazingly narrow **Somerset Bridge** (p129). The **Royal Naval Dockyard** (p134) marks the island's west end with a plethora of maritime sites, including the island's largest history museum.

Stroll among Victorian architecture on Front St, City of Hamilton (p55)

Stand atop the world's tallest cast-iron lighthouse at Gibbs Hill (p120)

Stay in the World Heritage–listed Town of St George (p71)

The **Arboretum** (p99) offers trails beneath a canopy of exotic trees, while **Paget Marsh** (p106) and **Warwick Pond** (p113) offer unspoiled native environments that will enthrall birdwatchers. The **Bermuda Aquarium, Museum & Zoo** (p90) presents a superb glimpse of the undersea delights around Bermuda and allows visitors to get up close to some cool creatures. For awesome underground sightseeing, explore the sparkling **Crystal Caves** (p87). And of course the green world in Bermuda includes some fine golf greens with splendid scenery, like the **Ocean View** (p101) and **Port Royal** (p123) golf courses.

Gaze on the flowering bird-of-paradise, Bermuda Botanical Gardens (p104)

GREG JOHNSTON

RAY TIPPER

Spot a yellow-crowned night heron at Spittal Pond Nature Reserve (p95)

Reflect at Palm Grove Garden (p99)

GREG JOHNSTON

Getting Started

This island does a stellar job of luring people to its shores and making the experience as easy as possible. Few visitors coming here need to bother with visas, and some don't even need to have valid passports (see p151 for details). Matter of fact, Bermuda is a popular last-minute getaway spot for many Americans.

Bermuda is an upmarket destination and would be a challenge for travelers on a very tight budget – there are no hostels, campgrounds or other facilities geared to backpackers. But even though food and accommodations prices are higher than in most other destinations, the bottom line won't necessarily strain your credit card limit. The average stay in Bermuda is five to seven days and airfares from the USA and Canada – the departure points of more than 90% of all visitors – are generally low, so the total cost of a vacation in this piece of paradise may actually compare favorably with other vacation options.

WHEN TO GO

Thanks to the warming effects of the Gulf Stream, Bermuda enjoys a mild, agreeable climate all year round. In terms of tourism the island has two seasons. The 'summer season' refers to the months of April through October, when Bermuda enjoys its warmest air and water temperatures and sees perfect conditions for swimming, snorkeling and diving. It's also the most vibrant time on the island, with a lively hotel scene, greater entertainment options and more visitors milling about. In the warmest months, July to September, the average high temperature is 85°F and the average low is 75°F. Midsummer is also the muggiest time of the year, and if you're not used to high humidity (which averages 84% in August) it can be a bit uncomfortable – though jumping in the pool will certainly cool things off.

One caveat for summer: it's also the hurricane season, particularly the months from August through October. Although Bermuda lies outside the main hurricane track that wracks the Caribbean, it does occasionally get whapped, most famously in 2003 when Hurricane Fabian gave the island's south coast a direct hit, taking more than a few roofs with it. So watch the forecast – www.weather.bm is a great resource for storm-watching.

See the Climate Chart (p142) for more information.

DON'T LEAVE HOME WITHOUT...

- Sunblock and good sunglasses to handle those dazzling pink sands
- A bathing suit, packed into your carry-on bag – if your luggage doesn't make it, you can still spend the first afternoon in the water
- A tie, and perhaps even a jacket, for men who want to dine at the island's fanciest digs
- A good pair of walking shoes for thoroughly exploring the streets of St George and Hamilton
- Some coffee and a few food staples, allowing self-caterers to put off a trek to one of Bermuda's pricey grocery stores on arrival
- A bungee cord to strap down a small bag in the basket of your moped, securing it from wind and the hands of a potential drive-by thief
- Your own snorkel, mask and fins if you plan to do much snorkeling
- Dive certification cards and logbooks for those who want to plunge deeper

The 'winter season' is from November to March, when daytime highs average around 70°F. This time of year is too chilly for swimming and many water-activity companies suspend operations for at least part of the season. Winter temperatures are a delight, however, for playing golf or tennis, hiking and general sightseeing. Also on the plus side, there are fewer visitors to compete with – actually no cruise ship visitors at all – so getting a table at your favorite restaurant will be a lot easier. And most hotels drop their rates in winter, so you can find tempting deals, even at the nicest resorts. If you want to time your visit with specific events, take a look at the Festivals & Events section (p144).

COSTS & MONEY

No doubt about it, Bermuda is an expensive destination. The island's high cost of living is reflected in everything, including accommodations. Once service charges and taxes are added to the tariff, there are barely a handful of places to stay in Bermuda where travelers can squeak by for $100 a night. At the midrange there are several attractive choices hovering around $200, and opting for a cushy resort will easily run to twice that.

If you plan to stay seven days or less, look into package tours that include both airfare and hotel, as they often work out more cheaply than buying the airfare and paying for the hotel separately. Although it's not heavily advertised, many tour operators can also create individualized 'package tours' for stays of longer than seven days – so even if you're staying for a couple of weeks, this may be an option to explore.

Most of the food consumed in Bermuda is imported, and prices are generally about 50% higher than those in the USA. Travelers lunching at local eateries and self-preparing most other meals in their guesthouse kitchen might get by for around $35 a day, while those opting to eat at resorts should expect to average close to $100 a day for meals. Families traveling together will fare best by getting an apartment-style place with a full kitchen – lunch deals abound in Bermuda, so eating out in the day is economical but you'll save a bundle by having breakfast and dinner at home.

TRAVEL LITERATURE

Several books about Bermuda offer a good read while providing insights to the island. The following are recommended. If you don't get a chance to grab one of them before you get on the plane, they can be picked up at bookstores in Bermuda after you arrive.

The Last Pink Bits by Harry Ritchie is a lighthearted, insightful account of Ritchie's recent travels in Bermuda and other scattered outposts that comprise the last remnants of the once-formidable British empire. A fun read.

Tracey Caswell, a transplanted Canadian, puts her advice for newcomers in *Tea with Tracey,* and it's an amusing read for visitors too. Get the scoop on lizards, etiquette and scooters from an insider's perspective.

Mark Twain and the Happy Island is a vivid account of Bermuda, through the eyes of Twain, conveyed by Elizabeth Wallace, who kicked around the island with America's foremost traveler.

For an escape into pure fiction, pick up *Bermuda Grass* by Keith Miles. A golf course architect goes to Bermuda to lay out the greens and gets involved in a web of sex, murder and mystery.

Bermuda Triangle Mystery Solved, by Lawrence David Kusche, provides an interesting read for those fascinated with the mysteries of vanished ships and planes in the world's spookiest quadrant.

LONELY PLANET INDEX

Liter of gas $1.45

Liter of bottled water $1.20

Pint of lager in pub $5

Souvenir T-shirt $18

Ice cream cone $3

HOW MUCH?

Bowl of fish chowder $5

One day of motor-scooter rental $70

Cup of tea at teatime $3

Average one night at B&B $160

Glass-bottom-boat cruise $50

TOP FIVES

Pampering Hotels

Bermuda enjoys a well-earned reputation for cozy little hotels and cottage colonies that coddle guests in style. The Royal Palms is a Victorian-era delight on the outskirts of the City of Hamilton. The other four places are intimate seaside gems sporting their own private beaches.

- Cambridge Beaches (p133), Sandys Parish
- Pompano Beach Club (p124), Southampton Parish
- Ariel Sands Beach Club (p101), Devonshire Parish
- Pink Beach Club & Cottages (p97), Smith's Parish
- Royal Palms Hotel (p66), Pembroke Parish

Festivals & Events

Bermuda may be small but it loves a party. The island offers a plethora of events throughout the year, some centering around sailing, some rooted in the island's culture and history, and others just plain fun. See the Festivals & Events section (p144) for a look at it all.

- Cup Match (p145), August
- Bermuda Music Festival (p145), October
- Bermuda Culinary Arts Festival (p145), November
- Peppercorn Ceremony (p144), April
- International Race Weekend (p144), January

Top Sightseeing Attractions

Whether you're looking to immerse yourself in a thoroughly colonial setting, want to spend the day at one of the world's most beautiful beaches or are ready to stroll about lovely gardens, it's all close at hand.

- Town of St George (p71)
- Royal Naval Dockyard (p134)
- Horseshoe Bay (p120)
- Bermuda Aquarium, Museum & Zoo (p90)
- Bermuda Botanical Gardens (p104)

INTERNET RESOURCES

Bermuda Department of Tourism (www.bermudatourism.com) Official government site with downloadable brochures.

Bermuda Online (www.bermuda-online.org) Comprehensive information on scores of subjects about Bermuda.

Government of Bermuda (www.gov.bm) Connects to government departments and official topics.

Limey in Bermuda (www.limeyinbermuda.com) Run by an expat Brit, this opinionated site delves into all things Bermudian.

Lonely Planet (www.lonelyplanet.com) Online guide with up-to-date topics and the Thorn Tree forum where you can ask other travelers what they think.

Royal Gazette (www.theroyalgazette.com) Local news online from Bermuda's top newspaper, including upcoming events and a searchable archive.

Itineraries
CLASSIC ROUTES

BERMUDA'S WESTERN SIDE
Two Days

This 40-mile loop through Bermuda's west begins at the Royal Naval Dockyard's attractions, takes you along Bermuda's finest beaches and visits some popular sights. With a very early start it could be done in one day, but it's much more relaxing to do it over several days.

From the City of Hamilton, take the ferry to the **Royal Naval Dockyard** (p134). Explore the extensive collections at the **Bermuda Maritime Museum** (p136) and enjoy fantastic views from its fortress walls. Then head over to the **Dockyard Glassworks & Bermuda Rum Cake Company** (p138) to watch glassblowers and sample homemade cakes. Hop on a bus to **Somerset Village** (p129) for a slice of traditional Bermuda and a fine waterview lunch at **Salt Rock Grill** (p133). Then make your way down to explore **Scaur Hill Fort** (p131). Upon leaving Sandys Parish, keep an eye out for **Somerset Bridge** (p129), the world's smallest drawbridge. Next climb up to **Gibbs Hill Lighthouse** (p120) for an unbeatable panorama and a spot of tea at the **tea room** (p125). From there, move on to **Horseshoe Bay** (p120), the most popular of Bermuda's knockout pink-sand beaches. If you're up for a walk, take the breathtaking **South Shore Park Trail** (p122) that runs past hidden coves to magnificent **Warwick Long Bay** (p113). Now make your way to the **Bermuda Botanical Gardens** (p104) and stroll around the fragrant grounds. While you're there, pop in to the splendid **Masterworks Museum of Bermuda Art** (p106), and if it's a Tuesday or Friday, take a walk through **Camden** (p107), the premier's residence.

BERMUDA'S EASTERN SIDE

Two Days

From the City of Hamilton, take the ferry to the **Town of St George** (p71), enjoying the fine coastal views along the way. The ferry docks at Ordnance Island, where a **statue** (p73) of Bermuda's founder Sir George Somers welcomes you to this history-steeped town. Enjoy the sights of nearby **King's Square** (p73), the heart of it all, and then wander about the old cobblestone streets and pop into some of the town's interesting museums. From there, head up to **Tobacco Bay** (p81), where you can take a swim or don snorkel gear for some underwater sightseeing. Next, explore the run of coastal forts that helped put St George on the map as a World Heritage site. First up and grandest is **Fort St Catherine** (p80), now set aside as a museum, followed by **Alexandra Battery** (p81) and **Gates Fort** (p81).

After St George head to the island of St David's to savor some of the island's freshest seafood at the harborfront **Black Horse Tavern** (p84). Continue on to **St David's Battery** (p83), where you can scramble around an impressive clifftop fort, and then climb **St David's Lighthouse** (p84) for a superb 360° view. The village of **Bailey's Bay** (p87) is next: take a tour beneath the hanging stalactites in the awesome **Crystal Caves** (p87) and stroll the curious grounds of **Blue Hole Hill Park** (p88). Now treat yourself to a drink at the **Swizzle Inn** (p89) before continuing on to the last stop, the splendid **Bermuda Aquarium, Museum & Zoo** (p90), Bermuda's most visited sightseeing attraction.

This tour through Bermuda's easternmost parishes – St George's and Hamilton – combines the island's best-preserved historic area with fine natural sites. It covers about 50 miles in all.

TAILORED TRIPS

SNORKELING BERMUDA

Bermuda has three snorkeling beaches, all of which conveniently have concession stands where you can rent snorkel gear. On the western side, **Bermuda Snorkel Park** (p137) sits beneath the towering fortress walls of the Royal Naval Dockyard and not only teems with colorful fish but also has colonial-era cannons dotting its sea floor. **Church Bay** (p122) in Southampton Parish is a beauty with a nearshore coral reef that attracts large rainbow parrotfish. **Tobacco Bay** (p81) shores up the snorkeling scene on the eastern end of Bermuda with pinnacle-like formations and coral gardens. Now that you've gotten your toes wet and your interest in the deep piqued, consider one of these uniquely Bermudian experiences: don a helmet instead of a mask and take a walk on the sea floor with a **helmet dive** (p39) or join one of the **snorkeling cruises** (p40) from Hamilton or St George that sail out to shallow shipwrecks.

HITTING THE GREENS

Bermuda's a golfer's paradise and you could easily spend your whole vacation on the greens. All of the courses have interesting topography and water views. A great place to start is **St George's Golf Club** (p76), where the scenery is often compared to California's famous Pebble Beach. **Ocean View Golf Course** (p101) lives up to its billing for views and is a fun, quick course popular with islanders. Next, test your skills with Bermuda's toughest opening hole at **Belmont Hills Golf Club** (p115). Also highly rated is nearby **Riddell's Bay Golf & Country Club** (p115), with snug fairways that require precision shots. Now you've earned a relaxing day on the gently sloping greens of the **Fairmont Southampton Golf Club** (p123), with short fairways that are a putter's dream. Finish off at the island's most popular course, the **Port Royal Golf Course** (p123), a Robert Trent Jones beauty with dramatic cliffside holes.

The Authors

NED FRIARY & GLENDA BENDURE

Ned and Glenda love traveling to islands and have written several guidebooks covering widely scattered island destinations, from the well-trodden Caribbean to remote Micronesia. Still, among the scores of islands they've explored, there are few they look forward to returning to more than Bermuda. They were first turned on to the island by a friend who had spent several years there working with the Bermuda News Bureau – his stories of island hospitality whetted their appetite, and Bermuda pole-vaulted to the top of their 'next trip' list. They've been to the island several times since, exploring it from top to bottom. They're the authors of the first two editions of Lonely Planet's *Bermuda*, as well as several newspaper stories on this delightful destination for the *Cape Cod Times*.

Our Favorite Trip

We typically head first to the Town of St George (p71) – it's so solidly historic that it's easy to imagine you're on the set of a colonial-era movie. Our favorite green retreats in the midst of suburbia are Paget Marsh (p106) and Spittal Pond (p95). Best of all are those powdery pink beaches – we love to take a morning walk along South Shore Park Trail (p122) between Horseshoe Bay and Warwick Long Bay, stopping to swim at a secluded cove along the way. And we always spend some time snorkeling, following those tropical fish around. A day of sightseeing in the City of Hamilton (p46) invariably ends with a dark 'n' stormy on one of those restaurant balconies overlooking the harbor.

CONTRIBUTING AUTHOR

David Goldberg, MD, wrote the Health chapter (p159). He completed his training in internal medicine and infectious diseases at Columbia-Presbyterian Medical Center in New York City, where he has also served as voluntary faculty. At present he is an infectious diseases specialist in Scarsdale, New York, and the editor-in-chief of the website MDTravelHealth.com.

Snapshot

Not surprisingly, weather has become a big topic on the island since Hurricane Fabian smashed into Bermuda in August 2003, killing four people and causing a whopping $300 million in damage. An entire wing of the Wyndham Beach Resort was swept into the sea and the roof of the exclusive Fairmont Southampton blew right off. Homes suffered similar damage, especially along the storm-battered south shore. The whole thing took Bermudians by surprise, since a storm of this size hadn't hit the island in 75 years.

It took more than a year to get things back in order but physical signs of damage are now relatively few. The way islanders think, however, has markedly changed. If you're in Bermuda during the hurricane season, expect to hear plenty of talk about storms. Islanders have become big storm-watchers, and many can tell you the exact locations of hurricanes sweeping across distant places in the Atlantic. From June to October the most-watched channel on TV is the Bermuda weather station, which now broadcasts 24 hours a day!

On the political front, in 2004 Alex Scott, who leads the ruling Progressive Labour Party (PLP), officially reopened the dialogue on the topic of independence from Britain. Since then there's been some discussion on the pros and cons, but little on any specific approach to breaking ties with the crown. It makes for interesting chatter over coffee at the lunch counter, but polls indicate the majority of islanders are currently against independence, and many would actually favor even closer ties to Britain.

Overseas financial institutions that operate out of Bermuda because of tax opportunities have become a backbone of the economy and now provide many of the best-paying jobs on the island. They pump so much money into the island that Bermuda now has an astounding $3.75 billion GDP.

However, for working-class people not plugged into the hottest sector of the economy there are downsides. Housing prices have soared to the point where the average single-family home sells for almost a million dollars, and many people are forced to take second jobs just to keep pace. In response to the tight housing market, several of the island's smaller hotels have closed and are being converted to condos, and locals say they're worried that tourism, once the leading sector of the economy, will spiral downhill as a consequence. Of course, for those who manage to trade in a job waiting tables for a high salary as an insurance actuary, the switch from a service economy to a white-collar one doesn't seem like such a bad thing.

On a lighter note there's cricket (the game, not the bug!), which sweeps the island every summer. At the height of it all during the August Cup Match (p133), don't expect to hear anything but cricket buzz – the fervor is so gripping that work is suspended for two days, while everyone dons their team colors and heads to the match.

FAST FACTS

Population: 62,000

Percentage of blacks/whites: 61/39

Annual number of tourists: 465,000

Unemployment: 3%

Inflation: 3.4%

GDP: $3.75 billion

Motor vehicles per sq mile: 2222

Number of medal-winning Olympians: 1

Golf courses per sq mile: 0.39

Highest/lowest temperature (°F) on record: 91/44

History

A speck in the remote mid-Atlantic, Bermuda was well outside early migration routes and remained unsettled before its discovery by European explorers.

Bermuda takes its name from Spanish sea captain Juan de Bermúdez, who sighted the islands around 1503. The Spanish, in search of gold in the Americas, took no interest in colonizing the sparse island chain. In fact, there is no indication that the Spanish ever deliberately landed on Bermuda in the 16th century, although misadventures at sea cast them ashore at least a few times.

Spanish galleons sailing between Cuba and Spain commonly set a course north past Florida and then east out to sea. Although the extensive reefs surrounding Bermuda posed a potential hazard to their ships, there were no other islands in the mid-Atlantic that sea captains could use to take bearings, so Bermuda became a vital navigational landmark. Once Bermuda was spotted, the ship's course could be reset east-northeast to follow a straight line to the Azores and Spain.

In fair weather, sailing past Bermuda was usually uneventful. However, powerful storms occasionally swept ships off their intended course and onto Bermuda's shallow reefs. Scores of Spanish ships, their hulls loaded with bullion, never completed their journey home from the New World. Today you can see some of the gold booty recovered from the wrecks at the Bermuda Underwater Exploration Institute (p63).

The treacherous reefs gained such a reputation among mariners that by the mid-16th century Bermuda was appearing on Spanish charts with the nickname 'Islas Demonios,' or 'Isles of Devils.'

> Bermuda is the oldest continually inhabited English settlement in the New World.

EARLY SETTLERS

On June 2, 1609, Admiral Sir George Somers of the Virginia Company set sail from England with nine ships carrying supplies and colonists to the recently established British settlement at Jamestown, Virginia.

Somers, who was in command of the flagship *Sea Venture*, got caught in a fierce storm and lost contact with the rest of his fleet. The *Sea Venture*, badly damaged by the storm, shipwrecked on a reef three-quarters of a mile off Bermuda's eastern shore. Using skiffs, all 150 people on board managed to safely come ashore.

The castaways salvaged wreckage from the *Sea Venture* and began construction of two new ships. Aware of the gloomy Spanish accounts of the island, the shipwrecked Brits expected the worst, but instead found Bermuda surprisingly agreeable. Native cedar trees provided timber for the new ships, palmetto palms supplied thatch for shelters and the abundant nearshore fish proved easy to catch.

In 1610, the two new ships, the *Deliverance* and the *Patience*, set sail to continue the journey to Jamestown, leaving a couple of men behind on Bermuda to establish an English claim.

Back in England, the officers of the Virginia Company took a keen interest in reports on the island's suitability for colonization. The fact

> Although the name failed to stick, the British christened the islands the Somers Islands in honor of the English admiral who shipwrecked here.

1503	1609
Bermuda is first sighted by Spanish explorer Juan de Bermúdez	Admiral George Somers shipwrecks on Bermuda's shoals with 150 passengers and spends the rest of the year on the island

that Bermuda **was uninhabited** weighed heavily in its favor, especially in light of the **Indian sieges that** decimated the Jamestown settlement. The Virginia **Company amended** its charter to include Bermuda in its New World **holdings, and** organized a party of 60 settlers to establish a permanent colony there.

The settlers landed on Bermuda in 1612, led by Governor Richard Moore, an able carpenter who went about building the village of St George. In 1620, the parliamentary State House (p75), which can still be seen today, began to hold meetings of the colonial legislature.

In the 17th century, Bermudians ran a sea-salt business in the Turks Islands, with nearly 1000 Bermudian colonists and slaves working 900 miles from home.

Bermuda was divided into parishes, each named for a stockholder of the Virginia Company, and plots of land were leased to settlers. Crops were planted, but agriculture was limited by the shallowness of the topsoil and the reliance upon rainwater as the sole water source. In the end, Bermuda became reliant upon food imports from the American colonies to augment its meager harvests.

The Virginia Company ruled Bermuda like a fiefdom, telling people what crops to grow, monopolizing trade and forcing those who violated their rules into indentured servitude. Over time, the settlers grew weary of the restrictions and took their case to London, where they successfully sued to have the charter rescinded in 1684. Bermuda was then ruled as a British crown colony in much the same vein as the American colonies.

Slavery, the norm on British colonies, was introduced to Bermuda in 1616. Although the vast majority of slaves came from Africa, there were also Mahican Indians taken from the American colonies. The Atlantic crossings were so brutally inhumane that many of the slaves, chained in the ships' suffocating hulls, died en route.

The dehumanizing conditions continued after arrival, permeating every aspect of life and even following into death. Slaves were buried in their own part of the cemetery, away from whites, and you can still see walls separating the two as you stroll around old churchyards such as St Peter's (p73) in the Town of St George.

Slavery was abolished in Bermuda 31 years earlier than in the United States of America.

Degrading as the conditions were, they were not as horrendous as in other New World colonies. Most of the slaves in Bermuda did not end up toiling in sweltering fields, but were put to work as servants, construction workers and sailors. Some became skilled tradespeople and were able to pass their skills on to their children, assuring them opportunities in the trades long after the end of slavery.

By the early 1800s, the antislavery movement was gaining widespread support. The British Parliament passed legislation in 1807 that outlawed

SINK OR HANG

The witchcraft hysteria that swept Europe and America in the 17th century hit Bermuda as well. The first death sentence imposed upon a 'witch' in Bermuda was in 1651, when a woman accused of evildoing was given a 'trial' in which her feet and hands were tied and she was thrown into the ocean.

The fact that the woman managed to float 'confirmed' she was indeed a witch, and she was subsequently hanged. Bermudians continued searching for witches in their midst until the hysteria ended in the 1690s.

1612	1616
The first permanent English settlers arrive on Bermuda and begin building the Town of St George	The first slaves are brought to Bermuda

THE ONION PATCH

Onions were first planted in Bermuda in 1616, though large-scale cultivation did not start until the 1830s. By the late 19th century, exported Bermuda onions had become so well known, particularly in New York markets, that Bermuda was nicknamed the 'Onion Patch' and Bermudians themselves were sometimes lightheartedly referred to as 'Onions.'

The onion biz ground to a halt as competition from 'Bermuda onions' grown in Texas swamped North American markets in the early 1900s. And a loss of Bermuda farmland to growing numbers of homes and hotels sealed the demise of onion exports. Indeed, there are indications that as early as 1908, Bermuda was importing the famed 'Bermuda onions' from Texas!

the sale of slaves, and phased out slavery itself over a broader period. By 1834 all slaves in Bermuda were emancipated.

BRITISH–US INFLUENCES

Historically, Bermuda was often put in a tight spot as it struggled to balance its close trade relationship with America against its political bonds with Britain.

During the War of 1812, the British Navy used Bermuda as a base to launch the Chesapeake Bay Campaign that torched the US White House and much of Washington DC. The Americans took revenge where they could. Under the rules of war practiced during the period, American ships were free to confiscate the cargo of any ship flying the British flag. Bermuda provided lucrative booty for American privateers, who made an easy catch of Bermuda's merchant fleet, devastating the island's trade-dependent economy.

The US Civil War (1861–65), on the other hand, provided a boon for Bermuda, which was thrust into the lucrative role as a center for blockade-runners. The Confederacy depended upon the sale of cotton to England's clothing mills to finance its rebellion, but had become forced to employ small, fast vessels to outrun the gunboats of the northern navy. These vessels could not handle transatlantic shipping, so Bermuda became an intermediate port. The Town of St George enjoyed unprecedented prosperity, its waterside warehouses overflowing with goods, its shops and taverns catering to mariners carrying fat wads of cash. Traders made fortunes until the northern forces became victorious in 1865 and Bermuda, which had sided with the south, saw its shipping industry all but collapse.

During WWII, Bermuda's strategic mid-Atlantic location made it a center for Allied military and intelligence operations. It was a port for Britain's Royal Navy, which patrolled the Atlantic for German submarines that threatened vital US–UK shipping lanes. The USA also established a substantial presence in Bermuda, most notably with the construction of an air base on St David's Island. The base, some 1040 acres in all, was so large it added 1.25 sq miles to the island in the form of reclaimed land, boosting Bermuda's total landmass by more than 5%.

Rogues & Runners: Bermuda and the American Civil War by the Bermuda National Trust provides a colorful account of St George's heyday, complete with period photos.

Fascinating historical documents, photographs and period maps can be found at www.rootsweb.com/~bmuwgw/bermuda.htm.

POSTWAR CHANGES

In the wake of WWII, many of the old colonial assumptions that prevailed in the British Empire were called into question. In Bermuda, long-held political and economic preferences given to white males, at the expense of women and blacks, came under fire.

Although blacks were granted the right to vote in the 19th century, franchise qualifications kept them from achieving significant political power. Indeed, in the 100 years between emancipation and WWII, only a dozen blacks were elected to parliament. Women, on the other hand, were completely blocked from the political arena until 1944, when they got the right to vote. Even then, voter registration for both sexes was restricted to property owners, leaving fewer than 3000 Bermudians eligible to vote.

Blacks in Bermuda faced policies of segregation similar to those in the USA – with the exception that Bermudian blacks were well entrenched in the trades. In the 1950s, buoyed by their clout in the trade movement, black Bermudians began to emerge as a political and social power to be reckoned with.

In 1959, intent on putting an end to segregation, blacks boycotted movie theaters and restaurants, forcing those businesses to accept integration. Under pressure, hotels and other businesses that had practiced discriminatory hiring began to open job opportunities to blacks.

In 1960, a grassroots movement called the Committee for Universal Suffrage started a campaign to extend voting rights to the 75% of the adult population that didn't own 'qualifying property.' Conservatives, unable to block the movement, settled for an amendment to the legislation giving property owners the right to cast two votes. Still, in the 1963 general election, every adult Bermudian could finally vote.

Before universal suffrage was introduced, Bermuda's political arena so narrowly represented the interest of white landowners that it was free of political parties and rival platforms. In 1963, the first political party in Bermuda, the Progressive Labour Party (PLP), formed to represent the interests of nonwhite Bermudians.

The PLP won support from newly enfranchised voters and captured six house seats in 1963. Many of the remaining independent members, wary of the potential bloc vote that the PLP could cast, united to form a counter party, the United Bermuda Party (UBP), which appealed to businesspeople.

Duncan McDonald's Another World? Bermuda and the Rise of Modern Tourism *provides a vivid understanding of how Bermuda came to be the hospitable sanctuary it is today.*

The most comprehensive and authoritative history book on Bermuda is The Story of Bermuda and Her People, *by William S Zuill – and it's a good read too.*

TWAIN AND THE PRINCESS

Princess Louise, daughter of Queen Victoria and wife of the Governor General of Canada, is credited with putting Bermuda on the map for North American tourists. Anxious to escape cold Canadian winters, the princess paid an extended visit to Bermuda in 1883. The press took note of her stay, and journalists, including perennial traveler Mark Twain, followed in her wake. In 1884, Bermuda's first seaside resort – named, not surprisingly, the Princess Hotel – opened in Hamilton.

In his golden years, Twain himself became a frequent traveler to Bermuda, making annual journeys to the island. It was, in fact, the last place he ever visited; Twain set sail from Bermuda just nine days before his death in 1910.

By the early 20th century, Bermuda was becoming a trendy winter destination for 'snow birds,' who flocked aboard steamers sailing from New York. The winter crossing, when stormy Atlantic seas are common, was rough enough that Twain compared his journey to 'going through hell' in order to reach paradise.

1884	1941
The first seaside resort – the Princess Hotel – opens for visitors	Bermuda becomes a key military base for American forces patrolling against German U-boats in the Atlantic

COME AND GONE

In March 1941, British authorities intent on having the USA develop Allied bases on Bermuda signed a 99-year lease giving the US military a substantial chunk of Bermudian real estate. Bermudians, who were not privy to the negotiations, were so taken aback by the lengthy term of the lease and the magnitude of territory involved that rumors Bermuda was on the verge of being taken over as a US possession ran wild.

While the USA had no intention of laying claim to Bermuda, its presence did bring rapid change to the sleepy colony. Scores of Bermudians found work on military construction projects, including the building of Bermuda's first airport. The US military introduced the widespread use of motor vehicles, which had previously been forbidden from Bermuda's streets. After the war, the airport opened to civilian traffic (yes, it's the very airport you land at today), giving islanders easy access to the US East Coast and opening Bermuda up as a weekend getaway for American tourists.

With the end of the Cold War, US bases in Bermuda no longer filled any legitimate military need. In September 1995, the USA ended its military presence in Bermuda, returning 1330 acres, some 10% of Bermuda's total landmass, to the island government.

Under encouragement from Britain, the UBP, PLP and independent parliamentary members joined together to produce a constitution, which took effect in 1968. The new constitution provided for full internal self-government on domestic matters from health to immigration, leaving control of security, defense and diplomatic affairs to the crown.

QUESTION OF INDEPENDENCE

After hammering out a constitution, independence from Britain became the dominant issue in island politics. Both political parties took at least tepid stances supporting independence but in August 1995, when it was finally put to a vote, a mere 25% of Bermudians voted in favor of breaking ties with Britain. In the end many Bermudians were apprehensive about the potential costs of independence.

Bermuda's long history of political and social conservatism undoubtedly played a role in the vote. Employment concerns also weighed into the decision to stick with the status quo, as many of the foreign companies operating in Bermuda let it be known they found security in the current system of British law.

With its absence of corporate taxes, Bermuda lures an ever-growing number of overseas financial operations to its shores. Over 300 international companies maintain at least a limited physical presence in Bermuda, including mutual funds services, investment holding firms and companies specializing in reinsurance, a type of insurance that protects conventional insurers against natural disasters. Among them are such heavyweights as Tyco, XL Capital and ACE Insurance. In addition, some 13,000 international businesses have no presence on the island but are registered in Bermuda, mostly to gain shelter from tax authorities and regulators elsewhere.

Bermuda is one of just a handful of remaining British overseas dependencies that include scattered outposts like the Falkland Islands and volcano-ravaged Montserrat.

In 2000, Unesco designated the historic Town of St George as a World Heritage site.

1963	1995
For the first time all adult Bermudians have the right to vote	Bermudians resoundingly vote against independence from Britain

The Culture

THE NATIONAL PSYCHE

Bermudians are generally quite conservative and pride themselves on old traditions. They like to make conversation on many contemporary topics, and will play the devil's advocate, but in the end they don't embrace abrupt changes. Perhaps nothing personifies this attitudes more than the vote about independence from Britain. In the years leading up to the vote, political leaders voiced support for independence and talk on the street leaned the same way, but when people finally slipped into the privacy of the voting booths 75% of them voted to keep things the way they were.

Traditional British influences permeate many aspects of society. Politicians and judges still wear powdered wigs, bobbies direct traffic, afternoon tea is a ritual and a pint of ale at the local pub is a common way to cap off a day's work. Cricket is Bermuda's most popular sport. Fashion and manners, not surprisingly, remain conservatively British.

But there is a distinct island flavor to it all. There's a friendliness and warmth to people. They will readily strike up a conversation with a stranger on the bus. And they're not rushed…as a matter of fact, getting there in a good mood is more important than getting there on time. Indeed, some Western businesspeople in Bermuda have recently coined the term 'Bermuda time' to mean 15 minutes later than the appointed time.

The head of state is Britain's Queen Elizabeth II. She appoints a governor to represent her in Bermuda, but the role is largely symbolic.

LIFESTYLE

Things do change in Bermuda, though ever so slowly. Families are getting smaller; the average size of a household has dropped from three people in 1980 to just 2½ people today. Because of spiraling housing costs, people don't leave home at a young age, and it's not uncommon for 30-year-olds to still be living with their parents.

Religion plays an important role in Bermudians' lives, and three out of four people opt to marry in the church. Still, marriage is not as universal as it's been in the past and some 40% of children are now born out of wedlock. Partly as a response to what some islanders see as a slip in moral values, fundamentalist religious sects are winning over members from more liberal churches.

Bermuda banned automobiles in 1906 after a mufflerless car spooked several horses, and it managed without them until 1946 when automobile ownership was finally legalized.

DOS & DON'TS

- Do be polite. Courtesy goes a long way in Bermuda. Never stop someone on the street for directions without first greeting them with 'good morning' or 'good afternoon.' Even ordering a drink from a bar should be prefaced with a friendly greeting.
- Don't wear bathing suits or skimpy beachwear any place other than the beach or swimming pool. Nude and partially nude (topless for women) bathing are not permitted anywhere in Bermuda.
- Don't be impatient. Things go a bit slower in Bermuda and people don't like being prodded. Be abrupt with the waiter and instead of your food arriving quicker, it may take even longer to arrive.
- Do tip the taxi driver. A 15% service charge is added to the bill at some restaurants, but if it's not, that's an appropriate tip to leave.
- Don't leave the water running. Most of Bermuda's household water comes from rain catchments, and it's scarce, so residents are very sensitive to conservation attitudes.

BERMEWJAN CHINWAG

Bermudians speak English with a local lilt that resembles that of some Caribbean islanders, and with a predominantly British accent.

Bermudian slang is colorful, lively and gives an interesting glimpse into the way folks relate to everyday friends and family. Its use is still common among islanders even though it's not nearly as widespread today as it was in decades past, in part due to the pervasive influence of overseas media, particularly American TV. Don't expect to hear much slang in formal settings, such as at the hotel front desk or in shops and restaurants, where polite proper English is the norm. Walk by a construction site where workers are chatting among themselves, however, and the conversation will inevitably be peppered with bits of the local vernacular.

With Bermudian slang you'll find a few distinct peculiarities. The interchange of 'w' for 'v' is not uncommon, so that 'welcome' is often pronounced as 'velcome.' Sometimes 'ing' is short-ened to 'in' ('wedding' thus becomes 'veddin') and the ending 'th' is sometimes spoken as 'f' ('with' becomes 'vif').

'Um, um' at the start of a sentence is used a delay tactic, like 'uh… ' or 'let me see.'

Common island expressions include:

ace boy best buddy; used when talking about a good friend

axe to ask, such as 'axe and I'll tell you'

back of town also known as de block; the northern back streets of the City of Hamilton, around Court St

bailin bathing suit

Bermewjan Bermudian

black short for the island-made Gosling's Black Seal Rum

black and coke a drink made of Gosling's Black Seal Rum and Coca-Cola

blinds a pair of sunglasses

boss form of addressing friends, as in 'hey, boss, what's up?'

burr beer

byes an gals boys and girls

chinwag chat, have a conversation, gossip

chyl-up knock up, or get your girlfriend pregnant

crucial couldn't be better, excellent

de Rock the Rock (referring to all of Bermuda)

deddy and mummy one's parents

ease me up give me a break

full hot drunk. And then there's half hot, meaning just a little drunk

get hot going out to tie one on, get drunk

going tawhn going to town (meaning going to the City of Hamilton)

greeze food, quick eats, as in 'I'm going out for some greeze'

gribble to be cranky or ornery, as in 'why you so gribble?'

guvmit Bermuda's government

have an attitude in a bad mood

how you sound what's wrong?

missin daydreamin', not paying attention

shrew having intercourse, going all the way; sometimes 'shrew de trees'

took licks got banged up in a fight

vexed pissed off

waxed angry; another term for vexed

woffless totally without merit

Bermudians tend to be conservative on social issues and tolerance for alternative lifestyles has never been widespread – simply put, Bermuda is not the most comfortable place to be a firebrand radical, embrace a hippie lifestyle, espouse atheism, or be openly gay, for that matter. Perhaps this is in part because the population is so small that anything different sticks out like the proverbial sore thumb.

A mild undertone of chauvinism still exists in some circles but women have made great strides in the workplace and in political arenas. Some make it all the way to the top to be CEOs, but as a group they are still underrepresented.

Bermuda's workplace is fully racially integrated, but some refer to it as a 'nine to five' integration, noting that many folks, particularly in the older generation, tend to socialize with people of their own race.

The average income is $44,000 and the median household income is $72,000. The middle class makes up about 50% of the population, and the rest is evenly divided between the wealthy and the lower class. Not

Traditional Bermudian weddings have two cakes. The bride's is a fruitcake decorated with silver leaf; the groom's is a pound cake with gold leaf.

SHORT AND DAPPER

You may have to stifle a giggle at your first sight of a businessman decked out in short pants and tall socks – with a bit of hairy knee showing through – but it's all very right and proper in Bermuda.

Unlike other places around the world where this nearly knee-length style of shorts is equated with casual wear, in Bermuda its namesake shorts are an element of formal dress for men. The rest of the outfit consists of knee socks, a dress shirt, a dapper tie and a smart-looking jacket – all essential parts of the whole. It's got to be put together with style, too. The shorts and jacket should be different colors – pink is a favorite hue – while the socks can complement either.

The shorts, incidentally, were inspired by British soldiers in tropical outposts such as India, who took to trimming the lower half of the legs off their trousers to make their uniforms more bearable in the heat. By the early 20th century, British soldiers stationed in Bermuda were wearing such shorts as standard uniform, and in the years that followed the more upscale Bermudian version began to make an appearance.

Today, Bermuda shorts are standard wear for male bankers, insurance executives, government officials and other conservatively dressed community leaders.

---

surprisingly, the wealthy tend to own waterfront property or live near the fanciest golf courses. Lower-class neighborhoods are found at the north side of the City of Hamilton but are also scattered around the island. Most people in Bermuda do live in those charming pastel houses you see everywhere – it's just that in the richer areas they're fancier, bigger (often mansion-like) and better maintained, while in the less well-to-do neighborhoods they are smaller, closer together and more likely to need a fresh coat of paint. There are no pockets of abject poverty in Bermuda, however, and no real ghettos. Travelers may run into the occasional panhandler, especially in Hamilton's 'back of town,' but it's not very common.

Bermudians find dignity in all sorts of work. Driving a taxicab is not a low-life job; as a matter of fact, it's not unusual to find a retired executive driving a cab part time. The trades are unionized, and organized labor has a lot of clout. And there's a distinctive Bermudian angle to how they go about their business. Bus drivers, for instance, may stage a partial-day strike if they're unhappy with contract negotiations but they'll typically wait until mid-morning to stop the buses and then resume their runs in time to pick up the children when school gets out for the day.

Drugs are considered the big spoiler in Bermudian society today and illegal drug use has been on a rapid rise. It's affected people's lives in a lot of ways; thefts and house burglaries, once rare, have increased significantly in recent years. And reports of violent crime among drug users and gang members are now common news items in the local papers.

> Celebrities are paid scant attention in Bermuda. Islanders consider it rude to ask for autographs and totally uncouth to gawk.

> More billionaires have second homes in Bermuda, per capita, than in any other place in the world.

POPULATION

Bermuda has no large urban centers. Nonetheless, as it has a limited amount of space, the population density is one of the world's highest. But the bottom line is, it's a small population. With just 62,000 residents, Bermuda would rank as a small town in most countries.

The population is fairly evenly scattered around the island, with 18% of all residents living in Pembroke Parish, which contains the City of Hamilton. The other eight parishes each contain approximately 8% to 14% of the total population.

SPORTS

No sport fires up passions more in Bermuda than the game of cricket. It's the primary spectator sport played between April and September, with matches taking place at cricket fields around the island every Sunday. Just turn to the sports section of any local paper for details and schedules.

Football (soccer) and rugby are the most popular spectator sports from September to April. Local competitions take place around the island every Sunday, with the biggest meets for both sports held at the National Sports Centre (p102) in Devonshire.

Bermudians also take a keen interest in major sailing events and golf tournaments; see p144 for more on major sporting events.

MULTICULTURALISM

Three-quarters of all people living on the island were born in Bermuda. Of those who are foreign-born, about 30% were born in the UK, 25% in the USA, 12% in the Azores or Portugal, 10% in Canada and 10% in the Caribbean.

Blacks, most of whom are the descendants of slaves, have been in the majority since colonial times and comprise 61% of the population. Most of the remainder of the population is white, but there's also a small minority that is of Native American descent. The races get along in relative harmony and workplaces are well integrated, though the top executive positions still go disproportionately to whites.

The Bermuda National Trust's website at www .bnt.bm has information on the island's cultural heritage.

MEDIA

Bermuda has a free independent press. Local TV programming is limited, government-funded and careful not to offend any of its constituents. For instance, you'll seldom see anything critical of unions, and even an impromptu bus strike might go unreported on the nightly news.

RELIGION

The majority of islanders are Christian but there's a shift taking place from the established old-guard sects to more charismatic evangelical churches. The number of people affiliated with the Anglican church has dropped to 23% (from 45% in 1970), though it remains the largest denomination. This is followed by Roman Catholic at 15%, African Methodist Episcopal at 11% and Seventh-Day Adventist at 7%. Other houses of worship in Bermuda include Methodist, Jehovah's Witness, Baptist, Pentecostal and Christian Science.

If you happen to be in Bermuda on Good Friday, you might be surprised to find the skies above the beaches teeming with colorful kites. Kite-flying is a traditional family activity on that day.

WOMEN IN BERMUDA

Considering Bermuda's conservative past, and the fact that women didn't even have the right to vote until 1944, Bermuda has made impressive strides in women's issues. Girls and boys have similar educational opportunities, with a level playing field when it comes to funding for sports and academic scholarships. Female executives are commonplace in both Bermudian and multinational companies. And they've made such an impact on the political front that two of Bermuda's last three governments have been led by female premiers.

Bermudian law requires that a woman wear a cover-up over her bikini top when she's more than 25 yards from the beach.

ARTS
Dance

Gombey dancing, unique to Bermuda, has roots in West African tribal music and also incorporates influences from Christian missionaries, the British military and, most visibly, Native Americans.

A Gombey group traditionally consists of men and boys, referred to as a 'crowd.' The young boys are called 'warriors' and wear short capes and carry wooden tomahawks. Older boys are called 'Indians' and carry bows and arrows, and the head males, or 'chiefs,' wear long capes, carry whips and command the show. The capes of all the dancers are brightly colored and decorated with sequins, yarn fringe and trailing ribbons. Their tall headdresses are ornamented with glitter and peacock feathers. Long sleeves, gloves and masks cover dancers from head to toe.

Military influence can be found in the use of a fife, whistles and snare drums. To the uninitiated, the Gombey dancers may just look like wildly costumed characters acrobatically jumping to loud music, but in fact the dancing is choreographed to specific rhythms. Pantomimed segments often portray stories from the Bible, such as Daniel in the lion's den.

Gombey dancers traditionally take to the streets on Boxing Day and New Year's Day; when islanders hear the drums they pour out of their homes to watch the dances. These days, they are also frequent performers at festivals, including the City of Hamilton's Harbour Nights (p59), held each Wednesday in summer.

The Masterworks Foundation's website at www.masterworks .bm has information on the arts.

Painting & Sculpture

Bermuda's pastel houses and gentle landscapes have long inspired both local and international artists. Among the more renowned artists who painted in Bermuda are Americans Georgia O'Keeffe, whose best-known island works depict banana flowers and banyan trees; Winslow Homer, who painted numerous Bermudian seaside scenes; and Andrew Wyeth, whose work focused on the people of Bermuda. The island's two main galleries – the Bermuda National Gallery (p51) and the Masterworks Museum of Bermuda Art (p106) – both have works by these artists.

One of Bermuda's best-known contemporary watercolorists is the late, prolific Alfred Birdsey, whose art still fills galleries both on the island and abroad. Two other well-known local watercolorists are Jill Amos Raine and Carole Holding.

Bermuda's most highly regarded contemporary sculptor is Desmond Fountain, who casts graceful, life-size figures of female nudes and playing children in bronze. His sculptures can be seen at Hamilton's city hall.

Bermuda's Architectural Heritage, a series of beautifully illustrated volumes by the Bermuda National Trust, is the definitive look at the island's period buildings and the people responsible for them.

Architecture

One of the first things to strike visitors upon arriving in Bermuda is the charming uniformity of the homes on the island – quaint cottages painted in pastel hues with stepped white roofs.

Although it may seem that the houses were designed solely for their pleasing aesthetics, their unique qualities are a consequence of local conditions, both in terms of available building material and the island's reliance upon rainwater.

Architecture – Bermuda Style by David Raine provides a solid background to understanding the characteristics of Bermuda's unique style of building.

Houses are built of local limestone. The roofs are cleverly designed to gather rainwater and direct it via angled stone gutters into a catchment tank that provides the residents with drinking water. The bleached-white color of the roofs is the result of their being painted with a limestone wash that acts as a water purifier. The appearance of these bright, textured roofs has earned them the nickname 'cake icing.'

The simplicity of the homes, free as they are of exterior embellishments, is necessitated by the smooth limestone surfaces. Jalousied wooden window shutters provide the main ornamental feature. One decorative indulgence is the 'eyebrow,' an inverted letter V above the windows of some homes.

THE SHAKESPEARE CONNECTION

When the first English castaways washed up on Bermuda's shores in July 1609, they may well have set the stage for William Shakespeare's final work, *The Tempest*. Shakespeare is thought to have begun work on that play in 1610, after the first reports of the *Sea Venture*'s wreck in a tempestuous storm appeared in England.

It seems that Shakespeare, who knew several of the shareholders of the Virginia Company expedition, probably had a copy of the account entitled 'A Discovery of the Bermudas, otherwise called the Isle of Devils' at his disposal when he wrote the play. Although the plot of *The Tempest* is not set in Bermuda, the description of the storm and shipwreck bear a close resemblance to the events surrounding the ill-fated *Sea Venture*. Indeed, in Act 1, Scene II, Shakespeare appears to make a direct reference to the islands with a mention of the 'still-vex'd Bermoothes.'

Keep an eye out too for the moongate, a round limestone gate thought to be of Chinese origin, often found at the entrance to Bermuda gardens. Passing through the moongate is traditionally said to bring good luck.

Literature

Bermuda can claim ties to a number of significant 20th-century writers who either vacationed or lived on the island.

Peter Benchley, who has a second home in Bermuda and helped establish the Bermuda Underwater Exploration Institute (p63), wrote his first blockbuster, *Jaws*, while in Bermuda. He found a setting for a second novel, *The Deep*, while diving in Bermuda with treasure hunter Teddy Tucker, who became the inspiration for the novel's main character. Benchley also used Bermuda for the setting of his suspense novel *Beast*.

James Thurber (1894–1961), author and cartoonist for the *New Yorker* magazine, wrote the fairy tale *The 13 Clocks* and other stories during long stays on the island. He was a frequent contributor to *The Bermudian* magazine.

Nobel prize–winner Eugene O'Neill (1888–1953), who had a place in Warwick Parish, wrote a number of works while in Bermuda, including *Mourning Becomes Electra* and *Strange Interlude*.

Munro Leaf (1905–76), an author and illustrator of books for children, had a home in Somerset. He wrote *The Story of Ferdinand,* about a Spanish bull, while living in Bermuda in the 1930s.

Filmed and set in Bermuda, Peter Benchley's movie *The Deep* (1977), starring Jacqueline Bisset and Nick Nolte, has some great underwater photography and weaves a suspenseful tale about dangerous treasure pillaged from a sunken ship.

Environment

THE LAND

Sitting by itself in the isolated North Atlantic, Bermuda enjoys a wide berth from its neighbors. The nearest lies 570 miles away at Cape Hatteras, North Carolina. And even though many people unfamiliar with Bermuda often mistakenly connect it with the Caribbean, nearly a thousand miles of ocean separate Bermuda from its tropical Caribbean neighbors to the south.

Bermuda is closer geographically to chilly Nova Scotia than it is to the tropical Caribbean.

Bermuda is composed of a cluster of some 150 small islands, which collectively total just 21 sq miles in area. The eight largest islands – St George's Island, St David's Island, Bermuda Island (or the 'main island'), Somerset Island, Watford Island, Boaz Island, Ireland Island North and Ireland Island South – are connected by causeways and bridges so that they form a continuous fishhook-shaped land that stretches 22 miles in length. In contrast, its width averages less than a mile across, and at its widest it barely reaches two miles. Together these eight connected principal islands contain more than 95% of Bermuda's landmass.

It's an amazingly small place. No matter where you start from you could walk across the width of Bermuda in less than an hour and with an early start you could trek from one end of the island cluster to the other in a day.

Bermudians tend to treat the connected islands as a single geographic entity and commonly refer to Bermuda simply as 'the island.' Only about a dozen of Bermuda's other tiny islands are inhabited. Most of the uninhabited islands are little more than rocks, and some are so small that there's not a general agreement, even among government departments, as to the exact number of islands in the colony!

The island has one of the world's highest concentrations of limestone caves.

Formed about 100 million years ago by a now-extinct underwater volcano, the islands are the uppermost tips of a pyramid-shaped mountain mass whose base extends 12,000ft from the sea floor.

The islands have a limestone cap, which is composed of coral deposits and the bodies of billions of shell-bearing creatures that gradually built up around the edges of the submerged volcanic peaks. From a combination of accumulating deposits and lowering sea levels, the mountaintops eventually emerged as islands and gave rise to the fringing coral reefs that surround them. Over time the action of the surf has pounded the limestone shells and coral into grains of sand that have amassed in the numerous bays and coves along the shoreline, giving Bermuda a generous string of sandy beaches.

Bermuda has a mildly undulating terrain, with its highest point reaching just 259ft.

IN THE PINK

Bermuda's sand is made up of particles of coral, marine invertebrates and various shells, but it takes its distinctive light pink hue from the bodies of one particular sea creature, a member of the order *Foraminifera*. A marine protozoan abundant on Bermudian reefs, foraminifers have hard, tiny shells that wash up on shore after the animal within the shell dies. These pink shell fragments provide the dominant color in what would otherwise be a less-distinctive confetti of bleached white coral and ivory-colored calcium carbonate shells.

WILDLIFE

Because of its remoteness, Bermuda's land was only lightly colonized by animals. Its most abundant wildlife has always been creatures that fly and creatures that live in the sea.

Animals

Bermuda has no native land mammals. The endemic Bermuda rock lizard *(Eumeces longirostris)*, a brown skink, was the only nonmarine land animal in Bermuda prior to human contact. Critically endangered, it fares poorly in altered environments and is now largely restricted to remote coastal cliffs and uninhabited islands.

You will, however, see many colorful introduced lizards scurrying about. Most predominant are the Jamaican anole *(Anolis grahami)*, which puffs out a showy orange throat sac as a territorial warning; the Warwick lizard *(A. leachii)*, a foot-long lizard with golden eye rings; and the Somerset lizard *(A. roquet)*, identifiable by its black eye patches. Enjoy them and get as close as you like – all of the lizard species are harmless. And there are no snakes, poisonous or otherwise, in Bermuda.

Despite those loud nocturnal peeps, Bermudians are fond of their whistling tree frogs. There are two species: *Eleutherodactylus johnstonei*, which is about 1in long, and the slightly larger but less common *E. gossei*. Both are brown, live in trees close to the ground and were introduced to Bermuda near the end of the 19th century. The frogs create a musical chorus of loud, bell-like whistles that fill the night from April to November, as long as the night temperature is above 68°F. Because of their size and habitat you're unlikely to ever see one, but they are immortalized on earrings and trinkets sold in nearly every shop on the island.

The giant toad *(Bufo marinus)*, imported from Guyana in 1875 to control cockroaches, is more visible but unfortunately it's most often seen squashed flat on the road, hence its local nickname 'road toad.'

BIRDS

Land birds made an easy catch for the early English colonists and now only a single endemic species survives: chick of the village *(Vireo griseus)*, a subspecies of the white-eyed vireo. This small olive and yellowish bird that has spectaclelike circles around its eyes has shorter wings than its continental counterparts, having lost its need to fly long distances. The vireo can be spotted in parks and wooded areas.

Of the introduced species now common to Bermuda, the most conspicuous is the kiskadee *(Pitangus sulphuratus)*, a noisy yellow-breasted flycatcher often spotted on hotel grounds. The kiskadee was introduced from Trinidad in 1957 in hopes of bringing the lizard population down so that beetles introduced to prey on cedar-scale insects would have a better chance of getting established.

Other common land bird species include starlings, sparrows, European goldfinches, catbirds and mourning doves. Two other birds, the northern cardinal and the eastern bluebird, suffered declines with the loss of cedar habitat and increased competition from kiskadees, but are on the comeback thanks to conservation efforts.

Although Bermuda's resident species may be limited, the island hosts a great variety of migrant birds. The checklist of some 350 birds includes three dozen warblers, numerous shorebirds, and herons and ducks.

Although it's a migrant, many Bermudians consider the white-tailed tropicbird, known in Bermuda as the longtail, to be their national bird. The longtail's arrival is always a welcome harbinger of spring. They nest

The Bermuda Aquarium, Museum & Zoo's website at www.bamz.org has lots of information on island conservation issues.

The Bermuda Audubon Society's website at www.audubon.bm has loads of information on the island's nature reserves, best birding spots and the like.

in the cliffs around the island and can be seen gracefully swooping and gliding along the shore from March to October. In addition, sandhill cranes and a number of other exotic birds, such as the Pacific fairy tern, make the occasional visit.

In spring, storm petrels, jaegers, terns and four species of shearwaters pass by, often in flocks that number in the thousands. The peak of the spring seabird migration occurs in May and June.

Still, fall is the most varied time for sighting birds, with the migrations reaching their peak in October. At that point, most of the shorebirds and herons and some of the land birds, ducks and coots have arrived. Among the more interesting birds spotted during the fall migration are ospreys, ring-necked ducks, double-crested cormorants, eastern wood peewees, yellow-bellied sapsuckers, scarlet tanagers and rose-breasted grosbeaks.

MARINE LIFE

The waters surrounding Bermuda harbor an astonishing variety of marine life. Because Bermuda is so far north, it may amaze some visitors to find that many of the tropical fish common to the Caribbean can also be spotted in Bermuda. The waters radiate with scores of brilliant species including rainbow parrotfish, clown wrasses and elegant butterflyfish.

Bermuda enjoys the most northerly coral reefs in the world.

The key to all this marine life is Bermuda's coral formations, which grow in the clear shallow waters surrounding the islands. These are the northernmost corals found in the Atlantic and owe their existence to the warm ocean currents carried north by the Gulf Stream. In all, Bermuda has nearly 50 species of coral running the gamut from hard brain coral to wavering sea fans and other soft corals.

In addition to all those pretty fish, Bermuda's coral reefs also harbor menacing-looking creatures, including green moray eels that grow up to 10ft long. Although moray eels may provide a bit of a shock to snorkelers who suddenly come upon them, typically they are not aggressive, and the intimidating mouth-chomping motions they make are not meant for defense but are simply a breathing mechanism that pumps water across their gills. Three other species of eels are found in Bermuda's waters: the speckled moray, brown moray and conger eel.

Bermuda's waters also hold brittle stars, sea horses, sea spiders, sea cucumbers, sea hares, sea anemones, sea urchins, squid, conchs, slipper lobsters and spiny lobsters.

Bermuda's Marine Life by Wolfgang Sterrer, the former director of the Bermuda Biological Station for Research, is the authoritative tome on everything that wiggles in the sea. It has lots of dazzling color photos.

Red land crabs, active along the shoreline at night, make telltale burrows in dunes above the beach, particularly along the south shore. The females release their larvae into the ocean at least once each summer, often on nights following the full moon.

Humpback whales, migrating north from the Caribbean, can sometimes be seen off the south shore in March and April, and dolphins and porpoises are sometimes found in deeper waters as well. Green sea turtles, hawksbill turtles, loggerhead turtles and leatherback turtles are occasionally spotted near the reefs.

A great place to go for an introduction to Bermuda's marine life is the Bermuda Aquarium, Museum & Zoo (p90) in Flatts Village, where you'll find tanks identifying nearly 200 species of fish and coral.

ENDANGERED SPECIES

Hundreds of miles from the nearest landmass, Bermuda's flora and fauna evolved in an isolated environment with limited competition and few predators. Consequently, when the first human settlers arrived on the scene 400 years ago, they had a devastating impact.

Free-roaming pigs, believed to have been left by passing sailors in the 16th century, and rats, cats and dogs introduced by the first permanent settlers in the 17th century, spelled havoc for many species of endemic plants as well as ground-nesting birds. Other species met their demise through the direct action of humans.

One bird that offers a haunting testimony to species devastation is the Bermuda petrel, or cahow *(Pterodroma cahow)*. These quail-size seabirds were abundant when the first settlers landed, but they had no natural fear of people. Diego Ramirez, the Spanish captain who spent three weeks in Bermuda in 1603, noted that his men were able to make a ready catch of thousands of the plump little birds. When the English arrived six years later, they too developed an appetite for the cahow. The birds made such an easy take – indeed, they would even land on the colonists' arms – that they all but disappeared within a few decades.

Bermuda Petrel: The Bird That Would Not Die by Francine Jacobs gives a fascinating account of the comeback of the cahow, the bird that went unseen for centuries.

Biologists were astounded when after three centuries without sightings, the cahow, which was officially listed as extinct, was rediscovered in 1951. Subsequent research identified 20 nesting pairs of the birds on four small uninhabited Castle Harbour islets. Although environmentalists were initially encouraged, the islands were found to be a marginal habitat for the ground-nesting birds, as rats preyed upon their eggs and the soil was so eroded that it was no longer sufficient for digging nests in. The cahows had adapted by nesting in natural holes in the cliffs, but they had to compete for these nesting sites with the more aggressive longtails. Because the longtails nested later in the season, the cahows were sometimes forced to abandon their nests before they had a chance to rear their chicks.

To create more favorable odds for survival, special baffles were installed in the opening of the cahows' cliffside nesting holes, reducing the size of the entrance to prevent the larger longtails from entering. In addition, naturalists created artificial nesting burrows, hollowed into the islands' rocky surfaces and roofed with concrete, in the hopes of returning the cahows to ground-level burrows and reducing competition with the longtails. In conjunction with these efforts, rats and other predatory mammals were eradicated from the four islets where the cahows nest.

Bermuda lays claim to being one of the most isolated places in the world.

The cahow, which lays only a single egg each year, is making a slow, precarious comeback. There are currently an estimated 70 nesting pairs of cahows, and they are still one of the rarest kinds of seabirds in the world.

ROOTS OF THE BOTANICAL GARDEN

The rhizomes of the arrowroot plant *(Maranta arundinacea)* yield a nutritious, easily digestible starch that's an ideal thickener for gravies and puddings. In modern times, less-expensive cornstarch has largely replaced arrowroot in the kitchen, but in days past, arrowroot was a leading Bermudian export.

One of the largest arrowroot factories in Bermuda was built by Henry James Tucker, the mayor of Hamilton in the mid-19th century. Tucker lived in Camden (p107), a plantation house at the current Bermuda Botanical Gardens (p104), and the arrowroot factory, where the starch was soaked from the plants and dried in the sun, was built at the back of the house. The arrowroot starch he produced was prized in both England and America for its superior quality.

Although arrowroot starch is no longer produced in Bermuda, Tucker's arrowroot factory still stands, and has been renovated with its original works spruced up and part of the building turned into the Masterworks Museum of Bermuda Art (p106).

Plants

Bermuda, with its subtropical frost-free climate, is abloom with colorful flowers year-round. Since temperatures usually stay within the range of 50°F to 90°F, tropical plants imported from the West Indies thrive here, and so do many of the flowers found in temperate climates.

In all, about a thousand different flowering plants can be found in Bermuda. Some of the more common are bougainvillea, hibiscus, oleander, morning glory (called 'bluebell' in Bermuda), poinsettia, nasturtium, passion flower and bird-of-paradise. Old-style roses – including multiflora, tea and bourbon varieties – have remained popular since the 1700s and can be seen in gardens all around the island.

One of the few endemic flowers is the Bermudiana (*Sisyrinchium bermudiana*), a tiny blue-purple iris with a yellow center and grasslike leaves, which resembles the blue-eyed grass of North America. It blooms from mid-April to late May. Also keep an eye out for prickly pear cactus, which produces Bermuda's only native fruit and can be found near the seaside forts in St George's.

The endemic Bermuda cedar (*Juniperus bermudiana*) was the most predominant tree on the island until 1942, when a scale insect was accidentally introduced and an epidemic spread like wildfire. Within a decade, more than 95% of the island's cedar trees had succumbed to the blight.

Biological controls, including the release of insects that prey upon the scale insect, were introduced in an attempt to stop the devastation. Over time, those Bermuda cedars that did survive developed a resistance to the scale insect. Seeds from these healthy surviving trees have been intensely propagated in recent years as part of a community-wide campaign to bring the cedar back from near-extinction, and the trees once again dot the landscape throughout the island.

For a close-up view of Bermuda's varied flora, the Bermuda Botanical Gardens (p104) in Paget is a great place to start – there you'll find the widest variety of both native and introduced species.

NATIONAL PARKS

The island was a latecomer in developing a public park system and consequently there are no grand government-owned parks. But considering Bermuda's scarcity of open space, the government's done an admirable job since 1986, when legislation was enacted establishing a national parks system to protect, maintain and enhance the natural and historic character of environmentally sensitive areas.

Bermuda now has dozens of parks and nature reserves, collectively accounting for nearly 1000 acres. All together nearly 10% of Bermuda's land is set aside as parkland and nature reserves.

Although none of the parks are extensive, a handful of properties – most notably Spittal Pond Nature Reserve, the Bermuda Botanical Gardens and South Shore Park – are large enough to provide an hour or so of uninterrupted walking.

Bermuda has 2992 people per square mile, a population density more than three times greater than Japan's.

ENVIRONMENTAL ISSUES

Despite great strides forward in recent years, the island's environment is still troubled by past mistakes and present pressures. Bermuda is small with limited resources and a relatively high population density. Those conditions, along with the need to accommodate half a million visitors every year, inevitably cause stress on the environment.

In the waters surrounding Bermuda, overfishing practices have already decimated many reef-fish species, scallops and other edible marine life.

The Nassau grouper, for example, which was once the mainstay of the island fishing industry, has been fished to commercial extinction. Turtle hunting, still prevalent until the 1960s, was responsible for wiping out Bermuda's entire nesting green sea turtle population.

In the past few decades islanders have become keenly aware of environmental issues, and have taken many steps to turn the decline around, ranging from introducing natural history into the school curriculum to enacting strict regulations protecting marine life.

Bermuda's marine environment is now one of the most carefully safe-guarded in the world. The 1966 Coral Reef Preserves Act set up marine preserves that protect plants and fish in substantial tracts of Bermuda's reef waters. Subsequent marine protection orders have extended coverage to other environmentally sensitive areas by restricting fishing, spearfishing and the taking of lobsters.

Other programs to restore native fauna are also making headway. To the delight of bird-watchers, the yellow-crowned night heron has been successfully brought back and is now a common sight in marshy areas. The cahow, an endemic seabird once thought to be extinct, is on the comeback, and a concerted effort in setting up islandwide nesting boxes has once again made the eastern bluebird a part of the landscape.

In terms of environmental aesthetics, Bermuda has long been in the vanguard – it remains totally free of polluting heavy industry and does not allow billboards or neon signs. The use of public buses and ferries is encouraged, and the ownership of cars is strictly limited. Only one automobile is permitted per household – regardless of the number of drivers in the family! Bermudians have been known to concoct creative schemes to circumvent the spirit, if not the letter, of the law – such as dividing a home into two separate apartments – but that only stands as testimony to how effective the law actually is.

Although open space is at a premium, Bermuda nonetheless maintains a growing number of parks and nature reserves and is making efforts to restore some of the unpopulated islands, particularly Nonsuch Island, to their precolonial ecology.

The island's two most influential private preservation groups – the Bermuda National Trust and the Bermuda Audubon Society – have joined forces to buy up tracts of some of the most environmentally sensitive land on Bermuda. Two of their recent projects, in what's now dubbed the 'Buy Back Bermuda' campaign, have been the purchase and establishment of Warwick Pond and Paget Marsh nature reserves, preserving two of the finest birding areas on the island.

Island roads are so narrow that the Volkswagen Beetle is banned in Bermuda because its chassis is too wide.

Outdoor Activities

HIKING

Bermuda's numerous parks and nature reserves provide plenty of opportunities for short walks. The best hiking destinations are the areas with the greatest acreage, most notably Spittal Pond Nature Reserve (p95) in Smith's Parish and South Shore Park (p122) in Southampton and Warwick Parishes.

Railway Trail

In land-scarce Bermuda, the longest walking trails aren't found in government parks and nature reserves, but are along the now-buried tracks that once carried Bermuda's narrow-gauge railway. The railway, which began operations in 1931, never gained in popularity, and the last train was retired in 1947. After that, most of the track was simply abandoned, though a few sections were lost to modernization – most notably a 3-mile stretch around the City of Hamilton that was widened into roadway.

In 1984 the government, realizing what a unique opportunity they had, set aside the remaining sections of the old rail line for foot and bridle paths. In all, these encompass some 21 miles of trail, from Somerset Village at the West End of Bermuda to St George's at the East End.

The Railway Trail is not a single continuous route; there is a significant break between Paget and Devonshire Parishes, as well as shorter breaks here and there where hikers briefly have to walk along a vehicle road until the Railway Trail starts up again. Some sections are open only to hikers, bicyclists and horseback riders, but other parts are open to scooters as well.

The government publishes a nifty pocket-size booklet, *Bermuda East to West*, which details all seven sections of the trail, complete with maps and tidbits about nature and interesting historical points encountered along each section. The free booklet can be picked up at tourist offices in Bermuda.

The Railway Trail makes a traffic-safe route for joggers. Joggers should use caution when running in other areas, as many Bermudian roads are narrow, with heavy traffic, no sidewalks and the occasional blind curve.

If you want to take a good companion along on the trail, pick up a copy of *Hiking Bermuda* by Cecile and Stephen Davidson, which details 20 of the best nature walks and trails on the island.

Organized Walks

The **Rock Ramblers** (☎ 238-3438), a local eco-heritage group, meets for an interpretive walkabout on the first Sunday of each month. Visitors are

---

BERMUDA INTERNATIONAL RACE WEEKEND

The big running event of the year is the Bermuda International Race Weekend, held annually on the second weekend of January. It centers around the running of two races on the Sunday: the Bermuda International Marathon, a 13-mile looped route, run twice, that begins on Front St in Hamilton; and the Bermuda International Half-Marathon, held concurrently but covering only one loop of the course.

Activities begin Friday evening on Front St in Hamilton with children's competitions and a series of mile-long invitational races for elite runners and local celebrities. The evening is capped off with music by the Bermuda Regiment Band.

Saturday's event is the 10K Run & Charity Walk, a 10km race and a concurrent noncompetitive walk along the north shore starting at the National Sports Centre in Devonshire.

Entry fees are $40 for the marathon and a bit less for the other events. Information and an entry form can be obtained from the **Bermuda Marathon Committee** (www.bermudatracknfield.com).

welcome and it's a great way to meet islanders and learn more about Bermuda's ecology and culture. There's no charge, though donations are appreciated and go to help environmental causes. Locations change; look for the schedule in the 'Calendar' section of the *Royal Gazette*.

Tim Rogers of **Bermuda Lectures and Tours** (☎ 234-4082; adult/child $15/10) leads informative walking tours at various locations around the island. The tours, which focus on architecture and history, typically begin at 10am, last 1½ hours and cover about 2 miles. Private tours can also be arranged with Tim Rogers.

BIRDWATCHING

Bermuda can be a delight for birders, though timing is key. With just 22 species of resident birds nesting in Bermuda, the peak birdwatching seasons are during the spring and fall migrations. During those periods more than 200 species of migratory birds wing their way to Bermuda, including numerous species of warblers, herons, sandpipers, stilts and seabirds.

One of the finest all-around birdwatching sites is Spittal Pond (p95), Bermuda's largest nature reserve. Paget Marsh (p106) offers unsurpassed opportunities to see herons up close. With its wooded margins and vast mud flats, Warwick Pond Nature Reserve (p113) is the ideal place to spot both woodland birds and waders. Somerset Long Bay Nature Reserve (p132) is another prime locale for sighting shorebirds and ducks.

A Checklist and Guide to the Birds of Bermuda, by David B Wingate, has species descriptions and charts on the seasonal distribution and abundance of birds.

For more information on birdlife in Bermuda, see p29.

The best book on the market for birders is *A Birdwatching Guide to Bermuda,* by Andrew Dobson, which has more than 2000 photos and lots of details on where and when to see each species.

TENNIS

Bermuda has scores of tennis courts, some at hotels and available only to their guests, and others open to the general public. If you plan to play much tennis, you might want to bring your own equipment; however, most places that have tennis courts also rent racquets and sell tennis balls. Lessons are available at many resort facilities. On all courts in Bermuda, proper tennis attire is preferred (tennis shoes and whites), and on some it is mandatory.

Fees are typically charged on a per-hour, per-person basis, ranging from $8 to $12.

Tennis courts open to the public can be found at WER Joell Tennis Stadium (p66) in Pembroke Parish, north of the City of Hamilton; Grotto Bay Beach Hotel (p89) in Hamilton Parish; Elbow Beach Hotel and Horizons & Cottages in Paget (p108); Port Royal Tennis Club and the Fairmont Southampton hotel, both in Southampton (p124); and Willowbank Hotel (p133) in Sandys.

The private **Coral Beach & Tennis Club** (☎ 236-2233) in Paget, which has clay courts and is considered the island's top tennis facility, is open only to members or by introduction from a member.

TENNIS, ANYONE?

The game of tennis, which originated in England in 1872, was played for the first time in the Western Hemisphere in 1873 at the Bermuda home of Sir Brownlow Gray, the island's chief justice.

Mary Outerbridge, a guest at the Gray home, was so enthralled by the game that she carried a pair of racquets with her on a trip from Bermuda to New York. She is credited with introducing tennis to the USA, in 1874.

Schedules and information on tennis tournaments are available from the **Bermuda Lawn Tennis Association** (☎ 296-0834; www.blta.bm).

GOLF

With scenic ocean vistas on nearly every green, golfing just doesn't get much better than this. In all, Bermuda has eight golf courses, each with its own distinct character.

Of course, each is still thoroughly Bermudian, so you'll need to maintain a certain air of propriety. All of the courses require 'proper golf attire,' which means shirts must have collars and shorts must be Bermuda-shorts length (to the knees); jeans, cutoff pants and sleeveless shirts are not allowed. So sharpen up and look your natty best!

Five of Bermuda's courses are public and three are private. What are they like? The Fairmont Southampton Golf Club (p123) has short fairways with heavily bunkered greens that require skillful iron work, rather than sheer power. Pick a day with calm weather, though, because the winds can get blustery on this hillside resort course. The nearby Belmont Hills Golf Club (p115), completely redesigned in 2003, offers a challenging run for the money with slender fairways, blind second shots and multi-tiered greens.

The Ocean View Golf Course (p101), the closest course to the City of Hamilton, is a local favorite, especially with city folks taking a workday break to sneak in a quick round. The tamest of all Bermuda's greens, it's only nine holes but can be played as 18. Ocean View is a government-run course, as are two beautiful Robert Trent Jones–designed courses: Port Royal Golf Course (p123) in Southampton, on the western end of the island, and St George's Golf Club (p76), on the eastern end. Port Royal is a jewel with stunning views, challenging tees and cliff-side holes that help rank it among the best public golf courses in the world. St George's, one of the few golf courses anywhere that can boast being within the boundaries of a World Heritage site, offers panoramic views of old Fort St Catherine and the turquoise seas beyond.

Bermuda's three other courses are private members clubs with restricted access to nonmembers. Riddell's Bay Golf & Country Club (p115), Bermuda's oldest course (1922), sits on its own narrow peninsula with breathtaking views and tight fairways that demand a sharp eye and a steady swing. It has some set times each week when nonmembers are allowed to play.

Bermuda's newest championship course, Tucker's Point Golf Club (p85), allows nonmembers to make reservations within 48 hours of their desired tee time on a space-available basis. It features greens with Tiff Eagle Bermuda grass, challenging contours and enough hazards to keep it interesting for the most skillful of golfers.

Bermuda's top-ranked course, the Mid Ocean Golf Club (p85), is also the most exclusive and the most difficult to get onto. Still, hotel concierges can sometimes make arrangements (being famous would help), so you may get lucky and get your chance to play a round behind Ross Perot.

Tee-time reservations for the government-run courses – Ocean View, Port Royal and St George's – can be arranged through an automated reservation system (☎ 234-4653) up to a year in advance. Reservations for the other courses are made directly.

Lessons are available at all courses, with the cost varying from $40 to $55 per half-hour. Bring a good supply of golf balls, but if you run short, they can be purchased at the courses for $40 to $60 a dozen.

Bermuda has more golf courses, per square mile, than anywhere else in the world.

Full-set club rentals cost from $25 to $40; left-handed and right-handed sets for both men and women are available at all courses. If you're thinking about bringing your own clubs to Bermuda, keep in mind this isn't a place where you can rent a car and toss them in the back, and they won't fit on scooters or buses, so you'll need to plan for a taxi between the golf courses and your hotel.

Golf tournaments, generally held from September to June, are open to both islanders and visiting golfers and are listed on p144. For more information, contact the **Bermuda Golf Association** (☎ 295-9972; www.bermudagolf.org).

HORSEBACK RIDING

For a different way to see the more remote south shore beaches, consider a horseback ride. The best time is in the early morning, before any beachgoers have arrived, as there's an almost meditative serenity along the trail.

You can't hire a horse to go off on your own in Bermuda, but Spicelands Riding Centre (p115) in Warwick offers guided rides along the scenic trails in South Shore Park.

BEACHES & SWIMMING

Bermuda abounds in beautiful pink-sand beaches. Matter of fact, there are so many of them that most high-end hotels have their own little private strand just for their guests. But fret not, there are more than enough public beaches to keep any beachgoer enthralled.

Beaches can be found all around the island but the finest run is unquestionably at South Shore Park, a 1.5-mile-long coastal park that encompasses a string of secluded coves sandwiched between two glorious bookend beaches. Its eastern boundary begins in Warwick Parish with the expansive Warwick Long Bay (p113), a half-mile-long unbroken stretch of pink sand, and the western boundary runs just beyond picturesque Horseshoe Bay (p120) in Southampton Parish. The coastal South Shore Park Trail (p122) links the beaches, making exploring fun and easy. No matter where you're staying in Bermuda, consider including an outing here in your plans.

Other notable beaches include Elbow Beach (p106) in Paget Parish, a beautiful mile-long strand that's a favorite with beachgoers from the City of Hamilton; John Smith's Bay (p96) in Smith's Parish, which often has calm waters when westerly winds kick up the surf elsewhere around the island; and Shelly Bay Beach (p87) in Hamilton Parish, which is a favorite with families because of its shallow waters and playground facilities.

In the tourist season, lifeguards are stationed at Horseshoe Bay in Southampton Parish and John Smith's Bay in Smith's Parish.

No beaches in Bermuda – even the secluded ones – allow nude or seminude sunbathing.

DIVING

Everyone knows Bermuda abounds with shipwrecks but many people are surprised to discover the waters here also harbor splendid coral. Despite its islands' northerly location, the combination of shallow water and warm ocean currents support a thriving reef system. Bermuda boasts 24 species of hard coral, including brain coral and tree coral, and another two dozen species of soft coral, including wavering sea fans and sea whips.

Although hundreds of miles of cool water separate Bermuda from the Caribbean, many species of tropical fish common to the Caribbean can also be found feeding among the corals in Bermuda. Some of the more

Be aware that the stinging Portuguese man-of-war (p143) is sometimes found in Bermuda's waters from March to July.

As a rule, Bermudians take their first swim of the year on Bermuda Day, May 24.

colorful fish you can expect to see include the clown wrasse, queen angelfish, rainbow parrotfish, spotted puffer, foureye butterflyfish, blue tang, orange spotted filefish and green moray eel.

There are five dive operations in Bermuda: Blue Water Divers (p107) at the Elbow Beach Hotel and at Robinson's Marina (p132); Fantasea Bermuda (p53) in the City of Hamilton and at Wyndham Bermuda Resort (p123); Triangle Diving (p89) at the Grotto Bay Beach Hotel; Dive Bermuda (p123) at the Fairmont Southampton; and Deep Blue Dive (p66) in Pembroke Parish. All are good reputable operations, and three of them – Fantasea, Dive Bermuda and Blue Water Divers – have been awarded the PADI 5-star rating.

Although dive shops operate year-round, the most popular season is from May to October, when the water temperatures are a comfortable 75°F to 86°F. From November to April, water temperatures range from 65°F to 71°F and full wet suits are de rigueur. Although the water is chilly, one plus of winter diving is the excellent visibility, reaching up to 200ft, compared with about 100ft in the warmer summer months.

Most dive operations take a break in winter (generally two to four weeks in January or February), when things are slower. Because these breaks vary by operation and year, it's a good idea to make reservations well in advance if you're planning to dive in the winter.

Wreck Dives

Bermuda is a wreck diver's dream, its treacherous reefs scattered with three centuries of shipwrecks. Because the reefs are relatively shallow, many wreck dives are suitable for both novice and intermediate-level divers. And since most wrecks are on the reef, a wreck dive in Bermuda typically doubles as a reef dive. Keep in mind that you should never dive inside a shipwreck unless you have specialized training and are under the supervision of a qualified wreck- and antiquity-diving expert.

The *Constellation,* a four-masted schooner that provided the inspiration for the *Goliath* in Peter Benchley's novel *The Deep,* is a favorite among wreck divers. The ship, which is now widely scattered along the ocean floor at a depth of only 30ft, was en route from New York to Venezuela when it diverted to Bermuda for mechanical repairs in 1943. On the approach to the island, just 7 miles northwest of the Royal Naval Dockyard, a current carried the 192ft schooner into the reef, where – laden with a cargo of cement – it sank into a watery grave.

In shallow water, less than 20yd from the *Constellation,* sits the wreck of the *Nola,* also referred to in Bermuda as the *Montana,* one of its aliases. The 236ft paddle steamer was built in England to serve as a blockade-runner during the US Civil War. Launched in 1863, it made it only as far as Bermuda, where it sank on the reef during its maiden voyage to the Confederate South. Some sections of the ship, including the paddle wheels, remain intact and are readily visible even from a glass-bottom boat.

The *Cristobal Colon,* a 500ft Spanish luxury liner that went aground in 1936, is the largest ship ever to wreck in Bermudian waters. Because the cruise ship grounded on the reef, rather than sinking, it was an easy target for pilferers. Although the authorities salvaged items during the day, scores of other islanders came aboard after nightfall and made off with everything from chandeliers to plumbing fixtures.

In 1937 the 250ft Norwegian cargo ship *Aristo* sighted the still-intact *Cristobal Colon* in a position that made it appear to be sailing straight up through the reef, and the captain set his course to follow. By the time he recognized his error, the *Aristo* had a lethal gash in its hull.

One of the most valuable artifacts ever recovered from a Spanish galleon, a gold cross studded with emeralds, was found off Bermuda in 1955 but stolen 20 years later just before Queen Elizabeth II arrived to inaugurate the museum it was to be displayed in.

CONSIDERATIONS FOR RESPONSIBLE DIVING

Dive sites tend to be located where the reefs display the most beautiful corals and sponges. It takes only a moment – an inadvertently placed hand or knee, or a careless brush or kick with a fin – to destroy this fragile, living part of our delicate ecosystem. You can help preserve the ecology and beauty of the reefs by following certain basic guidelines while diving:

- Never drop boat anchors onto a coral reef, and take care not to ground boats on coral.
- Respect the integrity of shipwrecks, which are marine archaeological sites that are protected from looting by law.
- Practice and maintain proper buoyancy control, and avoid over-weighting. Be aware that buoyancy can change over the period of an extended trip, and adjust your weight as required. Use your weight belt and tank position to maintain a horizontal position.
- Avoid touching living marine organisms with your body and equipment. Coral polyps can be damaged by even the gentlest contact. Never stand on or touch living coral. If you must hold on to the reef, touch only exposed rock or dead coral.
- Take great care in underwater caves. Spend as little time within them as possible, as your air bubbles can damage fragile organisms. Divers should take turns inspecting the interiors of small caves or under ledges to lessen the chances of damaging contact.
- Be conscious of your fins. Even without contact, the surge from heavy fin strokes near the reef can do damage. When treading water in shallow reef areas, take care not to kick up clouds of sand, which can easily smother the delicate reef organisms.
- Secure gauges, computer consoles and the octopus regulator so they're not dangling – they are like miniature wrecking balls to a reef.
- Resist the temptation to collect or buy coral or shells. Aside from the ecological damage, taking home marine souvenirs depletes the beauty of a site and spoils other divers' enjoyment.
- Ensure that you take home all your trash and any litter you may find as well. Plastics in particular pose a serious threat to marine life.
- Resist the temptation to feed fish. You may disturb their normal eating habits, encourage aggressive behavior or feed them food that is detrimental to their health.
- Minimize your disturbance of marine animals. Don't ride on the backs of turtles, as this can cause them great anxiety.

During WWII the US military used the *Cristobal Colon* as a target ship, literally blowing the vessel in two, with one half settling on either side of the reef. The *Aristo*, on the other hand, stands intact, its forward deck still holding a fire truck and other cargo that it was carrying to Bermuda. Both boats sit in about 50ft of water.

In the same general area is the *Taunton*, a 228ft freighter that sank, weighed down with a load of American coal, as it arrived in Bermuda in 1920. Just 20ft beneath the surface, it's a good wreck dive for novices.

One of the newest and most intact of the shipwrecks is the *Hermes*, a 165ft freighter that was built during WWII. In the early 1980s, after the *Hermes* was abandoned in Bermuda, the government decided to scuttle the boat and turn it into a dive site. First they stripped the hatches and other potential hazards so that it could be used safely for penetration dives, and then they towed it out to sea. The boat sits upright in 80ft of water about a mile south of Warwick Long Bay.

Helmet Diving

Find diving a bit daunting but still dream of walking along the ocean floor? Then you're in the right place. Bermuda's helmet dive operations provide visitors the chance to jump below the surface of the water without mastering any diving skills. In fact, you don't even have to know how to swim and children as young as five years can join.

Participants don a headpiece, called a helmet, that has a clear face plate and works on a similar premise to a glass held upside-down in water. The helmet rests atop one's shoulders and is connected to a hose that pumps in fresh air from the boat above. The 'dive,' which lasts about 30 minutes, occurs at the sandy edge of the reef in about 10ft of water, allowing fish to be viewed up close.

Up to 30 people can go out with the boat, but generally only six people go underwater at any one time. The entire outing lasts about 3½ hours. There's a shower on the boat, and wet suits are provided when the water temperature drops below 80°F.

Two companies in Bermuda, one on either end of the island, offer helmet diving daily from April to November.

Greg Hartley's Under Sea Adventure (p132) departs from Sandys Parish and has the advantage of going a bit further offshore, where the water tends to be clearer. Bermuda Bell Diving (p92) departs from Flatts Inlet in Smith's Parish.

SNORKELING

Snorkeling, like swimming and diving, is far more popular in the summer months, when the waters are at their warmest.

For excellent snorkeling right from the beach, head to Church Bay (p122) in Southampton Parish or Tobacco Bay (p81) in St George's Parish, near of the Town of St George. A bit less spectacular but very convenient is the Bermuda Snorkel Park (p137) at the Royal Naval Dockyard. Snorkel sets can be rented beachside at all three of these locations as well as at dive shops and resort beach huts.

There are many other beaches where you'll find coastal outcrops that harbor colorful fish – essentially any rocky shoreline in calm waters is a potential snorkeling site.

Still, the very best and most pristine snorkeling spots are too far offshore to be reached without a boat. So if you really want a dazzling underwater experience take a snorkeling cruise. Another plus is that snorkel cruises typically include a visit to a shipwreck – an easy task, since most of Bermuda's many wrecks crashed along coral reefs.

Although dive companies will take snorkelers along to snorkel above the reefs while the divers are beneath the surface, you're better off taking a cruise designed specifically for snorkelers. These head to shallow reefs where you can easily view the fish from the surface, rather than peering down at coral through 20ft to 40ft of water, which commonly happens when you go out with divers.

Most of the snorkeling cruises are combination sightseeing tours; some use glass-bottom boats. All include complimentary use of snorkeling equipment and a bit of instruction for first-time snorkelers.

The main snorkeling season is from May to October. Some tours begin as early as April and continue into November, but they only operate if they have enough customers to make it worthwhile – so the farther from summer, the fewer the outings offered. It's best to make reservations at least a day in advance to secure your place during busy times and to let operators know they have customers during slow periods.

Snorkeling cruises generally last 3½ to four hours. However, if you're going along primarily for the snorkeling, it's a good idea to ask how long will be spent in the water, as this can vary among tour companies.

FISHING

If you're a fisher, Bermuda offers year-round action but conditions are generally best from May through November.

Game fish found in deeper waters include Atlantic blue marlin, white marlin, blackfin tuna, yellowfin tuna, skipjack tuna, dolphinfish (not the marine mammal), wahoo, great barracuda, almaco jack and rainbow runner.

In the interest of Bermuda's conservation efforts, sport fishers are encouraged to tag and release game fish, particularly marlin and other billfish, unless they're being taken for food.

Boat charters are available for deep-sea fishing by either the half-day or full day. Rates vary according to the size of the boat, trip location, number of people on board etc. To charter the whole boat, expect to pay about $700 for a half-day, $1000 for a full day. Individuals who join up with a group typically pay $100 for a half-day, $150 for a full day. Prices include all fishing equipment; lunch and beverages are not included. Charter boats can be booked through **Bermuda Sports Fishing Association** (☎ 295-2370) or **St George Game Fishing & Cruising Association** (☎ 297-8093).

Those who want to try their luck at fishing from shore can rent rods, reels and tackle from Windjammer Watersports (p137) and Somerset Bridge Water Sports (p133), both in Sandys Parish. No licenses or fees are required to fish from shore; catches can typically include gray snapper, great barracuda, bonefish and pompano.

The highly prized marlin, a spectacular fighting fish with a long swordlike bill, is most prevalent from June through August.

KAYAKING

This is the perfect way to break away from the beach scene and see Bermuda's varied coastline from a whole new angle. You can paddle along peaceful mangrove-lined shorelines, visit nearshore islands or make your own outing. Most places that rent kayaks have singles and also doubles in case you want to make it a romantic outing with your sweetheart.

Singles typically cost $15 to $20 an hour and doubles $20 to $30 an hour, but you can often get steep discounts for longer rental periods; for instance, a four-hour rental typically costs just a bit more than double a one-hour rental. Kayaks can be rented at various seaside locales around the island and in most cases you can just hop in and paddle away.

Among the kayak rental operations are Fantasea Bermuda (p53) in the City of Hamilton and at the Wyndham Bermuda Resort (p123); Blue Hole Water Sports (p89) at Grotto Bay Beach Hotel; Blue Water Watersports (p107) at the Elbow Beach Hotel; Somerset Bridge Water Sports (p133) at Robinson's Marina; Pompano Beach Club Watersports Center (p123) in Southampton; Windjammer Watersports (p137) at the Royal Naval Dockyard; and the Bermuda Snorkel Park (p137), also at the Royal Naval Dockyard.

And if you don't want to set off on your own, you can join a kayak tour. Three companies offer three distinct tours and each one of them begins with a quick lesson in kayaking skills, so they're open to novices and experienced paddlers alike. Fantasea Bermuda offers an eco-oriented tour that visits remote areas and unpopulated islands. Blue Water Watersports provides a kayak tour that includes snorkeling over a reef and shipwrecks. Kayak Bermuda (p77) in the Town of St George paddles past small islands and makes time for swimming and sunbathing on the beach.

Although no one is likely to rent you one, a quirky local favorite is the Bermuda dinghy, a 14ft sailboat handcrafted of Bermuda cedar, driven by oversized sails and infamous for its tendency to capsize.

SAILING

If you know how to handle a small sailboat and want to head off on your own, there are several options. Rentals are available at Blue Hole Water

Sports (p89) at Grotto Bay Beach Hotel in Hamilton Parish; Blue Water Watersports (p107) at the Elbow Beach Hotel and at Rance's Boatyard (p107), both in Paget; Pompano Beach Club Watersports Centre (p123) in Southampton; and Windjammer Watersports (p137) at the Royal Naval Dockyard.

SIGHTSEEING CRUISES

If you've only seen Bermuda from land, you've only seen half of what it has to offer. Take a cruise to get a whole new angle on its beautiful coastline. Opt for a cruise boat that has a glass bottom and you'll be able to view coral and fish – even shallow shipwrecks. A variety of trips depart from the City of Hamilton (p53) and the Town of St George (p77).

Food & Drink

Bermuda being surrounded by water, it's no surprise that the lion's share of its cuisine revolves around seafood. Whether it's diced into traditional fare, grilled with a daub of fruit salsa or sliced into sashimi – expect to see plenty of fish.

STAPLES & SPECIALTIES

Don't leave the island without trying Bermuda fish chowder, a tangy red concoction made with fresh fish, typically rockfish or snapper, and flavored with local black rum and sherry peppers sauce. Don't be surprised if you see an eye staring back at you as you dig your spoon into the bowl, since the traditional way to cook chowder includes the heads.

The most common side dish served with Bermudian-style meals is peas 'n' rice. Portuguese immigrants introduced Portuguese bean soup to Bermuda in the mid-19th century and this steamy treat of spicy *liguicia* and red beans has been a staple ever since. Other popular everyday foods include johnnycakes, which are cornmeal griddle cakes, and codfish cakes, a savory grilled patty made of mashed codfish, potatoes and a pinch of curry. You can order codfish cakes on their own, but the most popular way to enjoy them is in a bun as a quick lunchtime sandwich.

Bermudians also love thick slabs of fresh fish. Fish sandwiches, made of fried fish fillets, are as popular here as hamburgers are elsewhere.

The most traditional meal is the Sunday codfish breakfast, a huge affair to linger over, which consists of codfish, eggs, boiled Irish potatoes, bananas and avocado, with a sauce of onions and tomatoes. Although it's most commonly served up in homes, there are a handful of local restaurants that offer this meal as well.

DRINKS
Nonalcoholic Drinks

As might be expected with their English heritage, a lot of Bermudians fancy a cup of tea, especially as a midafternoon break served with finger sandwiches and pastries. If you're a coffee drinker, fret not, as coffee is readily available as well.

Ginger beer is a distinctively Bermudian carbonated soft drink brewed right on the island. Don't confuse it with the pale ginger ale found elsewhere – this is a tangy, full-bodied ginger drink with a kick.

Bottled water, both generic spring water and the carbonated variety, is readily available at grocery stores throughout the island.

Alcoholic Drinks

Gosling Brothers, one of Bermuda's oldest companies, has been blending spirits on the island since the 1860s. Their cornerstone product is Gosling's

Everyone's favorite cookbook is *Bermudian Cookery*, by the Bermuda Junior Service League, which has recipes for a wide variety of tasty local dishes.

Island-caught lobsters are available in Bermudian restaurants from September to March only – order a lobster at any other time and it's flown in from Maine.

TRAVEL YOUR TASTEBUDS

Bermuda has a couple of unique dishes. Its shark hash, which makes its way onto island menus, is made of chopped-up shark bits mixed with potatoes and pan fried. Less common these days but big in colonial times was rockfish maw, made from the stomach of a rockfish stuffed with spicy pork and vegetables. For a refreshing light drink, try shandy, a mixture of nonalcoholic Bermuda ginger beer and alcoholic lager beer that can be ordered in any pub.

Black Seal Rum, a dark rum which, until World War I, was sold from the barrel using recycled wine bottles, the cork sealed with black wax – hence the name. If you pick up a bottle of Black Seal, take note that these days it comes in standard 80 proof as well as a fire-breathing 151 proof.

If you really want to tingle your tastebuds, order up a dark 'n' stormy, a two-to-one mix of carbonated ginger beer with Black Seal Rum – it's so popular among locals it's sometimes dubbed Bermuda's national drink.

Black Seal Rum is also the main ingredient in Bermuda's famous rum swizzle, which is far and away the favored drink of island visitors.

Go to www.blackseal.com to find tantalizing recipes with island flavor.

Gosling produces three liqueurs as well: Bermuda Gold, Bermuda Banana Liqueur and Bermuda Coconut Rum. The one that gets the most attention is Bermuda Gold, which is made from loquats and comparable to an apricot brandy. It's commonly served straight on ice, with a twist of lemon (called a shipwreck) or with orange juice (a royal blossom).

CELEBRATIONS

On Good Friday virtually every family sits down to a breakfast of codfish cakes accompanied by sticky-sweet hot cross buns.

For traditional Christmas fare there's cassava pie, made with a cake-like batter that contains the grated root of the cassava plant, stuffed with a meat filling and baked. The cassava bears special significance to Bermudians, as it's credited with having helped the early settlers get through periods of famine.

WHERE TO EAT & DRINK

Bermuda is a diner's delight. At the more moderate end, there are simple eateries dishing out good local food and places with full menus of English pub-grub fare spiced up with Bermudian specialties like fish chowder. Of course, Bermuda has excellent fine-dining options, ranging from waterview seafood restaurants to classic jacket-and-tie establishments in historic settings. And naturally there are all sorts of international foods as well – you're never far from an Italian restaurant in Bermuda, and Japanese sushi made from fresh local fish is all the rage.

With the exception of a sole KFC in the City of Hamilton, there are no fast-food-chain eateries anywhere in Bermuda.

If you're looking to mingle with the locals over solid Bermudian fare, veer away from hotel restaurants as well as those areas smack in line with the cruise ship gangplanks. Look instead for backstreet holes-in-the-wall and stand-alone diners where working-class folks pile in at lunch. Try such favorites as the Spot (p56) or Dorothy's Coffee Shop (p58) in the City of Hamilton, Angeline's Coffee Shop (p78) in the Town of St George, Monty's Restaurant (p68) in Pembroke, Island Cuisine (p125) in Southampton and New Traditions (p133) in Sandys.

VEGETARIANS & VEGANS

Bermuda has no purely vegetarian restaurants, but the island shouldn't prove too difficult for vegetarians, as there are plenty of cafés serving

---

BERMUDA RUM SWIZZLE

Although every Bermudian bartender has his or her own twist, the basic rum swizzle starts out like this: mix 4oz of dark rum with 3oz of pineapple juice, 3oz of orange juice, 1oz of grenadine or other sugar syrup, the juice from one fresh lemon and a couple of dashes of Angostura bitters. Put it all in a container with crushed ice, shake it until there's a head, pour into a pair of tall glasses and garnish them with slivers of orange. If you prefer, you can substitute a lime for the lemon.

BERMUDA'S TOP FIVE

- **Black Horse Tavern** (p84; St David's Island) Superb local seafood, super local ambience
- **Hog Penny** (p56; City of Hamilton) Traditional pub setting, great Bermuda fish chowder
- **Aggie's Garden** (p68; Pembroke Parish) Cozy café serving homemade, organic, island-grown food
- **Fourways Inn** (p110; Paget Parish) Manor house setting; creative food and service to match
- **Cafe Gio** (p77; Town of St George) Excellent fusion cuisine with a water view

---

good salads, and many restaurants have vegetarian options among their main courses.

Vegetarians won't go wrong heading to Aggie's Garden (p68) in Pembroke or Paradiso Cafe (p57) in the City of Hamilton. Supermarkets for self-catering are found all around the island and most have delis with some vegetarian offerings; especially notable are the Marketplace (p58) in the City of Hamilton and Miles Market (p68) in Pembroke, both of which have outstanding takeout buffets where you can pile your plate high with fresh salads and hot veggie dishes.

HABITS & CUSTOMS

Bermuda is very Western in its eating customs, with three meals a day. Meal times are similar to those in the USA, with the evening meal being the largest. The usual restaurant tip is 15%, which most restaurants automatically add to the bill – if not, add the tip yourself.

When it comes to fine dining, Bermuda remains somewhat traditional – not to the degree it used to be, but a few top-end restaurants still require a jacket and tie at dinnertime for men. Smoking is not banned from most of Bermuda's restaurants, but more and more eateries have set aside non-smoking sections and a few have gone totally smoke-free.

In *Tastes of Bermuda*, food writer Ed Bottone shares some of his favorite dishes and gives you the scoop on what's cookin' in local restaurants.

City of Hamilton

CONTENTS

HIGHLIGHTS

- Savor a bowl of fish chowder with rum at the classic **Hog Penny** Pub (p56)
- Explore hilltop **Fort Hamilton** (p52) with its winding dungeons and garden-filled moat
- Soak up some local history at the superb little **Bermuda Historical Society Museum** (p51)

Fort Hamilton ★

Bermuda Historical Society Museum ★

★ Hog Penny Pub

■ POPULATION: 987   ■ AREA: 0.5 SQ MILES

Virtually everything in Bermuda revolves around the City of Hamilton. Whether you're talking politics, commerce or geography, Hamilton is the hub of it all. This is where people head to attend to business, do some serious shopping or spend a night on the town.

Hamilton manages to look quaint and traditional on the one hand and bustling and cosmopolitan on the other. You can casually linger over a rum swizzle at a century-old waterfront restaurant while international business executives power lunch at the next table; order yourself local rockfish with peas or opt for the sushi; take a horse-and-carriage ride along the mansion-lined waterfront; or hop on a scooter and get tied up in rush-hour traffic.

Hamilton's pulse is Front St, a harborfront road lined with pastel-colored Victorian buildings in bright lemon, lime, apricot and sky blue. Many of them have overhanging verandas, where you can wine and dine as you watch the boats ferry across the harbor.

In addition to laying claim to the main government offices, and the handsome buildings that house them, Hamilton has a handful of other interesting sightseeing spots. But perhaps more than anything, it's the plethora of restaurants that attracts visitors to the city. Fully half of all of Bermuda's eateries are in the City of Hamilton and the choices run the gamut from delightful little cafés to impeccable fine-dining restaurants.

Because Hamilton serves as a central terminus and transfer point for island buses, you will visit it frequently if you use the public bus system. Note that Hamilton is commonly called 'town' by Bermudians, so 'going to town' means, without a doubt, going to Hamilton.

HISTORY

The city is named for Sir Henry Hamilton, the Bermuda governor (1788–94) who advocated for the building of a town in the central part of Bermuda in order to have a settlement convenient to all islanders. The new town adopted the motto *Hamilton Sparsa Collegit* ('Hamilton has brought together the scattered'), which can still be seen scrolled across the town's coat of arms.

In 1790 the grand design of Hamilton was laid out, with 50ft-wide streets in a neat grid pattern that covered an area of about 150 acres and spread north half a dozen blocks from a new commercial harbor. By 1795 the town had taken shape and the first municipal elections were held in the new town hall.

The idea of a central town caught on like wildfire. Hamilton prospered and grew so quickly that in just two decades enough people had migrated there to make Hamilton the biggest town in Bermuda. Political power swung in this direction as well, and in 1815 the capital was relocated from the Town of St George to Hamilton. In 1897 Hamilton's status was changed from that of a town to a city. To this day it remains Bermuda's one and only city.

Although hardly more than 1000 people live in the narrow boundaries of the city itself, nearly a quarter of the island's population lives within 2 miles of the city.

ORIENTATION

Hamilton is an easy town to explore. The center of activity is along Front St, where you'll find the lion's share of restaurants and shops, as well as the tourist office and the ferry and cruise ship terminals. Most anything of interest that isn't along Front St is within the first three blocks inland of it. The public bus terminal is along Washington St at the east side of City Hall.

Maps

The Bermuda Department of Tourism's free *Bermuda Handy Reference Map* has an inset

CITY OF HAMILTON

A   **B**   **C**   **D**

INFORMATION
Bank of Bermuda	**1** E3
Bank of Bermuda	**2** B5
Bermuda Book Store	**3** B5
Bermuda Public Library	**4** B4
Bookmart	**5** B4
Cable & Wireless	**6** C3
General Post Office	**7** D3
Immigration Headquarters	**8** D4
Internet Lane	**9** C4
Logic	**10** C4
Meyer-Franklin Travel	**11** D3
Perot Post Office	**12** B4
Phoenix Drug Store	(see 5)
Police Station	**13** D4
Quickie Lickie Laundromat	**14** A3
Twice-Told Tales	**15** B5
Visitors Service Bureau	**16** B5

SIGHTS & ACTIVITIES
Bermuda Cathedral	**17** D3
Bermuda Historical Society Museum	**18** B4
Bermuda Island Cruises	**19** B5
Bermuda National Gallery	**20** B3
Bermuda Society of Arts Gallery	(see 20)
Birdcage	**21** B5
Cabinet Building	**22** E4
Cenotaph	**23** E4
City Hall	**24** B3
Fantasea Bermuda	(see 19)
Hayward's Snorkelling & Glass Bottom Boat Cruises	(see 19)
Old Town Hall	**25** E4
Royal Bermuda Yacht Club	**26** A6
Sessions House	**27** E3

EATING
Barracuda Grill	**28** C4
Bob's Ice Cream	**29** D4
Cafe on the Terrace	(see 66)
Chopsticks	**30** F4
Coconut Rock	**31** C4
Deli	**32** C4
Dorothy's Coffee Shop	**33** D4
Down to Earth	**34** D4
Fresco's Restaurant & Wine Bar	**35** D4
Hamilton Ice Queen	**36** B4
Harbourfront	**37** B5
Hog Penny	**38** C4
Hungry Bear	**39** D4
Kathy's Kaffee	(see 63)
La Trattoria Deli	**40** C4
La Trattoria Restaurant	**41** C4
Lemon Tree Cafe	**42** B4
Lobster Pot	**43** A4
Marketplace	**44** C3
Mediterraneo	**45** D3
Monte Carlo	**46** B3
Paradiso Cafe	**47** B4
Porch	**48** D4

Serpentine Rd

Dundonald St — **60**

61

To Admiralty
House Park (1.7mi)

**Victoria
Park**

65

Park Rd

● **14**

46

Victoria St — **20** City Hall **24**

City Hall

To Bernard Park (0.6mi);
Blackwatch Pass (0.8mi);
North Shore Rd (1mi)

Victoria St

17
**Bermuda
Cathedral**

● **11** **45**

59

Church St

Church St — **6** **44**

Richmond Rd

36 **62**

**Windsor
Place**

57

40 **41** **53** **10**

**Washington
Mall**

8 ●

15

Gorham Rd

43
● **83**

**Par-la-Ville
Park**

P

4 ● **18**

● **5**

**Walker
Arcade**

9

Reid St

50 **34** **76**

**The
Emporium** **63**

35 **39** **75**

13
**Police
Station**

31 **38** **28**

71 **70** **69** **49** **56**
58 **48** **55**
29

12
42 **72**
3 ●

73

52 **66**
64 **67**
79

Front St

**No 6 Cruise Ship
Terminal**

● **21**

77 **78**

● **82**

**No 1 Cruise Ship
Terminal**

37

80

Pitts Bay Rd

68 **2** **74** **16**

19 **Ferry
Terminal**

To Fairmont Hamilton
Princess (0.3mi)

26 ●
Park

Hamilton Harbour

Ferry to/from Lower Ferry (4min)

Albouy's
Point

Ferry to/from Royal
Naval Dockyard (30min)

Ferry to/from Salt Kettle Wharf (12min);
Ferry to/from Darrell's Wharf (20min);
Ferry to/from Rockaway Wharf (20min);
Ferry to/from Somerset Bridge Wharf (30min);

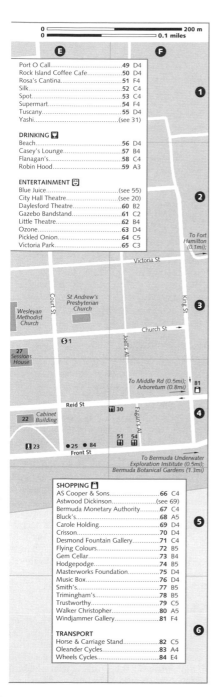

map for the City of Hamilton that shows the central roads, sightseeing attractions and handy details such as the locations of public toilets and bus stops.

INFORMATION

Bookstores

Bermuda Book Store (☎ 295-3698; 3 Queen St) Small but select, with an extensive collection of books about Bermuda.

Bookmart (☎ 295-3838; 3 Reid St) Bermuda's best and biggest bookstore, with a good selection of books about Bermuda as well as international best-sellers.

Twice-Told Tales (☎ 296-1995; 34 Parliament St; 🕙 8am-5:30pm Mon-Fri, 11am-4pm Sat) Sells used books at reasonable prices and also has rare 1st-edition books about Bermuda.

Emergency

Lifeline (9am-5pm ☎ 236-0224, 5pm-9am ☎ 236-3770) This 24-hour hotline provides counseling for those in need.

Police station (☎ 292-1458; 42 Parliament St) For ambulance, police and fire emergencies call ☎ 911.

Internet Access

Bermuda Public Library (☎ 295-2905; Par-la-Ville Bldg, 13 Queen St; 🕙 8:30am-6pm Mon-Thu, 10am-5pm Fri, 9am-5pm Sat) Free, but half-hour limit each day. Anyone with a photo ID can sign up for Internet access, but expect to wait for a free computer.

Internet Lane (☎ 296-9972; The Walkway, 55 Front St; per 30min $6; 🕙 9am-7pm) Several set-ups available, including private booths.

Kathy's Kaffee (☎ 295-5203; 69 Front St; per 15min $2; 🕙 8:30am-5pm Mon-Thu, 8am-4am Fri & Sat; 😺) Only one computer but it's often available and offers the cheapest online rates.

Logic (☎ 295-2255; 10 Burnaby St; per hr $10; 🕙 8am-6pm Mon-Fri, to 9pm Wed, 9am-5pm Sat) This is the place to go for business folk who don't want distractions.

Twice-Told Tales (☎ 296-1995; 34 Parliament St; per 15min $3; 🕙 8am-5:30pm Mon-Fri, 11am-4pm Sat) If you want a cybercafé setting where you can buy coffee and pastries, this cozy place fits the bill.

Laundry

Quickie Lickie Laundromat (☎ 295-6097; 74 Serpentine Rd; 🕙 6am-10pm, to 6pm Sun) Just northwest of the city center, this laundromat has coin-operated washing machines and dryers.

Libraries

Bermuda Public Library (☎ 295-2905; Par-la-Ville Bldg, 13 Queen St; 🕙 8:30am-6pm Mon-Thu, 10am-5pm

---

HAMILTON IN TWO DAYS...

On Day One, start your morning rubbing elbows with the locals at the **Spot** (p56), Hamilton's oldest eatery. From there head over to City Hall, where you'll find the island's best **art museum** (opposite) and several other sites of interest. Then walk to the **Bermuda Cathedral** (p53) and climb the steeple for the city's grandest view. Take a look into **Sessions House** (p52) and the **Cabinet Building** (p53) as you head down to the waterfront to do a little window shopping and appreciate the classic pastel-colored buildings that house the island's fanciest shops.

On Day Two pick up some luscious French pastries at the **Lemon Tree Cafe** (p58) and enjoy them on a bench at adjacent **Par-la-Ville Park** (p53). While you're there, take a look at Bermuda's oldest **moongate** (p53) and pop into the **Bermuda Historical Society Museum** (opposite). Then walk up to **Fort Hamilton** (p52) and explore its bastions, gardens and fine views. End the day with dinner at one of the city's top-notch **restaurants** (p56).

Fri, 9am-5pm Sat) Has a good reference collection of books about Bermuda and a place where you can sit and read British and American newspapers. From September to June it's also open to 7pm Monday through Thursday and from 1pm to 5pm Sunday.

Medical Services

The island's **general hospital** (p104) is nearby in Paget parish.

Phoenix Drug Store (☎ 295-3838; 3 Reid St) The largest of several pharmacies in the city center.

Money

Bank of Bermuda (🕑 9am-4:30pm Mon-Fri) Near the ferry terminal (☎ 299-5232); cnr Court & Church Sts (☎ 299-5329) Both branches have 24-hour ATMs.

Post

General Post Office (☎ 297-7893; 56 Church St; 🕑 8am-5pm Mon-Fri, 8am-noon Sat) The only Bermuda post office with Saturday hours.

Perot Post Office (☎ 292-9052; 11 Queen St; 🕑 9am-5pm Mon-Fri) Closer to the waterfront, this quaint little place is Bermuda's original post office.

Telephone

Cable & Wireless (☎ 297-7022; cnr Church & Burnaby Sts; 🕑 9am-5pm Mon-Fri) The main phone company office, this place sells phonecards, provides fax services and has booths in the lobby that offer privacy for making calls. Public phones are readily available elsewhere around town and use the same phonecards.

Internet Lane (☎ 296-9972; The Walkway, 55 Front St; 🕑 9am-7pm) Rents cell phones for $2.50 a day, plus usage charge, which is about 30 cents a minute in Bermuda and 50 cents a minute to the USA or UK.

Toilets

Public toilets can be found in numerous spots around the city, including at the south side of the tourist office, in the cruise ship terminals and on Victoria St near the bus terminal.

Tourist Information

Visitors Service Bureau (☎ 295-1480; 8 Front St; 🕑 9am-5pm Mon-Sat) This tourist office distributes free island maps and brochures, provides information on current happenings in Hamilton, and sells phonecards and transportation passes.

Travel Agencies

Meyer-Franklin Travel (☎ 295-4176; 35 Church St) A reliable full-service agency.

DANGERS & ANNOYANCES

The north side of Hamilton, known as 'back of town' or 'backside' by islanders, is not well regarded for safety, particularly after dark. Back of town has higher-than-average issues with violent crime, theft and drugs. Simply put, it is best to avoid walking at all in the area north of Victoria St at night, and even during the day it's not wise to carry a purse or other obvious valuables. The roughest area is around Court St.

Also note that the heavily walked section of Pitts Bay Rd between town and the Fairmont Hamilton Princess has seen its share of purse snatchings. One precaution to thwart drive-by snatchers is to carry your bag close to your body, away from the road.

SIGHTS

All of Hamilton's sightseeing attractions, with the exception of Fort Hamilton, are in the city center just a short walk from each other (see the Walking Tour p54). Fort Hamilton is on the northeastern outskirts of the city, about a 15-minute walk away.

City Hall

The sparkling whitewashed **City Hall** (☎ 292-1234; 17 Church St; admission free; 🕑 9am-5pm Mon-Fri, foyer open 9am-4pm) boasts a stylish Bermudian design that flawlessly blends historical and contemporary features. It was designed by Bermudian architect Wilfred Onions, built of local limestone and completed in 1960.

Exterior features include a prominent 91ft-high clocktower and pointy 'eyebrows,' a type of whimsical decorative detail that crowns the windows on the building's right side. If you step back a bit and look up to the top of the tower, you'll see a weathervane topped with a bronze replica of the *Sea Venture,* the boat that brought Bermuda's first settlers. The water fountain fronting City Hall contains two lifelike statues of playful children created by renowned Bermudian sculptor Desmond Fountain.

Inside, the foyer takes on a more classic look with an oil painting of Queen Elizabeth glaring down upon the portraits of the former mayors of Hamilton, some painted by Antoine Verpilleux, a French artist who retired to Bermuda in the 1930s. There's also interesting woodwork here. Stare up at the heavy chandeliers and you'll swear these oddities are made of concrete, but believe it or not it's actually Canadian pine. In contrast the staircase and doors are made of Bermudian cedar, a wood so lovely that it was nearly logged to extinction.

If you're interested in postage stamps, you can find Bermuda's best collection in the city office at the right side of the foyer. Known as the Benbow Collection, the stamps were donated by Colin Benbow, a former member of parliament and the current curator of the Bermuda Historical Society Museum.

BERMUDA NATIONAL GALLERY

Don't miss the **national gallery** (☎ 295-9428; www .bng.bm; 2nd fl, City Hall; adult/child $3/free; 🕑 10am-4pm Mon-Sat), which covers 350 years of island art and has a handful of notable international works as well.

The museum opened in 1992. Its initial collection is on display in the Hereward T Watlington Room. Here you'll find a 1632 etching *(Three Trees)* by Rembrandt, a bronze sculpture by Rodin and several European paintings spanning the 15th to 19th centuries. Exhibits include a portrait of American patriot Thomas Paine by George Romney and works by Thomas Gainsborough, Joshua Reynolds and Cornelius de Vos.

In the Ondaatje Wing you'll find paintings of Bermuda done by artists from the time of the early settlers to Alfred Birdsey, Bermuda's first modernist painter. There are also some fine examples of island-made cedar sculpture and silverwork.

In addition, the museum often has quality temporary exhibits of loaned art and occasionally offers lectures, film screenings and other art-scene events.

BERMUDA SOCIETY OF ARTS GALLERY

Another interesting place to browse on the 2nd floor of City Hall is the **Bermuda Society of Arts** (☎ 292-3824; www.bsoa.bm; admission free; 🕑 10am-4pm Mon-Sat), which displays and sells works by island artists. Many of these pieces, which include both abstract and realistic works, depict scenes of Bermuda through the media of watercolors, pastels and oils.

Bermuda Historical Society Museum

This wonderful little **museum** (☎ 295-2487; 13 Queen St; admission free, donations welcome; 🕑 9:30am-

---

THE GOODWILL AMBASSADOR

You might be surprised to be greeted at the Hamilton city limits by a cheery gentleman waving with both hands, blowing kisses and shouting, 'I love you.' No, he's not running for public office, nor has he slipped off the deep end. But he may well be the friendliest person in Bermuda.

Johnny Barnes, who is sometimes referred to as 'Bermuda's goodwill ambassador,' has been faithfully greeting the Hamilton morning commuters for more than 20 years. A retired bus driver, this spry octogenarian sporting a generous silver beard and a straw hat stands at the Crow Lane roundabout, just east of the Bermuda Underwater Exploration Institute (BUEI) from 5am to 10am each weekday morning.

If you happen to pass by outside of these hours, you can still be greeted by Johnny Barnes…in the form of a bronze statue, hands outstretched, on the ocean side of the road between the BUEI and the roundabout.

3:30pm Mon-Sat), which occupies the front rooms of Par-la-Ville, is run by Colin Benbow, the island's foremost historian. Not surprisingly, it has one of the most insightful museum presentations you'll find in Bermuda. It's a bit of a hodgepodge, but take the time to look around and you'll discover plenty to captivate.

Start in the lobby, where you'll find models of the ill-fated *Sea Venture* and the two ships that Admiral George Somers built to replace it. Tucked away in the same room is Somers' actual sea chest, made of Italian cypress, and the lodestone that Somers used to magnetize his compass (which obviously didn't serve him very well).

Other fun things to search out are the 1615 'hog money' shilling, a map of Bermuda drawn in 1622 and a 250-year-old bracket clock with a trio of musicians that play a jig on the hour. Tidbits of history that you may walk away from here with: Boer prisoners of war were interned on Bermuda in the late 19th century (their handicrafts are on display); and George Washington made a plea in 1775 requesting the support of Bermudians in the American struggle for independence (look for the letter in the corner of the lobby). There are plenty of quality antiques here as well, including two rooms of 18th-century furniture built of Bermuda cedar and pieces of period china painted by Josiah Wedgwood.

Fort Hamilton

With its panoramic views and its endless nooks and crannies, this hilltop **fort** (☎ 292-1234; Happy Valley Rd; admission free; ◷ 9:30am-5pm) is a thoroughly enjoyable place to explore.

Erected in the mid-19th century when tensions were rising between Great Britain and the USA, Fort Hamilton remains a steadfast testament to the era. Its immense ramparts are still mounted with muzzle-loader guns that were capable of firing a 400lb cannonball through an 11-inch-thick iron plate – more than enough penetration force to have sliced any iron-hulled vessel that sailed the seas. But as history would have it, no enemy ships ever appeared.

Today the fort is as much park as historic site. The south-facing ramparts offer a bird's-eye view of Hamilton Harbour. Take some time to scurry about in the fortification's dungeon-like magazine and you'll find gun embrasures, shell hoists, munitions storage rooms and the like. And don't miss strolling through the fort's narrow moat, which has been turned into one of Hamilton's more unusual gardens. Sandwiched between the steep walls of the fort's inner and outer ramparts, this dry moat is cool and shady with a luxuriant growth of ferns, bamboo and other tropical vegetation. Some of the plants are identified with name plaques.

Keep an eye out for the inconspicuous entrances to the magazine and moat, which are both to the left of the main fort entrance immediately after you cross the bridge over the moat.

If you're in Bermuda during the winter season (November through March), try to plan your visit to coincide with the colorful skirling performance held at midday on Mondays by the kilted bagpipers and drummers of the Bermuda Islands Pipe Band.

To get to the fort from the city center, walk east to the end of Church St and turn north on King St for a block; at the top of the hill make a sharp right onto Happy Valley Rd – the fort is about 150 yards further east. Although it's just a 15-minute walk from town, not many visitors come up to the fort, making it a quiet retreat from the city's hustle and bustle.

Sessions House

Hamilton's centerpiece building, the **Sessions House** (☎ 292-7408; 21 Parliament St; admission free; ◷ 9am-12:30pm & 2-5pm Mon-Fri), encloses the chambers for Bermuda's 40-member House of Assembly and its Supreme Court. Although the building dates to 1817, much of its grand appearance, including the landmark clock tower and Italianate ornamentation, were added in 1887 to mark Queen Victoria's golden jubilee.

Everything inside rings with Old World tradition. The House of Assembly meets on the 2nd floor, where the speaker of the house, outfitted in British-style wig and robes and flanked by paintings of King George III and Queen Charlotte, presides over the parliamentary debate. Members of the House are arranged Westminster-style in rows on either side of the chamber, with the two major parties facing each other.

House sessions, which are open to the public, are held at 10am on Friday from late October to late July. If you happen to be around at budget time (February and March), the House typically convenes on Monday and Wednesday as well and the debates get more heated as members vie for funding of their favorite projects.

Although it's of greatest interest when sessions are under way, the assembly meeting room can be visited throughout the year. Photography is allowed only when the House is not in session.

Cabinet Building

The **Cabinet Building** (☎ 292-5501; 105 Front St; admission free; ☉ 9am-5pm Mon-Fri), a stately 19th-century limestone edifice, houses the meeting chamber of Bermuda's Senate. Visitors are welcome to climb the steps to the 2nd-floor chamber and take a look at the round table where the 11 Senate members gather to conduct business. If you want to witness government in action, their sessions are open to the public and held at 10am each Wednesday from late October to July.

Although the chamber has been reserved for island government, the Cabinet's round table, whose shape gives members equal prominence, has served a more international role. In 1953 the table was dismantled and moved to a private location for a conference between Sir Winston Churchill and President Dwight Eisenhower. In 1971 the table was again borrowed, this time being taken to Government House (p65), for a meeting between Prime Minister Edward Heath and President Richard Nixon.

Par-la-Ville Park

This pleasant public **park** (admission free; ☉ 8am-6pm), a haven of birdsong in the city center, abounds with manicured lawns, blooming flowers and a variety of trees, including Bermuda cedar and a huge India rubber tree, both found at the east side of the grounds. The **rubber tree** (*Ficus elastica*), which casts shade onto the adjacent library, was planted by Hamilton's postmaster in 1847 using a seed sent from British Guiana. As is often the case with exotics, the tree hasn't fit its environment as well as it may appear – its extensive root system not only extends beyond the library and post office, but has spread clear down to the waterfront, eating its way through cement en route! Still, the tree's historic significance (Mark Twain

once quipped he was disappointed to see the tree didn't have a crop of hot-water bottles and rubber overshoes hanging from its branches) has thus far saved it from the ax.

Most people enter the park from busy Queen St, but one of the park's jewels is at the less-frequented southwestern tip of the property. Stroll over to the rear entrance of the park, which is off Par-la-Ville Rd, and you'll discover Bermuda's oldest moongate. A walk under this gracious stone arch, which spans the entry, will guarantee you a long spell of good luck.

Bermuda Cathedral

This Anglican **cathedral** (☎ 292-4033; Church St; admission free; ☉ 8am-5pm Mon-Sat), a weighty neo-Gothic building, is one of the city's most dominant landmarks. The original church that stood here dated to 1844 but was burned down by an arsonist. In 1894, the present reconstructed church was designated as a cathedral. Built of native limestone block, the cathedral has lofty arches and handsome stained-glass windows. But best of all, for a $3 donation you can climb the 157 steps to the top of the church tower for a sweeping 360-degree view of greater Hamilton; the tower is accessible from 10am to 3:30pm on weekdays.

ACTIVITIES

Several cruises and party boats depart from Hamilton Harbour.

Hayward's Snorkelling & Glass Bottom Boat Cruises (☎ 236-9894; departs from ferry terminal; 4hr tour $50; ☉ 9:45am & 1:30pm May-Oct) uses a 54-foot motorboat that has an easy-access platform for its snorkeling tours to the northwestern barrier reef and nearby shipwrecks. The captain of this ecologically oriented operation has done work with *National Geographic* and provides fascinating commentary.

Fantasea Bermuda (☎ 236-1300; www.fantasea .bm; 5 Albouy's Point; half-day dive from $65, 3hr boat tours $50; ☉ 9am-5pm) offers a full range of dives, cruises and water activities, and also rents out snorkel sets ($10). There's a boat tour to suit every taste, including kayak tours with an emphasis on ecology, a catamaran sail that includes snorkeling time and a traditional glass-bottom boat cruise.

'Party with the right attitude' is the motto of **Bermuda Island Cruises** (☎ 292-8652; departs from ferry terminal; adult/child $85/45; ☉ 7-10:30pm

FALL INTO SPRING

If you think Bermuda is a sleeper in the offseason, you're in for some surprises. From November 1 to March 31 the Bermuda Department of Tourism lures wintertime visitors with a special series of weekly activities. All of the fun things that follow are free – just show up and join the crowd.

At 10am on Monday, a guided walking tour of the City of Hamilton begins at the waterfront tourist office. At 11:15am there's a tour of the parliamentary Sessions House and at noon there's a colorful skirling ceremony at historic Fort Hamilton; both are included in the walking tour or can be taken in separately.

At 10:30am on Tuesday there's a 90-minute tour of the Bermuda Botanical Gardens in Paget Parish, beginning at the garden's visitor center; it's followed by a midday visit to Camden, the official residence of the premier. At 4pm on Tuesday, in the City of Hamilton, a spirited perform-ance by a troupe of costumed Gombey dancers takes place at the No 1 cruise ship passenger terminal.

On Wednesday, the Town of St George offers an hour-long walking tour from King's Square at 10:30am, ending with a greeting from the mayor in the town hall, and a midday reenactment of the ducking-stool punishment that was once meted out to gossipers.

Thursday features Bermuda's West End, with an hour-long walking tour of Somerset Village departing at 10am from the Somerset County Squire restaurant on Mangrove Bay. In the after-noon at 1:30pm, there's an hour-long guided tour of the Royal Naval Dockyard, leaving from the craft market.

On Friday it's back to the Bermuda Botanical Gardens in Paget Parish, with a garden tour beginning at 10:30am, followed by a midday visit to historic Camden house.

Saturday again features an hour-long walking tour of the Town of St George, starting at King's Square at 10:30am. As with the Tuesday tour, this includes a greeting from the mayor in the town hall and the midday ducking-stool reenactment.

Sunday's events take you back to the West End. If you're a nature lover, meet at the moongate at the Willowbank hotel at 2pm for a 90-minute guided walk around the meadows and woods of the Heydon Trust property. If you're a history buff, head instead to the Royal Naval Dockyard, where an hour-long walking tour of the Dockyard's period buildings begins at 2:15pm at the entrance to the craft market.

Tue, Wed, Fri & Sat May-Oct), which cruises to its own private island. This is hands-down the best of the party boats. If you're ready to let your hair down it's a fun carnival-style scene with a steel-pan band, limbo dancing, a beachside barbecue and an open bar.

WALKING TOUR

Hamilton's history comes to life on this walking tour that takes you to the city's top cultural and historical sites. The **tourist office (1**; p50) on Front St makes an ideal starting point. Walk out the back to **Albouy's Point**, where there's an inviting little grassy **park (2)** with benches and water views. The picturesque salmon-colored building at the west side of the park quarters the island's elite **Royal Bermuda Yacht Club (3)**.

From the park, walk back to the main road and continue to the intersection of Queen and Front Sts, where there's a colorful box that is used during rush hour by a bobby

(police officer) for directing traffic. With its metal posts and tiny roof, it's easy to see why it's nicknamed the **birdcage (4)**.

Heading north on Queen St, you will shortly come upon the **Perot Post Office (6)**, which occupies a classic Bermudian build-ing, whitewashed with black shutters, that was erected by Postmaster William Perot in 1842. As is duly noted on the bronze plaque fronting the building, it was here, in 1848, that Perot issued the first Bermudian post-age stamps. Although the main post office has long since moved to larger quarters, this historic building is such a treasured landmark that it still functions as a neigh-borhood post office.

Next to the post office is Par-la-Ville, a graceful Georgian-style house built in 1814 by William Perot, the father of the afore-mentioned Hamilton postmaster. The build-ing now houses the **Bermuda Historical Society Museum (8**; p51), and the family gardens have now been turned into **Par-la-Ville Park** (**7**; p53), which makes a wonderful place to stroll. You might want to pick up a couple of mouthwatering pastries at the adjacent **Lemon Tree Cafe** (**5**; p58) and enjoy them on one of the park benches.

Continuing north along Queen St, bear right onto Church St and you'll arrive at **City Hall** (**9**; p51), which houses two art galleries and has several other interesting features both inside and out.

Next on Church St is the lofty Anglican **Bermuda Cathedral** (**10**; p53), with its 144ft tower. An interesting tidbit – Queen Victoria wouldn't allow Hamilton to be recognized as a city until the cathedral's construction was completed in the 1890s.

As you continue on Church St, it's easy to see how the street picked up its name, as a church adorns every block. The **Wesleyan Methodist Church (11)** is followed by **St Andrew's Presbyterian Church (13)**, a pretty pink building that dates to 1846, which makes it the oldest church still standing in the city.

Heading south on Court St, you'll pass Bermuda's two stately 19th-century govern-ment buildings, **Sessions House** (**12**; p52) and the **Cabinet Building** (**14**; p53), both of which are open to the public.

At the east corner of Court and Front Sts is the **old town hall (15)**, which boasts one of the longest histories in Hamilton. It was erected in 1794 as a warehouse for customs, served as a chamber for the House of Assembly from 1815 to 1822 and was converted into Hamilton's City Hall in the late 19th century. It is currently used as the Registry of the Supreme Court.

Continue west along Front St to view the **Cenotaph (16)**, a war remembrance monument built of Bermuda limestone. The cornerstone was laid in 1920 by the Prince of Wales. The monument is a replica of the cenotaph that stands in Whitehall, London.

As you walk west on **Front St**, back toward the tourist office, you'll pass Hamilton Harbour on the left and the city's most fanciful Victorian buildings on the right. Now would be a good time to treat yourself to a refresh-ing drink at one of the atmospheric veranda restaurants overlooking the harbor – the **Pickled Onion** (**17**; p59) makes a perfect choice.

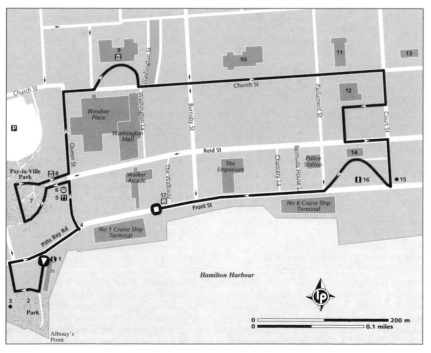

SLEEPING

There are no hotels or guesthouses within the strict boundaries of the City of Hamilton, but there are numerous places within walking distance of town; these are detailed on p66 in the Pembroke Parish chapter.

EATING

It may come as no surprise, but more than half of the restaurants in Bermuda are right here in Hamilton. Thanks in part to the ever-increasing number of foreign businesspeople setting up office in the city, the variety of food just keeps expanding. You can find everything from local island fare and English pub grub to fine French pastries and authentic Japanese sushi.

There's an active café scene, some excellent waterfront restaurants and several good foreign options. In addition to eateries listed here, see p68 for places on the west side of the city.

Restaurants

Hog Penny (☎ 292-2534; 5 Burnaby St; mains $15-26; ☽ lunch Mon-Sat, dinner nightly; ✗ ✵) With its dark pub interior and reliably good British, Bermudian and East Indian fare, this place is a perennial favorite. Not to be missed is the fish chowder ($6) spiced up with rum and sherry peppers sauce. Specialties include bangers and mash (sausages with mashed potatoes) and steak-and-kidney pie from the traditional pub menu. But really, everything from the Indian curries to the prime rib with Yorkshire pudding is a good bet here.

Fresco's Restaurant & Wine Bar (☎ 295-5058; 2 Chancery Lane; lunch $13-20, dinner $20-30; ☽ lunch Mon-Fri, dinner nightly; ✗ ✵) This atmospheric place offers a superb wine selection and a delectable fusion of Mediterranean and Bermudian influences. At lunch you can opt for lighter sandwich and salad fare or order from the dinner menu with indulgent choices like lobster minestrone and Bermuda wahoo grilled with palm hearts. Other dishes range from vegetarian risotto to rack of lamb.

Spot (☎ 292-6293; 6 Burnaby St; breakfast & sandwiches $7-12, dinner $13-17; ☽ 6:30am-10pm Mon-Sat; ✗ ✵) Bermuda's version of a neighborhood diner, the Spot has been serving solid Bermudian fare since 1941. It has perfected the double-decker club sandwich but also makes tasty veggie wraps, burgers and fish and chips. At breakfast you can order all the standards –

French toast, waffles and omelettes – along with a bottomless cup of coffee.

Coconut Rock (☎ 292-1043; 20 Reid St; dishes $9-18, desserts $5-8; ☽ lunch Mon-Sat, dinner nightly; ✗ ✵) A trendy meeting place, the Rock attracts a hip, young crowd. Standouts among the creative sandwiches are the vegetarian lentil burger with melted blue cheese and the 'C-Rock Sandwich' of grilled chicken breast with bacon and Swiss cheese. Other offerings include roast chicken, barbecued ribs and hot pastas. Or just hit the desserts, with temptations like honey-rum banana crêpes and a luscious lemon *tartufo*.

Harbourfront (☎ 295-4207; 21 Front St; sushi $5-12, lunch $10-20, dinner $20-30; ☽ 11:45am-4pm & 5-10pm Mon-Sat; ✗ ✵) Harborview dining and a varied menu that offers fresh seafood in every conceivable form, from sushi to lobster linguini, are the draw at this popular restaurant. It also gets a lot of return customers for its huge Angus rib-eye steaks. Come before 7pm for good-value early dinner specials, or between 5pm and 7pm for the discounted sushi-bar happy hour.

Barracuda Grill (☎ 292-1609; 5 Burnaby Hill; lunch $15-20, dinner $21-38; ☽ lunch Mon-Fri, dinner nightly; ✗ ✵) Classy and contemporary Barracuda's menu features great seafood, steaks and prime rib. For a romantic meal, start with oysters on the half shell ($12) and end with chocolate fondue for two ($14). Rumor has it Michael and Catherine like to dine here. Cool amber bar too.

Port O Call (☎ 295-5373; 87 Front St; lunch $10-15, dinner $15-30; ☽ lunch Mon-Fri, dinner nightly; ✵) With its upmarket nautical decor and delicious seafood, this is a favorite dining spot for Hamilton's well-heeled business crowd. In addition to fresh local fish and lobsters, the place does a knockout filet mignon. And the wine list is even more extensive than the menu, with more than 50 different vintages that can be ordered by the glass.

Porch (☎ 292-4737; 93 Front St; lunch $10-16, dinner $18-29; ☽ lunch Mon-Fri, dinner Mon-Sat; ✵) This restaurant takes its name from its 2nd-floor balcony dining room sporting a bird's-eye view of Hamilton Harbour. At lunch you'll find specialty salads and an array of sandwiches. Dinner is more eclectic with everything from satay chicken to rack of lamb. Ask about the early dinner special from 5pm to 7pm that pairs onion soup with black rum mahimahi for just $20.

Mediterraneo (☎ 296-9047; 39 Church St; dishes $10-18; ☯ 11am-3pm Mon-Fri & 5-11pm nightly; ☒) This cheery restaurant packs in a crowd with its delightful upstairs balcony and scrumptious menu of Mediterranean fare. In addition to a to-die-for seared tuna niçoise salad and a tantalizing calamari *fra diavoli*, it whips up lots of creative focaccia sandwiches, pastas and pizzas. You're sure to find something here that piques your interest.

Yashi (☎ 296-6226; 20 Reid St; à la carte dishes $4-8; ☯ lunch Mon-Fri, dinner Mon-Sat; ☒) This is the real deal – Bermuda's best sushi prepared by a Japanese sushi master in a serene setting that looks like it's right out of Tokyo. Tasty hand-rolled options include soft-shell crab, yellowtail tuna, fried tofu or smoked eel. There are also a couple of hot appetizers, such as shrimp tempura and deep-fried calamari. Wash it all down with steaming green tea or sake.

Tuscany (☎ 292-4507; 95 Front St; appetizers $5-14, mains $15-30; ☯ lunch Mon-Fri, dinner Mon-Sat; ☒ ☒) Dine beneath frescoes of Tuscan scenes or opt for the great outdoors on the balcony overlooking Front St. Either way you can feast on authentic Italian fare including tangy carpaccio, eggplant parmesan and beef tenderloin in a Tuscan wine sauce. And of course there is plenty of pizza and pasta as well.

Silk (☎ 295-0449; 55 Front St; dishes $17-26; ☯ lunch Mon-Fri, dinner nightly; ☒ ☒) Authentic Thai food has finally come to Bermuda. Aromas of ginger, garlic and lemongrass will pull you into this superb little restaurant. Specialties include snapper served on banana leaf, and crispy duck breast, while stir-fries and savory curries shore up the menu. Get a seat on the balcony for a view of the Front St action.

Monte Carlo (☎ 295-5433; 9 Victoria St; lunch $10-20, dinner $20-33; ☯ lunch Mon-Fri, dinner nightly; ☒ ☒) The food here masterfully blends the flavors of Italy and Southern France with a menu that runs the gamut from French onion soup to savory seafood bouillabaisse. The pan-seared duck with cranberry-plum sauce is an award winner but the pastas are innovative as well.

La Trattoria Restaurant (☎ 295-9499; 22 Washington Lane; lunch $11-15, dinner $15-28; ☯ lunch Mon-Sat, dinner nightly; ☒ ☒) Traditional red-brick decor and a wood-fired pizza oven are the hallmarks of this popular Italian eatery. The

scrumptious pizzas are packed high with toppings in a wide range of options from spicy seafood to classic pepperoni. Or select from the mains with hard-hitters like cheese-laden lasagna, grilled sirloin in wine sauce and blackened salmon with pesto.

Lobster Pot (☎ 292-6898; 6 Bermudiana Rd; lunch $10-28, dinner $25-33; ☯ lunch Mon-Fri, dinner nightly; ☒) OK, you guessed it, the specialty here is lobster. The top-of-the-line treat is the seafood-lover's feast, which includes half a lobster, mussels, crab claws, clams and shrimp simmered in saffron broth. Also worthy of note is the pan-fried local catch topped with bananas and almonds. A lobster tank and nautical decor set the tone.

Chopsticks (☎ 292-0791; 88 Reid St; lunch $10-15, dinner $12-17; ☯ lunch Mon-Fri, dinner to 11pm nightly; ☒ ☒) In Bermuda, if you think Chinese food you think Chopsticks. Hamilton's oldest Chinese restaurant serves good Cantonese fare and has a few Thai curries on the menu to boot. The spicy hot and sour soup ($4) is a delight, the curried vegetables are a spicy awakening and naturally there's a full menu of pork, beef and poultry dishes. The same tasty dishes can be ordered for take-out ($4 to $12).

Rosa's Cantina (☎ 295-1912; 121 Front St; appetizers $8-12, mains $12-22; ☯ 11:30am-11pm; ☒ ☒) Tex-Mex in Bermuda? Why not. For starters, try the cheese-stuffed jalapeño peppers, called 'iguana eggs' ($8), and wash them down with a frosty margarita. The menu includes all the regular favorites – burritos, quesadillas, enchiladas – as well as a handful of tasty vegetarian offerings and a 'L'il Texan' menu for kids.

Cafés

Paradiso Cafe (☎ 295-3263; 7 Reid St; breakfast $6-8, lunch $7-12; ☯ 7am-5pm Mon-Fri, 8am-5pm Sat; ☒) It's hands-down the best café in Hamilton. Even the finest restaurants can't beat the specialty salads here, which are crispy fresh and delightfully creative. Another treat is the grilled Tuscan chicken sandwich. The European-style pies and cakes make a perfect finish. Only catch is, unless you arrive before noon for lunch, you'll never get a table!

Rock Island Coffee Cafe (☎ 296-5241; 48 Reid St; pastries $3-5; ☯ 7am-6pm Mon-Fri, 8am-6pm Sat; ☒ ☒) The aroma of fresh roasting coffee wafts out the door letting you know you've found

Hamilton's finest java. This laid-back coffee shop not only fires its own beans but it makes unbelievably luscious strawberry pies – don't even try to resist! Relax in an easy chair and read the newspaper as you linger over your café au lait.

Lemon Tree Cafe (☎ 292-0235; 7 Queen St; pastries $3-5, sandwiches $6-10; ⏰ 7:30am-4pm Mon-Thu, to 3pm Fri) Sit out back in the shaded garden of this brilliant lemon-colored café and indulge yourself with the finest French pastries this side of Paris. The fruit tarts are absolutely sumptuous, while a wrap sandwich makes a delicious, healthy lunch choice.

Hungry Bear (☎ 292-2353; Chancery Lane; snacks $3-7; ⏰ 7am-3pm Mon-Fri; ☒ ☒) If you enjoy artsy, unhurried places, this espresso bar and café on Chancery Lane fits the bill. In addition to a full range of strong brews, people flock for the fresh scones, homemade soups and creative sandwiches.

Cafe on the Terrace (☎ 296-5265; 59 Front St; breakfast $4-7, lunch $9-13; ⏰ 9:30am-4:30pm Mon-Sat) Unwind over afternoon tea and scones ($8) while watching the action on Front St from this quiet veranda café. Fluffy breakfast omelettes and lunchtime sandwiches and salads are also available. Enter the AS Cooper & Sons department store and take the elevator to the 2nd floor.

Kathy's Kaffee (☎ 295-5203; 69 Front St; dishes $4-8; ⏰ 8:30am-5pm Mon-Thu, 8am-4am Fri & Sat; ☒) If you get the munchies after midnight on weekends then this perky little café in the back of the Emporium is the place to go. Expect inexpensive breakfast fare, homemade cakes and good sandwiches and gyros. And of course there's always a fresh pot of kaffee brewing.

Quick Eats

La Trattoria Deli (☎ 295-9499; Washington Lane; items $3-7; ⏰ 10am-4pm Mon-Sat) Join the office workers that queue up here for the best lunch deal in Hamilton. Strictly take-out, this hole-in-the-wall sells food prepared at the upmarket La Trattoria Restaurant across the lane. Choose from creative wrap sandwiches, huge pizza slices, lasagna and similar Italian items at bargain prices.

Dorothy's Coffee Shop (☎ 292-4130; 3 Chancery Lane; burgers $4, omelette breakfasts $5-8; ⏰ 7:15am-3:30pm Mon-Fri; ☒) The best burgers in Bermuda are served up here. It's just a simple breakfast and lunch spot, with stools set around an L-shaped counter, but it's so popular you may have to wait in line.

Bob's Ice Cream (☎ 292-5732; 95 Front St; cones $2.50-4; ⏰ 9am-5:30pm) If the heat's getting to you and you've a yearning for creamy rich ice cream, this is the place. For a treat, try the rum raisin, a flavorful local favorite.

Deli (☎ 295-5890; Washington Mall; items $3-6; ⏰ 8am-5pm Mon-Fri, to 4pm Sat) It's not fancy but this take-out counter serves up generous made-to-order sandwiches at unbeatable prices. Everything is fresh and wholesome. There are also simple salads.

Hamilton Ice Queen (☎ 292-6497; 27 Queen St; items $4-6; ⏰ 10am-midnight Mon-Sat, to 10pm Sun; ☒ ☒) Bermuda's version of a fast-food eatery, the Ice Queen is spotlessly clean and open long hours. Hamburgers, gardenburgers (vegetarian patties), fried chicken and soft-serve ice cream are the standard-bearers.

Groceries

Marketplace (☎ 295-6066; Church St; ⏰ 7am-10pm Mon-Sat, 1-5pm Sun) In addition to all the usual grocery items, this large, well-stocked supermarket has a good liquor section; fresh, inexpensive bakery items; and a superb self-service buffet ($6.75 per lb) with salads and two dozen hot dishes such as baked salmon and fried chicken.

Supermart (☎ 292-2064; 125 Front St; ⏰ 7:30am-9pm Mon-Sat, 1-5pm Sun) If you're down on Front St, the Supermart is a convenient choice and has offerings similar to those at the Marketplace.

Down to Earth (☎ 292-5639; 56 Reid St; ⏰ 9am-5:30pm Mon-Sat) Hamilton's biggest and best natural foods store carries everything from vitamins to trail mix and frozen foods. There's also a juice bar that whips up tasty tropical fruit smoothies ($4) that can be spiked with add-ins such as ginseng and bee pollen.

DRINKING

Hamilton offers an enticing variety of watering holes to quench any thirst. In addition to the places that follow, most of the city's better restaurants also have a bar.

Flanagan's (☎ 295-8299; 69 Front St; ☒) An Irish pub and sports bar on the 2nd floor of the Emporium, Flanagan's has rock 'n' roll music from 10pm to 1am most nights with a nice mix of locals, expats and tourists. If you're not up for dancing, you can hang in the adjacent sports bar, which serves up Irish brew on tap.

Casey's Lounge (☎ 292-9994; 25 Queen St; ⚇) This welcoming bar attracts a broad section of the island community and there's always something happening. It's mostly DJ music, geared to a different crowd on different nights. For instance, Saturday is the traditional ladies night, while on Wednesday and Friday it's a gay-friendly crowd.

Robin Hood (☎ 295-3314; 25 Richmond Rd; ⚇) British expats looking for a homey pub flock here, and it's not just for the UK brews – the pub grub is the real deal as well. And yes, you can watch cricket and European football (soccer) matches on the telly.

Beach (☎ 292-0219; cnr Front & Parliament Sts) This Front St bar offers the cheapest drinks in town, and its sidewalk tables make it a good people-watching spot. The big-screen TVs inside are often tuned to US sports programs, which draws lots of Americans who want to follow the action back home.

Hog Penny (☎ 292-2534; 5 Burnaby St; ☼ 11:30am-1am; ✕ ⚇) This atmospheric English pub, best known for its food, is also a fun place to come for a drink. It serves up tall schooners of English draught beer and a guitar duo plays most nights from 10pm to 1am. It tends to attract a slightly more subdued and refined crowd, but it's not at all stuffy.

In addition, **Fresco's** (☎ 295-5058; 2 Chancery Lane; ☼ lunch Mon-Fri, dinner nightly; ✕ ⚇) garden courtyard offers a romantic setting for lingering over a glass of wine, and **Coconut Rock** (☎ 292-1043; 20 Reid St; ☼ lunch Mon-Sat, dinner nightly; ✕ ⚇), which plays music videos, is a casual spot for enjoying a drink of any sort, from coffee to cocktails. If you're up for afternoon tea, **Cafe on the Terrace** (☎ 296-5265; 59 Front St; ☼ 9:30am-4:30pm Mon-Sat) in the upmarket AS Cooper & Sons department store is the place. For the island's best coffee, head to **Rock Island Coffee Cafe** (☎ 296-5241; 48 Reid St; ☼ 7am-6pm Mon-Fri, 8am-6pm Sat; ✕ ⚇).

ENTERTAINMENT

If you're up for dancing the night away, then Front St is the place to head. In addition to the clubs that follow, a couple of the bars listed in the drinking section – Flanagan's and Casey's – also have music and dancing. The City of Hamilton is also home to the island's main theaters. A great way to keep up-to-date on what's happening is to check the 'What's On Where' listings in the Lifestyle section of the *Royal Gazette* on Thursday.

Ozone (☎ 292-3379; 69 Front St, 3rd fl, Emporium; cover charge $10-20; ⚇) The city's hippest dance spot, Ozone attracts the singles crowd as well as other night owls, especially those in their 20s and 30s. The music is pumped up and runs the gamut from rock to R&B and techno. If you're hot on salsa dancing, come on Thursday, when the Ozone gets down and dirty with SalsaMania.

Blue Juice (☎ 292-1959; Bermuda House Lane; ⚇) This 'disco bar' behind Tuscany restaurant plays music videos and spins hip-hop, reggae and R&B. It's less boisterous than Ozone and tends to attract a well-heeled crowd.

Pickled Onion (☎ 295-2263; 53 Front St; ⚇) A friendly place that attracts visitors and locals in equal measure, this 2nd-floor restaurant pushes aside the tables to create a dance floor and rocks with live entertainment from 10:30pm to 1am nightly. It's typically R&B and classic rock, anything from Janice Joplin to Jimmy Buffett. It's also a wonderful place to enjoy an afternoon drink on its water-view balcony.

Victoria Park (☎ 298-5543; cnr Cedar & Victoria Sts) The Bank of Butterfield sponsors open-air concerts at the park's gazebo bandstand on some Sunday evenings during the summer months – mostly jazz but also rock, soul and island music. It's a fun family scene, with face painting for the kids and food stalls. The schedule varies each year.

City Hall Theatre (☎ 292-2313; 17 Church St) Plays, concerts and other performances are held in this 378-seat theater at City Hall, including some put on by big-name international artists during the Bermuda Festival in winter. Call for schedule and ticket information.

Daylesford Theatre (☎ 292-0848; 11 Washington St) Opposite Victoria Park, this small theater is the home of the Bermuda Musical and

---

HARBOUR NIGHTS

On Wednesday nights during the cruise ship season, Hamilton lures visitors into the streets by throwing a festival. From 6pm to 10pm Front St is closed off to traffic, and craft booths, Gombey dancers and food stalls take over. And of course the shops stay open late. It's very touristy, but fun and free.

Dramatic Society, which stages performances of Shakespeare, Chekhov and the occasional contemporary work.

Little Theatre (☎ 292-2135; 30 Queen St) This cinema in the city center shows first-run British and American movies.

SHOPPING

Hamilton offers Bermuda's greatest selection of shopping opportunities with a wide range of merchandise available, from simple souvenirs to fine art. Most of the shops are either right on Front St or within a block of it.

The island's largest department stores, **Trimingham's** (☎ 295-1183; 37 Front St), **Smith's** (☎ 295-2288; 35 Front St) and **AS Cooper & Sons** (☎ 295-3961; 59 Front St) are all in the block of Front St between Queen and Burnaby Sts. These are good places to get an idea of selection and costs, as they carry everything from Waterford crystal and international designer clothing to Bermuda shorts and Royall Bay Rhum cologne.

Arts & Crafts

Desmond Fountain Gallery (☎ 292-3955; 69 Front St, Emporium) If you're taken with those lifelike bronze statues fronting City Hall, you can pick up a version here for around $40,000. Fountain also makes some smaller pieces priced under $1000 and the gallery is fun to browse around even if you're not buying.

Carole Holding (☎ 296-3431; 81 Front St) If you want to take home memories of the island, Holding's pastel watercolors delightfully capture Bermuda scenes. The shop sells mostly prints and notecards at affordable prices, but there are also some originals for sale.

Masterworks Foundation (☎ 295-5580; Bermuda House Lane, behind 97 Front St) This nonprofit organization sells Bermuda-inspired prints, notecards and jewelry. One popular item is the collector-style china plates with paintings of Bermuda scenes.

Bermuda Society of Arts (☎ 292-3824; www.bsoa .bm; admission free; ☷ 10am-4pm Mon-Sat) On the 2nd floor of City Hall, this gallery sells artwork by resident and visiting artists, most with local themes. The mediums are varied, including watercolor, pastel, acrylic, oil and sculpture.

Windjammer Gallery (☎ 292-7861; 87 Reid St) This eclectic art gallery sells select original watercolors, oils and bronzes, as well as posters, prints, cards and calendars with Bermudian themes.

Collectibles

Bermuda Monetary Authority (☎ 295-5278; www .bma.bm; 26 Burnaby St) The national mint, which issues Bermuda's money, also sells collectors' notes and coins. At least one commemorative set, in gold or silver, is issued each year.

Bluck's (☎ 295-5367; 4 Front St) This shop has a fine collection of antiques, particularly fine china and crystal – period Waterford and Wedgwood are its specialty.

Stamp collectors can go to the Bermuda Philatelic Bureau window at the General Post Office (p50) to buy commemorative stamps.

Jewelry

Gem Cellar (☎ 292-3042; Walker Arcade, off Front St) This is a good place to find affordable charms and pendants with Bermudian motifs such as tree frogs, longtail birds and hog pennies, made right on the premises.

Walker Christopher (☎ 295-1466; 9 Front St) This one-of-a-kind shop sells fine antique jewelry, rare gems and such treasures as gold doubloons recovered from an 18th-century Spanish shipwreck.

Crisson (☎ 295-2351; 71 Front St) This high-end shop specializes in exclusive items such as Rolex watches, diamonds and international designer jewelry, but also has Bermuda-themed necklaces and bracelets.

Astwood Dickinson (☎ 292-5805; 85 Front St) This shop has a little bit of everything in the jewelry realm, ranging from island-themed pendants to Omega watches.

Souvenirs

Trustworthy (☎ 296-4164; cnr Front St & Old Cellar Lane) Operated by the Bermuda National Trust, proceeds benefit the trust's historical restoration projects. A fun place to browse, with a bit of everything – trinkets with Bermuda insignia, Bermudian cookbooks, sherry pepper sauce – you name it.

Flying Colours (☎ 295-0890; 5 Queen St) Looking for some quality souvenirs with Bermuda logos? Head here first. You'll find everything from porcelain coffee mugs to stylish T-shirts and tank tops sized for children and adults.

Hodgepodge (☎ 295-0647; cnr Point Pleasant Rd & Front St) Every tourist town has a shop that revels in kitsch. This place, adjacent to the tourist office, is chock-full of inexpensive mugs with Bermuda decals, sun hats, coral jewelry, painted wooden fish etc.

QUIRKY TRAVEL

So you think the days of horse and buggy (p156) or 10mph choo-choo trains are gone? Well, think again – Bermuda just doesn't give up that easily on tradition. Some of those same buggies that Mark Twain hopped on to get around town in days long past still carry passengers along the waterfront, right past the grand ole Princess hotel where Twain stayed. The traffic is certainly heavier than in Twain's day but the waterfront buggy ride is still an enjoyable way to cruise the west side of town.

As for the train, now that's just plain quirky. It's an open-air carriage, pulled by a small truck designed to resemble an old-fashioned train engine. Yes it looks a bit tacky, like a toy kiddies' ride in an amusement park, but heck, this is Bermuda and you're on vacation, so why not! The **Bermuda Train Company** (☎ 236-5972; tour $23) runs a 60-minute tour around the city and the botanical gardens at 10am on weekdays.

Music Box (☎ 295-4839; 58 Reid St) Here you will find the best selection of CDs by local musicians, ranging from steel-drum music to the Bermuda Regiment Band. For something really offbeat, try the recordings of Bermuda's tree frogs chirping through the night. A handy headphone setup allows you to sample tunes before deciding what you want to buy.

GETTING THERE & AROUND
To/From the Airport
It's a 30-minute taxi ride from the airport to the City of Hamilton. The taxi fare is about $25. Bus Nos 1, 2, 10 and 11, which take about 40 minutes to Hamilton and cost $4.50, stop in front of the airport terminal which is in St Georges Parish, but the bus is only practical if you're traveling very light, as bus rules require that your luggage fits on your lap.

Boat
Ferries (p154) leave from the terminal adjacent to the tourist information office on Front St. They connect Hamilton to St George, the Royal Naval Dockyard and places in Sandys, Southampton, Warwick and Paget parishes. For more information see the Getting There & Around sections of those chapters.

Bus
Of the 11 bus routes serving Bermuda, all except the St George–St David's route leave from the Hamilton bus terminal on Washington St. Consequently, if you're exploring the island by bus, you'll find yourself coming through the city frequently.

Ticket books and tokens and transportation passes (p155) can be purchased at the bus terminal information booth from 7:15am to 5:30pm weekdays, 8:15am to 5:30pm Saturdays and 9:15am to 4:45pm Sundays and holidays.

For information on getting to and from Hamilton from specific destinations see the relevant parish chapters.

Motor Scooter
Scooter rentals (p157) are available at **Wheels Cycles** (☎ 292-2245; 117 Front St), in the city center, and **Oleander Cycles** (☎ 295-0919; Gorham Rd), just off Bermudiana Rd. Scooter parking is clearly marked and easy to find along the main roads, including Front and Church Sts. There are no parking fees.

Taxi
Taxis are readily available along Front St near the cruise ship terminals and the ferry terminal, as well as on Church St just south of the bus terminal.

Pembroke Parish

HIGHLIGHTS

- Enjoy a delicious gourmet meal at the atmospheric **Ascots** (p68) restaurant
- Discover wonders of the marine world at the **Bermuda Underwater Exploration Institute** (opposite)
- Stay at one of the parish's smolderingly romantic **Victorian-era inns** (p66)

- POPULATION: 11,306
- AREA: 1.98 SQ MILES

Appearing like a sturdy thumb extending upward from the center of Bermuda, Pembroke has much to attract visitors. It abounds with water views, overlooking colorful Hamilton Harbour to the south, scenic Great Sound to the west and the open Atlantic to the north. It's short on sandy beaches, but that's never been enough to keep visitors at bay. Indeed, the very first resort ever built in Bermuda, the venerable Princess Hotel, wasn't erected on one of those glorious Warwick beaches but went up right here on stony Hamilton Harbour. And it became such a magnet for visitors that several of the elegant mansions lining the nearby waterfront opened as genteel inns. A testimony to the solid Bermudian hospitality that has been their cornerstone, many of these places still draw visitors who prefer traditional charm to a day at the beach.

That's not to say Pembroke is caught in some sort of time warp. To the contrary – this is the most vibrant and expanding parish in Bermuda. The same waterfront that's home to period inns bustles with new office buildings, and if you walk through the Princess Hotel you'll likely see more businesspeople than tourists. Almost all of the growing number of international companies that have flocked to Bermuda have set up in Pembroke.

Not surprisingly, the parish offers superb dining options; the quieter north shore has scenic coastal parks to explore; and the Bermuda Underwater Exploration Institute, at the southeast side of the parish, shouldn't be missed by anyone interested in the mysteries of the ocean.

The rest of the parish's many attractions, eateries and amenities – those within the City of Hamilton – are detailed in the previous chapter (p46).

Information
There's a **Bank of Butterfield** (☎ 294-2070; 90 Pitts Bay Rd) branch at the Waterfront building. Extensive services and amenities are nearby in the City of Hamilton.

Sights
BERMUDA UNDERWATER EXPLORATION INSTITUTE
The **Bermuda Underwater Exploration Institute** (BUEI; ☎ 292-7314; www.buei.org; 40 Crow Lane; adult/child $10.50/5.50, under 7 yrs free; ⏰ 9am-5pm Mon-Fri, 10am-5pm Sat & Sun) unravels the mysteries of the underwater world via an amazing array of exhibits and interactive displays.

A real eye-opener, the first hall reveals the history of diving. Take a look at the wooden dive bell invented by comet-finder Sir Edmund Halley in 1690; it resembles an inverted whiskey barrel with a peephole! Then there's a cool 19th-century hard-hat diving suit attached to a primitive air pump that looks like it was torn from the pages of a Jules Verne novel. And don't miss the full-scale model of the original bathysphere, the submersible chamber that William Beebe and Otis Barton used for their record-setting (3028ft) underwater descent off Bermuda in 1934.

Want to try things on for size? There's a cut-away of the bathysphere that you can jump into and a simulated dive that creates the sense of dropping some 12,000ft to the ocean floor. The latter is really a submarine-shaped elevator with a surround theater that shows giant squid passing by the portholes and pretends you've hit a time warp in the Bermuda Triangle. It jiggles and thumps for about seven minutes before 'landing' safely on the lower floor of the center, where there are, quite apropos, displays on deepwater creatures and shipwrecks.

A highlight here is the incredible gold coin and jewelry collection that has been recovered from Spanish galleons that wrecked upon Bermuda's hazardous reefs. Another curious exhibit, complete with morphine-filled glass ampoules, focuses on the *Constellation*, a four-masted schooner that went down during WWII. The ship became the subject of Peter Benchley's book *The Deep*,

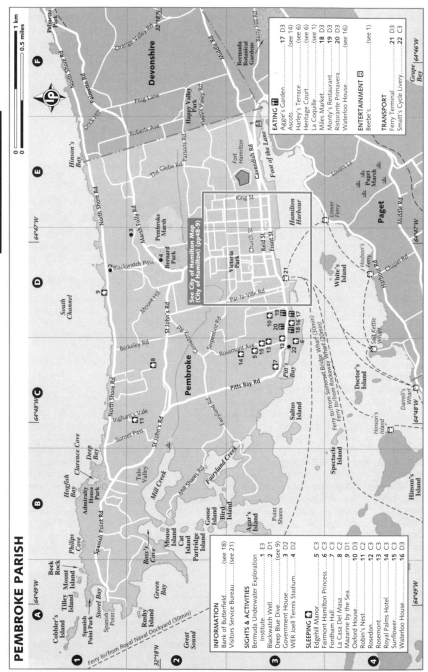

whose plot developed around recovering the wreck's cargo of opiates. But the *Constellation* was just one of scores of ships that sank to watery graves just off Bermuda's shores and there are so many recovered items – ranging from 16th-century guns to diamond-studded jewels – that only a fraction is on display. Amazingly, most of the items found here were recovered by just one islander, Teddy Tucker, during his 40-year diving career. Tucker and Benchley, incidentally, were two of the leading forces behind the development of the nonprofit Bermuda Underwater Exploration Institute.

BUEI is just a 10-minute walk east from the City of Hamilton. You could catch the gist of everything here in an hour, but it's better to give yourself at least double that to really absorb it all.

SPANISH POINT PARK

This very pleasant coastal **park** (Spanish Point Rd; sunrise-sunset) has fine views and a curious history. It served as a camp for Spanish sailors six years before the English ever set eyes on Bermuda. Both arrived the same accidental way. In 1603 a Spanish galleon passing Bermuda struck a rock on a nearby reef, forcing its captain, Diego Ramirez, to come ashore at Stovel Bay, where the crew stayed for three weeks to repair the ship to a seaworthy condition. It was the English who later discovered remnants of the camp and dubbed this northwestern tip of Pembroke Parish 'Spanish Point.'

Today, the north side of Stovel Bay has been turned into the 7-acre Spanish Point Park. The bay is a mooring area for small boats, and the park consists of manicured grassy lawns dotted with casuarina trees. A short, paved footpath leads from the bay to the tip of the point, where there's a clear view of the Royal Naval Dockyard's twin towers, which sit 2 miles across the Great Sound to the northwest.

You'll also see what looks like a shipwreck off the west side of the point; actually, it's an old dry dock that sank here in 1902. When the wind picks up, windsurfers launch from the park, but at other times the park is an ideal spot for picnicking.

ADMIRALTY HOUSE PARK

Once home to the admiral who served as the regional commander-in-chief of the British naval forces, **Admiralty House Park** (Spanish Point Rd; sunrise-sunset) is a 16-acre recreational area. A network of short trails leads through shaded woods filled with birdsong and along low cliffs with coastal views.

Admiralty House, built in 1812 as a naval hospital, was turned into the admiral's residence in 1816 and served that function until the late 1950s, when the navy withdrew and turned over the property to the island government. In 1974 the grounds were converted into Pembroke Parish's largest park. Some of the buildings previously used by the navy now house the offices of community groups.

The highlight of the coastal park is **Clarence Cove**, whose shallow waters and lovely little sandy beach make it a popular destination for families on weekend outings. The cove is just a five-minute walk along the winding path that leads north from the parking lot.

On the south side of the road, **Tulo Valley**, currently a parks department nursery, was originally the vegetable garden for Admiralty House. A tunnel, now blocked off, once connected the two areas.

BLACKWATCH PASS

Seems every hilly island has a road whose very construction taxes the imagination. In Bermuda the most impressive road engineering feat is unquestionably **Blackwatch Pass**, a tunnel-like pass cut more than 50ft deep into the limestone cliffs separating the north shore of Pembroke from the City of Hamilton. The pass is so steep that people turn their headlights on while driving through it during the day!

Along the north side of Blackwatch Pass, near the intersection with the Langton Hill road, you'll spot the site of **Blackwatch Well**, which is marked by a small enclosure. The well, now capped, was dug by British troops during a severe drought in 1849 to provide the area with a more reliable source of water.

GOVERNMENT HOUSE

The official residence of Bermuda's governor, **Government House** is generally not open to the public, but with its hillside location it can readily be seen from North Shore Rd. Built in 1892 on the 112ft Langton Hill, this stately stone house rimmed with verandas has more than 30 rooms. It was on the 33-acre estate grounds that governor Sir Richard Sharples, along with his bodyguard and the Great Dane that Sharples was walking, were gunned down by an assassin on March 10, 1973.

For more than a century, dignitaries visiting Government House have traditionally been invited to plant a tree ceremonially. More than 100 of these commemorative plantings dot the grounds, including a mango tree planted in 1880 by the future King George V, a princess palm planted by Ethiopian King Haile Selassie in 1963, and a queen palm planted by Queen Elizabeth in 1994.

Activities

TENNIS

WER Joell Tennis Stadium (☎ 292-0105; Bernard Park, Marsh Folly Rd; court per hr adult/child $8/4; ☼ 8am-10pm Mon-Fri, to 4pm Sat & Sun), a government-run facility, has three clay and five plexicushion courts. Racquet rentals cost $5 an hour, a ball machine can be rented for $45 an hour, and lessons are available at $60 an hour. At night, there's an additional $8 fee to light the courts.

DIVING

Deep Blue Dive (☎ 292-0080; deepbluedive@ibl.bm; 91 North Shore Rd; dive $65; ☼ 9am-5pm) operates out of Mazarine by the Sea guesthouse. This dive shop specializes in offering diving courses, with everything from a two-day crash course ($200) that gives you the basics of diving to an open-water certification course ($375) that takes four days and covers everything necessary to make you a registered diver.

Sleeping

Most of the places to stay in Pembroke are at the south side of the parish. Because this is also the closest accommodation to the City of Hamilton's business district, these places, particularly those with kitchen facilities, are often booked heavily by foreign businesspeople who sometimes reserve a unit for months at a time. The accommodations at the north side of the parish are a bit further afield and hence tend to be easier to book.

WEST OF HAMILTON

The western outskirts of the City of Hamilton has a waterfront dominated by the Fairmont Hamilton Princess hotel. Inland from the Princess is a quiet neighborhood of wealthy homes that includes several small hotels and guesthouses. Collectively, these hostelries offer a fine variety of accommodations, ranging from moderate to upscale. All are within a 10-minute walk of the city center.

Royal Palms Hotel (☎ 292-1854, in the USA ☎ 800-678-0783, in Canada ☎ 800-799-0824; www.royalpalms.bm; 24 Rosemont Ave; r winter/summer from $185/195; ✗ ✗ ✗) A real jewel, this intimate family-run hotel brims with pleasant personal touches and breakfast is included. The main house, a lovingly restored c 1903 mansion, has 13 guestrooms decorated with tasteful Victorian furnishings. A newer section, constructed in a similar period architectural style, has suites and cottages with kitchen facilities. The superb Ascots restaurant is located on site, so if you're around at lunch or dinner you're in for a treat.

Fairmont Hamilton Princess (☎ 295-3000, in the USA & Canada ☎ 800-441-1414; www.fairmont.com/ham

---

UNDERCOVER AT THE PRINCESS

Tourism ground to a halt in Bermuda during WWII, but that didn't mean the island's hotels were shuttered. On the contrary, they were brimming with activity as Bermuda, with its strategic mid-Atlantic location, became a center for Allied military intelligence operations.

The brain center of it all was the Princess Hotel, which was taken over by British intelligence agents, who turned the hotel's basement into their operations center. There, tucked out of view, scores of codebreakers interpreted correspondence passing between the USA and Europe in an effort to uncover Axis espionage operations and decode secret messages. At its height the operation employed more than 1000 people – many of them single English women who quietly left their towns in the UK and worked clandestinely at the Princess without any contact with friends and family back home.

Today, as you wander through the posh resort, you can imagine the hundreds of workers set up in their below-ground digs, painstakingly opening suspected mail without damaging the seal, examining the letter and then quickly getting it back into circulation.

ilton; 76 Pitts Bay Rd; r winter/summer from $259/349; ☒ ☒ ☒) As Bermuda's oldest luxury hotel, opened in 1884, this venerated place has hosted presidents, princes and such luminary travelers as Mark Twain. But don't expect cobwebs – this grand ole dame hasn't been sitting on its laurels. Now a favorite among high-end business travelers, the Princess does a fine job at combining period charm with modern conveniences, offering everything from voice mail to fitness facilities. The harborside locale is not suited for swimming, but free transportation is provided to its sister hotel, the Fairmont Southampton, where there's a splendid beach.

Sunflower (☎ 296-0523; inkdrops@northrock.bm; 31 Rosemont Ave; s/d $125/140; ☒) This cozy studio in the home of Tricia Thompson-Browne is compact but has full amenities including a 'micro-kitchen' suitable for preparing simple meals, and a shaded patio. The hospitality and decor are on par with pricier places in this exclusive neighborhood. All in all, if you don't need extra elbow room, Sunflower is a cheery affordable choice and there are no additional taxes or gratuities added to the bill.

Rosedon (☎ 295-1640, in the USA ☎ 800-742-5008; www.rosedonbermuda.com; 61 Pitts Bay Rd; r winter/summer from $150/210; ☒ ☒) This romantic hotel offers the inviting character of a genteel guesthouse. The grand main house, built in 1906, has a cozy living room with fireplace, where complimentary afternoon tea is served, and a couple of delightful 2nd-floor guestrooms with Victorian furnishings and four-poster beds. Equally comfortable but less atmospheric are the rooms in the modern two-story wings that flank the pool and gardens behind the house. Breakfast is included.

Oxford House (☎ 295-0503, in the USA ☎ 800-548-7758, in Canada ☎ 800-272-2306; www.oxfordhouse.bm; Woodbourne Ave; s/d winter $145/170, summer $165/190; ☒) Yep, another lovely mansion glowing with old-fashioned charm. This classic family-run B&B inn has lovely Victorian decor and attentive service that matches the setting. As a matter of fact, things are so nice here that the place consistently wins tourism awards. Breakfast is included.

Edgehill Manor (☎ 295-7124; www.bermuda.com /edgehill; 36 Rosemont Ave; s/d winter $140/160, summer $156/180; ☒ ☒ ☒) An agreeably down-to-earth atmosphere and comfortable rooms characterize this small guesthouse. The nine rooms vary, but each is pleasant and sports

full amenities including a refrigerator; a couple of rooms even have kitchens. Breakfast is provided. The upstairs rooms have balconies with fine hilltop views. Discounts are available for longer stays.

Waterloo House (☎ 295-4480, in the USA ☎ 800-468-4100; www.waterloohouse.com; 100 Pitts Bay Rd; r winter/summer from $210/265; ☒ ☒) Period decor and pampering service set the tone at this quiet harborside hotel just a few minutes west of central Hamilton. Part of the upmarket Relais et Chateaux chain, Waterloo House encompasses a restored 19th-century manor house and has 32 cushy rooms. For an extra $75 you can add on a stunning water view.

Fordham Hall (☎ 295-1551; fordham@northrock.bm; 53 Pitts Bay Rd; r winter/summer $140/150; ☒ ☒) This informal guesthouse occupies a 19th-century manor house just beyond the Princess hotel. The guest rooms are simple but the common areas include a spacious guest lounge and a breakfast room overlooking Hamilton Harbour. Breakfast is included in the price. One caveat – the guesthouse is on a stretch of busy Pitts Bay Rd that doesn't have a sidewalk, so the walk to town will be partly in the street. Breakfast is included.

Rosemont (☎ 292-1055, in the USA ☎ 800-367-0040; www.rosemont.bm; 41 Rosemont Ave; studio/apt $170/200; ☒ ☒ ☒ ☒) Popular with return visitors, the 47 units in this family-run apartment complex have all the conveniences of home, including full-size kitchens. Little extras include complimentary coffee and newspapers, and free local phone calls. The roomy apartments are spiffier than the studios and well worth the extra $30.

NORTH PEMBROKE

The following places are in residential neighborhoods north of the City of Hamilton. They are about 10 minutes from town by bus or scooter or 20 minutes on foot.

Mazarine by the Sea (☎ 292-1690; mazarinebythe sea@ibl.bm; 91 North Shore Rd; r winter/summer from $90/125; ☒) If you like water views, this comfy guesthouse, perched above the water's edge, has it all. You can literally walk down cliffside steps in the backyard and start snorkeling. There's no sandy beach but even the pool boasts an ocean view. And, oh yes, despite the affordable price the units have everything you'll need from kitchens to phones. Mazarine by the Sea shuts down for a month each year from mid-October through mid-November.

La Casa Del Masa (☎ 292-8726; fax 295-4447; 7 Eves Hill Lane; unit $130; 🗙 🖳) Set atop a small but steep hill, La Casa Del Masa will give your legs a little exercise and reward your eyes with a panoramic view of the north shore and the azure waters of the Great Sound. Spacious and modern, each of the three units has a bedroom with two double beds, a separate kitchen and full amenities. Guests share a patio and can enjoy a cook-out at the barbecue grill by the pool.

Robin's Nest (☎ 292-4347, in the USA ☎ 800-637-4116; robinsnest@cwbda.bm; 10 Vale Close; 1-/2-bedroom unit $125/175; 🗙 🗙 🖳) In a quiet neighborhood on a little side road, this place has four apartments that are neat as a pin and it's a good option if you want to be a bit off the beaten path. Lots of nice touches, such as ceiling fans (if you don't want to use the air-con) and cable TV.

Eating

All of the places listed in this section are just west of the City of Hamilton, with the exception of La Coquille, which is on the eastern outskirts of the city. In addition, visitors can take advantage of the full array of restaurants in Hamilton, which is within walking distance of most Pembroke accommodations.

RESTAURANTS

Ascots (☎ 295-9644; 24 Rosemont Ave; lunch $15-25, dinner $35-55; 🕑 lunch & dinner; 🗙 🗙) If you're looking for a splurge, this stylish restaurant in the Royal Palms Hotel is the place to head. The cuisine is award-winning, the service is unsurpassed and the wine list is among the island's best. The menu includes continental fare such as tarragon-grilled lamb, as well as local favorites, including a delicious pan-fried rockfish topped with bananas and rum. There are also a few vegetarian items on the menu and there's always a fresh fish-of-the-day special at lunch.

Aggie's Garden (☎ 296-7346; 108 Pitts Bay Rd; dishes $10-14; 🕑 10am-3pm Mon-Fri; 🗙) Café tables on the waterfront lawn and homemade organic dishes await the lucky diners who find their way to this delightful little spot. So incredible is the food here that heavyweights like *Food & Wine* magazine discovered owner/chef Judith Wadson's restaurant shortly after it opened. The ingredients change

seasonally with whatever's fresh, but such things as pumpkin-ginger soup and lemon-roasted chicken spice up a menu that also includes crispy fresh salads.

Monty's Restaurant (☎ 295-5759; 75 Pitts Bay Rd; breakfast & lunch $7-12, dinner $20-26; 🕑 breakfast, lunch & dinner; 🗙 🗙) A cheery lime-green interior and local food with a creative twist are the hallmarks of this island favorite. Breakfast features just about anything that can be done with an egg, and at lunch you'll find juicy burgers and tasty wrap sandwiches. There are lots of fun choices at dinner, including a delicious mango Caribbean chicken served with rice and peas.

La Coquille (☎ 292-6122; 40 Crow Lane; appetizers $15-20, mains $22-40; 🕑 dinner; 🗙 🗙) A quiet harborfront location and good French Provence cuisine make a winning combination for a romantic night out. Seafood is the pièce de résistance. If asparagus and lavender-marinated salmon or grilled tuna truffle in a merlot sauce sound good, then you're in for a treat. Ask about the four-course menu ($65). The restaurant is at the east side of the Bermuda Underwater Exploration Institute.

Waterloo House (☎ 295-4480; 100 Pitts Bay Rd; lunch $12-20, dinner $28-40; 🕑 lunch & dinner; 🗙) The formal English-style dining room at the Waterloo House hotel has a harbor view and a solid international menu. Dishes such as herb-crusted lamb and pan-seared tandoori sea bass are just a couple of the award-winning dinner options. Men are required to wear jackets and ties at dinner. Lunch, served on the harborside terrace, is a less fastidious affair.

Ristorante Primavera (☎ 295-2167; 69 Pitts Bay Rd; lunch $12-20, dinner $18-30; 🕑 lunch Mon-Fri, dinner nightly; 🗙 🗙) Traditional Italian fare, from cheese-laden lasagna to fresh seafood marinara dishes, is the specialty in this reputable restaurant. It has jumped on the sushi trend too, but stick with the Italian options and you won't go wrong.

Fairmont Hamilton Princess (☎ 295-3000; 76 Pitts Bay Rd; 🕑 lunch & dinner; 🗙) This elegant hotel has several restaurants, including the waterside Harley's Terrace for alfresco dinner dining and the lobbyside Heritage Court for light eats, cocktails and afternoon tea.

GROCERIES

Miles Market (☎ 295-1234; 90 Pitts Bay Rd; 🕑 7:30am-7pm Mon-Sat, 1-5pm Sun) Around the back of the

'Waterfront' building, this is hands-down the island's best grocery store, with an impressive selection of imported items ranging from Indian nan to free-range chicken. It's also a splendid place for take-out fare, with a deli making sandwiches and gourmet-quality grilled salmon, a superb salad bar and luscious bakery pastries and breads.

Entertainment

Fairmont Hamilton Princess (☎ 295-3000; 76 Pitts Bay Rd; 🏊) Join the crowd of businesspeople that flocks to Friday happy hour (5pm to 9pm) at Harley's Terrace for half-priced drinks, free hors d'oeuvres and reggae music. Nice harbor view too. The hotel's Heritage Court, overlooking the posh lobby, has piano music and a vocalist on the weekends.

Beebe's (☎ 292-6122; 40 Crow Lane) This sophisticated lounge at La Coquille restaurant is a great place to watch the yachts sail in and out of the harbor as you linger over a rum swizzle. On Friday and Saturday nights, there's a DJ and dancing.

For other entertainment in the nearby area, see p59.

Getting There & Around

BUS

Several buses (p155) run through Pembroke Parish, all departing from the bus terminal in the City of Hamilton. Distances are short, with the longest bus ride – between the City of Hamilton and Spanish Point – taking just 12 minutes.

Bus No 4 runs west from the City of Hamilton along St John's Rd to Spanish Point Park and returns to Hamilton along North Shore Rd. Monday to Saturday the bus runs at least hourly from 8am to 6pm, but on Sunday there are only half a dozen runs.

Bus No 11, which terminates in the Town of St George, connects the City of Hamilton with the northeast coast of Pembroke via Blackwatch Pass. Monday to Saturday the bus runs from 6:45am to 11:45pm, with departures every 15 minutes at the height of the day, but as infrequently as once an hour in the early morning and during the evening. On Sunday bus No 11 runs once an hour from 7:45am to 10:45pm.

MOTOR SCOOTER

Scooter rentals (p157) are available from **Smatt's Cycle Livery** (☎ 295-1180; Pitts Bay Rd), next to the Fairmont Hamilton Princess.

TAXI

Taxis (p157) line up at the Fairmont Hamilton Princess and can be waved down along Pitts Bay Rd.

St George's Parish

ST GEORGE'S PARISH

HIGHLIGHTS

- Stroll the cobbled streets of the **Town of St George** (opposite), with its profusion of historic sights

- Dine on freshly caught seafood at St David's waterfront **Black Horse Tavern** (p84)

- Snorkel over the underwater delights of **Tobacco Bay** (p81)

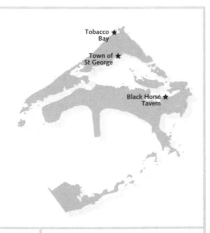

Tobacco ★ Bay

Town of ★ St George

Black Horse ★ Tavern

- POPULATION: 5451
- AREA: 2.14 SQ MILES

The parish of St George's embodies Bermuda's colonial past like no other place on the island. Indeed, some would argue like no other place anywhere. The centerpiece of Bermuda's easternmost parish is the historic Town of St George. Overlooking St George's Harbour, it was Bermuda's first capital and stands today as its most fascinating sightseeing area.

Established in 1612, the Town of St George is the oldest continually inhabited English settlement in the New World. Many of its original twisting alleys and colonial buildings remain intact, as do several forts. St George has done such an exceptional job of preserving its historic sites that in 2000 Unesco recognized the town and its fortifications as a World Heritage Site.

What is so unique about St George isn't simply that the town has preserved so many of its original buildings, but that it's done such a tremendous job of maintaining their original character in the face of changing times. The town has kept modern eyesores, such as overhead utility lines, to a minimum. Several buildings, from the town hall to the waterfront tavern, still have functions that reflect their original use.

The parish's other town, St David's, is a bastion of local tradition in its own right. It doesn't abound with historic buildings the way the Town of St George does, but it has deep roots that go back nearly as far. Most of the families living in the village trace their heritage to early colonial years and pride themselves on maintaining their legacy of living close to the sea.

The other side of St George's Parish is the exclusive community of Tucker's Town, which is located – somewhat confusingly – on the southwest side of Castle Harbour with no land connection to the rest of the parish. It has Bermuda's most expensive real estate and is a second home for some very wealthy folks, including a few prominent international billionaires.

TOWN OF ST GEORGE

No matter what direction you look in, this town exudes period charm. Some of its centuries-old buildings have been set aside as museums, but others continue to function as public meeting places, churches and shops. Even the names of the public ways – King's Square, Old Maid's Lane and Featherbed Alley, to name a few – conjure up images of the past.

St George has a pleasantly slow pace that sets it aside from the bustle of Hamilton, Bermuda's present-day capital. With the exception of outlying forts and beaches, all the main sights are within walking distance of the town center and are easily explored on foot. Be sure to give yourself a full day to appreciate all the town has to offer and treat yourself to lunch at one of those breezy harborside restaurants.

If you're touring in winter, consider coming on Wednesday, as it's the one day of the week when the Old State House and the Old Rectory are open to the public. If you're visiting in the summer, keep in mind that cruise ships dock at St George during the week so it tends to be less crowded on weekends.

Information
BOOKSTORES
Book Cellar (☎ 297-0448; 5 Water St) A quality little bookstore with books about Bermuda, travel literature and a choice selection of British and American novels.
Robertson's Drug Store (☎ 297-1736; 24 York St; ☻ 8am-7:30pm Mon-Sat, 4-6pm Sun) This is the place to pick up a wide range of foreign magazines and newspapers; it stocks some Bermuda-themed books as well.

EMERGENCY
Police station (☎ 297-1122; 22 York St) Centrally located in the heart of St George.

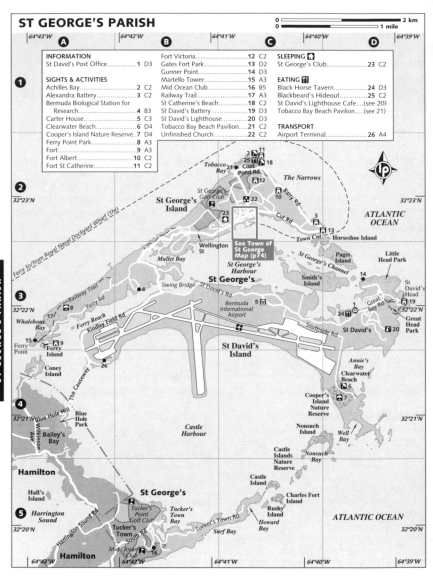

ST GEORGE'S PARISH

INFORMATION	
St David's Post Office.............1 D3	
SIGHTS & ACTIVITIES	
Achilles Bay.........................2 C2	
Alexandra Battery.................3 C2	
Bermuda Biological Station for	
Research...........................4 B3	
Carter House.......................5 C3	
Clearwater Beach..................6 D4	
Cooper's Island Nature Reserve..7 D4	
Ferry Point Park....................8 A3	
Fort...................................9 A3	
Fort Albert.........................10 C2	
Fort St Catherine................11 C2	

Fort Victoria......................12 C2	
Gates Fort Park..................13 D2	
Gunner Point......................14 D3	
Martello Tower...................15 A3	
Mid Ocean Club..................16 B5	
Railway Trail......................17 A3	
St Catherine's Beach............18 C2	
St David's Battery................19 D3	
St David's Lighthouse...........20 D3	
Tobacco Bay Beach Pavilion....21 C2	
Unfinished Church...............22 C2	

SLEEPING	
St George's Club..................23 C2	
EATING	
Black Horse Tavern...............24 D3	
Blackbeard's Hideout............25 C2	
St David's Lighthouse Cafe....(see 20)	
Tobacco Bay Beach Pavilion.....(see 21)	
TRANSPORT	
Airport Terminal..................26 A4	

INTERNET ACCESS
Cyber Caffe Latte (☎ 297-8196; 8 York St; per 15min $3; ☽ 7am-5pm) First-class cybercafé with good espresso and cushy chairs.

LAUNDRY
Tic-O-Matic Laundromat (☎ 293-9823; Shinbone Alley, north of York St; ☽ 7:30am-9pm Mon-Sat, to 6pm Sun)

MEDICAL SERVICES
Robertson's Drug Store (☎ 297-1736; 24 York St; ☽ 8am-7:30pm Mon-Sat, 4-6pm Sun) This large, well-stocked pharmacy is the place to get prescriptions filled.

MONEY
Bank of Bermuda (☎ 297-1812; King's Sq; ☽ 9am-4pm Mon-Fri)

Bank of Butterfield (☎ 297-1277; King's Sq; 9am-3:30pm Mon-Thu, to 4:30pm Fri) Both banks have ATMs that are accessible 24 hours.

POST
St George's Post Office (☎ 297-1610; 11 Water St)

TELEPHONE
There are pay phones at King's Square, including one inside the tourist office.

TOILETS
Public toilets are located east of the tourist office.

TOURIST INFORMATION
Visitors Service Bureau (☎ 297-1642; King's Sq; 9am-5pm Mon-Sat) The helpful staff here can pile you high with brochures covering all of Bermuda and provide local sightseeing information as well. It also sells bus tokens and passes. A second branch of the Visitors Service Bureau opens in the Penno's Wharf cruise ship terminal on mornings when cruise ships arrive.

Sights
KING'S SQUARE
Step into this quaint square, in the historic heart of St George, and it would be easy to imagine you'd entered the set of a colonial-era movie. **Town Hall** (☎ 297-1532; admission free; 10am-4pm Mon-Sat), erected in 1782 and decorated with the parish's colorful seal, crowns the square's eastern flank. This attractive building, where the mayor and council still meet, retains its original period character inside as well as out, with walls of Bermuda cedar and portraits of former mayors.

Another place to stick your head into is the **pillory and stocks** at the north side of the square. Now a photo op for tourists, they were once used to publicly chastise male residents who offended colonial mores with such misdeeds as excessive drinking and rowdiness.

Colonial women had their justice doled out on the south side of the square, in the form of the **ducking stool**. This odd contraption has a seat at the end of a long seesaw-like plank that's hung over the water's edge. Women accused of gossiping or other petty offenses had to endure the humiliation of being dunked into the harbor. These days it's more fun, with costumed actors reenacting the scene at noon on Wednesday and Saturday year-round and on additional days in summer.

Just west of the ducking stool, a little causeway leads to Ordnance Island, which once served as a British arsenal and now hosts a cruise ship dock and the public ferry. At the northwest side of the island, you'll be welcomed by a lifelike **statue of Sir George Somers**, Bermuda's shipwrecked founder, created by local sculptor Desmond Fountain. On the east side of the island is a **replica of Deliverance** (☎ 297-1459; adult/child $3/1; 9am-5pm Apr-Nov), the wooden ship that Somers built in 1610 in order to continue his journey to the Virginia colony of Jamestown. As happens to old ships, this replica could benefit from a little restoration, but you can walk through the boat's holds, where simple exhibits using mannequins give a glimpse of what life was like in these cramped quarters.

ST PETER'S CHURCH
Perhaps no building in town conveys a more thorough sense of history than **St Peter's Church** (☎ 297-8359; York St; admission free; 10am-4pm). One of the oldest Anglican churches in the Western Hemisphere, it dates to 1612, though much of the present church was added in the early 1700s.

It's a completely historic building with open beams of timber, hanging chandeliers and a wall of marble memorial stones whose curious epitaphs honor early governors, clergy and business leaders. In the east wing is the oldest piece of Bermudian furniture on the island: a red cedar altar made under the direction of the first governor.

Other early colonial period items are in the vestibule behind the main altar, where a vault with a glass door contains a silver chalice that's been in use by the church since 1625. The chalice is engraved with the coat of arms of the Bermuda Company, which bankrolled the early settlers, and a scene showing the ill-fated *Sea Venture* grounding on a rock.

More insights into the past can be found in the surrounding **churchyard**. Like St Peter's

ST GEORGE'S PARISH

BY GEORGE, I THINK I'VE GOT IT

Parish, island, town – all these names are bloody confusing. So here's the deal: St George's Parish is home to the island of St George's, which in turn is home to the Town of St George.

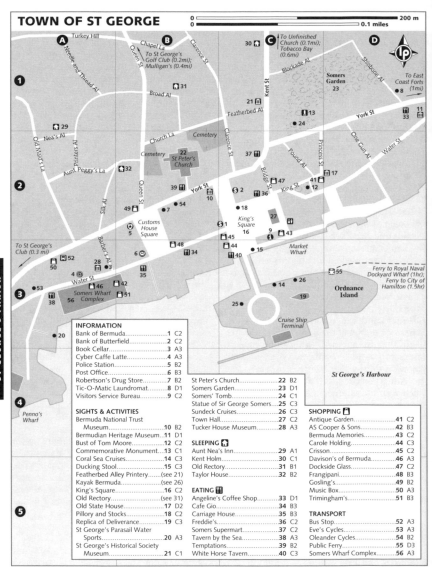

TOWN OF ST GEORGE

Church itself, it once had segregated areas for black and white parishioners, with the graves for slaves confined to the west side of the yard in the walled area closest to Queen St. On the church's east side is the grave of Sir Richard Sharples, the Bermudian governor who was gunned down in March 1973. The governor is buried alongside his bodyguard, Captain Hugh Sayers of the Welsh Guards, who was murdered by the same assassins on the grounds of Government House.

BERMUDA NATIONAL TRUST MUSEUM

If the walls could talk, this **museum** (☎ 297-1423; cnr York St & King's Sq; adult/child $4/2; ⏱ 10am-4pm Mon-Sat) would have some curious tales to tell. This well-preserved colonial structure was built as the Governor's House in 1700 by Bermuda governor Samuel Day, who was later jailed for placing the land title in his own name. In the mid-1800s it was turned into the Globe Hotel, and in 1863 it became the office for Major Norman Walker, an agent for the US Confederate government.

St George had an interesting role in the US Civil War as a transshipment center for Southern cotton headed to mills in England. Because of the Union blockade, swift steamships were employed as blockade-runners by the Confederacy to get the cotton as far as Bermuda, where it was transferred to more seaworthy cargo vessels for the transatlantic passage. St George enjoyed an unprecedented economic boom, its harbor bustling with North American ships and its waterfront warehouses piled high with cotton.

The upper floor of the museum focuses on the role Bermuda played during the US Civil War, mainly through displays delving into the nitty-gritty details of blockade-runners and war profiteering. Downstairs there's a model of the *Sea Venture*, the flagship that carried the first English settlers to St George, and a 12-minute video presentation on Bermudian history.

Add $1 to the admission fee and you can get a combination ticket that also allows entry to the Tucker House Museum in St George and the Verdmont Museum (p94) in Smith's Parish.

OLD STATE HOUSE

The **Old State House** (King St; admission free; ☉ 10am-4pm Wed), perched above the east end of King St, dates to 1620 and is the oldest building in Bermuda. Although modest in size, the building incorporates Italianate features and has a stately appearance from its former role as colonial Bermuda's parliamentary house. After the capital was moved to Hamilton in 1815, the Freemasons were granted the building as a meeting hall in exchange for the annual payment of a single peppercorn.

Over the years, the place slipped into disrepair but was thoroughly renovated and reopened in a grand ceremony officiated at by Prince Charles in 1970. If you happen to be in town on a Wednesday, you can view the ornate chamber where island lawmakers debated their causes for nearly two centuries.

On King St, in front of the Old State House, you'll find a little green space containing the **bust of Tom Moore**, an Irish poet who sojourned in Bermuda in 1804. Moore made a bit of a wave in town when he developed a crush on the 16-year-old wife of one of the Tuckers and immortalized her in a collection of poems, *Odes to Nea*.

ST GEORGE'S HISTORICAL SOCIETY MUSEUM

This well-presented **museum** (☎ 297-0423; cnr Kent St & Featherbed Alley; adult/child $5/2; ☉ 10am-4pm Mon-Fri Apr-Dec, 12am-4pm Wed Jan-Mar) does a fine job at recreating a sense of colonial days in this richly historic town. A portrait of the town's most famous resident, Sir George Somers, sits frozen in time above the fireplace. The rest of the museum, which resides in a 1730s house, is decorated with antique furnishings, including four-poster beds, a wood-fired oven, a 1644 Bible, period weapons, hand-blown bottles and the like.

In the basement of the same building, you'll find the **Featherbed Alley Printery**, where broadsides are still occasionally imprinted using a centuries-old press. Volunteers in period dress staff the museum and the printery and will cheerily show you around and point out intriguing little oddities.

TUCKER HOUSE MUSEUM

Walk through the door of the **Tucker House** (☎ 297-0545; Water St; adult/child $3/2; ☉ 10am-4pm Mon-Sat) and it's a bit like stepping back to 1775. That's the year that Henry Tucker, the colonial treasurer, purchased this place. Treasurers had deep pockets and the Tuckers were one of the most prestigious families in Bermuda. One unique aspect of this house is that it remains almost exactly as the Tuckers had it in the 18th century and provides a glimpse of that period through the life of just one family. The decor is unchanged and most of the furnishings, silver and china on display come from the Tucker estate.

The museum's collection includes numerous portraits of Tucker family members and priceless pieces of mahogany and Bermuda cedar furnishings. If you want to learn more, duck into the basement, where there's a little archaeological exhibit that details the history of the property.

Add $2 to the admission fee for a combination ticket that also allows entry to the

ST GEORGE'S PARISH

Bermuda National Trust Museum in St George and the Verdmont Museum (p94) in Smith's Parish.

OLD RECTORY

The **Old Rectory** (☎ 236-6483; 1 Broad Alley; admission free; ☼ 1-5pm Wed Nov-Mar) was built in 1699 by the notorious pirate George Dew, who fled the American colonies for Bermuda where he converted to the good life, becoming a church warden and lawyer. Dew knew a bit about construction and erected the house with a stone roof, rather than the less durable palmetto thatch that had been used previously on island homes. He built the walls from limestone quarried beneath the house foundation, a technique that also created a cellar in the process.

The Old Rectory takes its name from a later owner, Alexander Richardson, an English minister who was given the property in the mid-18th century as a wedding gift from the father of his Bermuda-born bride. Today it's still a charming little house with period furnishings, cedar ceilings and a solidly colonial character.

Now owned by the Bermuda National Trust, you can tour the interior of the house in two ways – either by staying there as a B&B guest (opposite), or by visiting on Wednesday afternoons in winter, the only time it's open to sightseers. At other times, view it from outside the gate.

BERMUDIAN HERITAGE MUSEUM

Dedicated to the history of black Bermudians, this earnest **museum** (☎ 297-4126; cnr York & Water Sts; admission $4; ☼ 10am-3pm Tue-Sat) tells the story of the struggle for equality in Bermuda.

Displays cover the impact of slavery from 1616, when the first two slaves were brought to Bermuda to dive for pearls, up until emancipation in 1834. Look for the story of Sally Bassett, a slave burned at the stake for allegedly poisoning slave owners though she insisted she was innocent, and the account of the *Enterprise*, a US slave ship blown off course into Bermudian waters, a fortuitous event for the 73 slaves who were set free under Bermuda law. Today thousands of black Bermudians can trace their ancestry to the descendants of the *Enterprise*.

Also detailed are the 'friendly societies' that were organized in the years surrounding emancipation to create economic and social opportunities for black residents. Other exhibits touch upon the barriers of segregation that black Bermudians encountered long after emancipation ended, and the extensive contributions of black Bermudians in fields ranging from the construction trades to cricket and government service.

UNFINISHED CHURCH

Although it looks like the ruins of a once-grand Gothic church, the **Unfinished Church** (north end of Kent St; admission free) is, in fact, the hollow shell of a 'new' Anglican church. It was intended to replace St Peter's, which had fallen into disrepair by the mid-1800s. Construction began on this replacement church in 1874 and piecemeal work continued for two decades. Meanwhile, bickering between parishioners – some who supported the new church and an increasing number who favored restoring St Peter's – eventually brought the project to a halt.

Although it was left abandoned before a roof ever went up, the ruins have come to represent another slice of history and the Bermuda National Trust now maintains the property. The trust has even done restoration work to stabilize the walls so visitors can stroll the grounds safely.

SOMERS GARDEN

This **park** (York St; admission free; ☼ 7:30am-7:30pm summer, to 4:30pm winter), the town's largest green space, offers some shady respite with tall royal palms and a monument erected in 1909 to commemorate the 300th anniversary of the founding of Bermuda by Sir George Somers. Admiral Somers, as islanders like to note, left his heart in Bermuda – and they mean this quite literally. Somers' heart, along with his entrails, lie at rest in a modest **tomb** at the southwest corner of the park. As was customary at the time, the rest of his body was packed into a barrel of alcohol and shipped back to England for burial in his hometown of Lyme Regis. Incidentally, Lyme Regis and St George are now twinned as sister cities.

Activities

GOLF

Don't let the affordable rates mislead you at the government-run **St George's Golf Club** (☎ 297-8353, reservations 234-4653; 1 Park Rd; greens fee $60; (☉ sunrise-sunset). This par-62, 4043yd course, built by Robert Trent Jones, is a beauty. It offers breathtaking views and just enough challenges to keep you focused. Ask about reduced rates after 3pm in summer and 1pm in winter.

KAYAKING

Kayak Bermuda (☎ 297-4223; Ordnance Island; tour $55; ☉ 9am-5pm Mar-Nov) runs a 3-hour kayak tour that paddles past unspoiled islands and allows time for swimming and sunbathing.

CRUISES

Sundeck Cruises (☎ 293-2640; Ordnance Island; tour $45; ☉ departures 9:30am & 1:30pm May-Nov) takes out a 60ft glass-bottom catamaran to shallow reefs for a 3½-hour snorkeling cruise. It provides all the goodies – all you need is a bathing suit and towel.

Coral Sea Cruises (☎ 335-2425; Ordnance Island; adult/child $25/15; ☉ departures 1:15pm Mon-Sat, also 11am Thu) operates a 60ft glass-bottom boat on a one-hour cruise to a coral reef. It's an easy and fun way to see Bermuda's colorful underwater world without getting wet.

PARASAILING

Feel like flying over the water? **St George's Parasail Water Sports** (☎ 297-1542; Somers Wharf; ride $50; ☉ 9am-5pm May-Oct) will strap a harness and sail onto you and zip you up and away for a 10-minute thrill ride across St George's Harbor.

Sleeping

Old Rectory (☎ 297-4261; oldrectory@northrock.bm; 1 Broad Alley; r with shared bathroom $100-150) This lovely historic building, which is owned by the Bermuda National Trust, has turned two of its rooms into a B&B. Staying in this authentically-preserved home is like plunging into another era, with rooms full of antique furnishings and a thoroughly colonial appeal. There's even an original fireplace in one of the bedrooms. Breakfast is included in the price. An unforgettable experience, especially for those who would like to soak up the rich sense of history that St George offers.

Taylor House (☎ 297-1161; mark@bermudagetaway .com; Aunt Peggy's Lane; winter/summer $100/130; ❄) A delightful split-level apartment in a c 1690 house, this place combines historic charm

with all the comforts of home. Downstairs there's a cozy living room and a kitchen equipped with every convenience imaginable. Upstairs is a roomy bedroom with a queen bed and a single bed. Both the living room and bedroom have cable TV, phones and ceiling fans. There's no housekeeping service, but the owner provides guests with clean towels and sheets as needed, and no service fees or taxes are added on to the bill.

Aunt Nea's Inn (☎ 297-1630; www.auntneas.com; 1 Nea's Alley; r winter/summer from $160/190; ❄ ❄) Attentive service and comfy rooms await at this upmarket B&B in a quiet residential neighborhood within walking distance of the town center. The rooms, most of which are in the 18th-century main house, boast antique furnishings, with either four-poster or sleigh beds, and some also have fireplaces and whirlpool baths. Guests have access to a TV lounge and limited kitchen facilities; breakfast is included.

St George's Club (☎ 297-1200; www.stgeorgeclub .com; Rosehill Hill St; r winter/summer from $180/325; ❄ ❄) It's as large as things come in this little town, but this hilltop condominium complex has an agreeable low-key layout that's in touch with its surroundings. The tone is serene, pampering and personable. The 70 units are comfortably furnished, each with a living room and complete kitchen and most with nice views of the town and surrounding sea. Facilities include a fitness center, three pools (one heated), tennis courts and a putting green.

Kent Holm (☎ 297-0528; Kent St; r/studio $75/95) Home hospitality is the hallmark at this small family-run guesthouse at the home of Grace Smith. Situated on the road to the Unfinished Church, it's a short walk to anywhere in the town center and about 10 minutes to Tobacco Bay. Choose between a straightforward room that has one double and one single bed and a small refrigerator, or a studio unit that is equipped with a full kitchen.

Eating

RESTAURANTS

Cafe Gio (☎ 297-1307; 36 Water St; lunch $9-16, dinner $15-29; ☉ lunch & dinner; ❄ ❄) This trendy place has a lot going for it: excellent food fusing Italian and island influences, an open-air waterfront patio and good service. The chefs know their stuff here. Favorites include the crispy calamari fritti, a mouth-watering crusted tuna which is seared on the outside and sashimi-like in the middle, and of course the local catch of the day. It also offers a full range of pizza and pasta.

Mulligan's (☎ 297-1836; 1 Park Rd; lunch $10-20, dinner $26-34; ☺ lunch & dinner; ☒) Perched above St George's Golf Club, this place does a nice job with anything that swims in the sea. The chowder is an award-winner, the grilled wahoo sandwich is a sure bet and the chef consistently prepares tuna the way it was meant to be. Good codfish cakes and salads too. It's easy to see why people come from all over the island to eat here.

Temptations (☎ 297-1368; 31 York St; items $2-6; ☺ 8:30am-5pm Mon-Sat; ☒ ☒) The best place for a quick bite in the town center, this simple eatery is a cross between a bakery and a café. You'll find reasonably-priced pies, cakes and pastries. A tasty house special is the chicken curry pie, or order a sandwich on your choice of breads. Temptations also doubles as the local ice-cream shop.

Angeline's Coffee Shop (☎ 297-0959; 48 York St; dishes $5-9; ☺ 7am-3pm Mon-Fri, to noon Sat & Sun; ☒) This is where the locals eat. And there's absolutely no fast food here – instead, everything is made to order as you watch. Sit at the counter as Angeline grills up hand-patted burgers, thick and juicy. The fish sandwiches, crispy and mounded high, are a meal in themselves.

Carriage House (☎ 297-1730; Water St; lunch $9-18, dinner $22-38; ☺ lunch & dinner; ☒ ☒) Old World atmosphere permeates this 18th-century building that used to serve as a storage house for horse-and-buggy carriages. Although it's best known as an upmarket candlelit dinner restaurant, they serve some reasonably-priced lunch deals as well, including sandwiches and a seafood plate of the day. At dinner expect continental fare such as rack of spring lamb, roasted duck and filet mignon.

White Horse Tavern (☎ 297-1838; King's Sq; lunch $10-16, dinner $25-40; ☺ lunch & dinner) You can get better food elsewhere, but for atmosphere and setting, it's hard to beat this popular place, which has a patio that literally hangs over the water. At lunch most people opt for the salads, sandwiches and pub grub; the steak and ale pie is a favorite. At dinner there's a full complement of meat and fish plates.

Tavern by the Sea (☎ 297-3305; 14 Water St; sandwiches $8-14, mains $13-30; ☺ 11:30am-10pm or later) This pub is a busy eating spot on sunny days, when people flock to its waterside patio. It's best known for its sandwiches and burgers, which run the gamut from vegetarian options to a bacon-cheeseburger or classic reuben (corned beef, sauerkraut and Swiss cheese on rye bread). The place also has specialty salads and pub grub such as shepherd's pie.

Freddie's (☎ 297-1717; King's Sq; mains $10-20; ☺ lunch & dinner) A sunny balcony overlooking the square, and decent prices, including a daily soup and sandwich special ($10) make this a good central budget place to take a break from your sightseeing.

GROCERIES

Somers Supermart (☎ 297-1177; 41 York St; ☺ 7am-9pm Mon-Sat, 8am-8pm Sun) This is the only place to buy groceries in town, but it's conveniently located with long opening hours.

Entertainment

In St George, the entertainment generally varies with the time of year, with the most activity occurring during the season when the cruise ships are in dock, from May to October. The rest of the year things quiet down dramatically, so it's best to call ahead or take a look in the local papers to see what's happening.

White Horse Tavern (☎ 297-1838; King's Sq) One of St George's main entertainment venues and a fine place to linger over a mug of frosty brew while looking out at the sea. On Monday, Tuesday and Wednesday nights during the cruise ship season it turns into a DJ nightclub after dinner and rocks until 3am, and throughout the year on Friday and Saturday nights there's live music.

Tavern by the Sea (☎ 297-3305; 14 Water St; ☺ 11:30am-10pm or later) This pub has happy hour from 5pm to 7pm on weekdays. During the cruise ship season, there's live entertainment (anything from karaoke to rock bands) into the wee hours of most nights.

Freddie's (☎ 297-1717; King's Sq) Downstairs in the restaurant of the same name, this smoky sports bar right on King's Square attracts a mixed crowd of locals and American expats who come to watch the big-screen satellite TV that tunes in to Boston-based baseball, football and basketball.

On Tuesdays during the summer months, St George holds Heritage Nights from 7pm to 9:30pm with craft and food stalls set up in King's Square, and live music and Gombey dancers, all geared to entertain cruise ship passengers in port at the time.

Shopping

There are lots of good shopping possibilities in St George. Hamilton's two main department stores – **Trimingham's** (☎ 297-1726; Water St) and **AS Cooper & Sons** (☎ 297-0925; Water St) – have branches at the Somers Wharf complex. These stores carry a wide variety of items, including top international brands of china, crystal, designer clothing, jewelry and perfumes. They also have swimsuits and local items such as Bermuda shorts and Royall Bay Rhum cologne.

Bermuda Memories (☎ 297-8104; 7 King's Sq) Adjacent to the tourist office, this shop sells quality watercolors by artist Jill Amos Raine, who focuses on Bermuda's historic buildings, pastel-colored houses and waterside scenes. In addition to the original paintings, there are also reasonably priced prints and notecards, all of which would make nice take-home memories of Bermuda.

Dockside Glass (☎ 297-3908; 3 Bridge St) A branch of the famous Royal Dockyard company, the shop sells handblown glass – everything from tiny tree frogs to large serving bowls – it also sells Bermuda-made rum cakes. Come in for a free cake sample and to watch the glassblower do her thing.

Frangipani (☎ 297-1357; Water St) For women who like pastel colors and lightweight cotton fabrics, this clothing shop is a real find, with lots of beachwear in tropical flower and fish designs.

Carole Holding (☎ 297-1833; King's Sq) This namesake shop features the Bermuda-themed watercolors of Carole Holding on everything from bone china mugs to T-shirts and frameable prints. The shop also sells other souvenirs such as jams, trinkets and Bermuda-made handicrafts.

Davison's of Bermuda (☎ 297-0348; Water St) Head here if you want to pick up Bermuda design T-shirts, polo shirts, beach bags and other casual gear.

Antique Garden (☎ 297-0901; 2 King St) This shop, fittingly in a centuries-old building, sells high-end antiques, both from Bermuda and the owner's travels abroad.

Music Box (☎ 297-0484; 8 York St; ☿ closed Mon) CDs and cassettes by Bermudian musicians are for sale here. Choose from steel bands, reggae groups, the Bermuda Regiment Band, and even tree frogs!

Crisson (☎ 297-0107; cnr Water & King's Sq) This jewelry shop carries imported watches, jewelry and gemstones as well as Bermuda-themed pendants and bracelets with sea turtles, dolphins and similar designs.

Gosling's (☎ 298-7339; cnr York & Queen Sts) If you're looking for wine and spirits, this liquor store carries a good variety, including its namesake Gosling's Black Seal Rum.

Getting There & Around
TO/FROM THE AIRPORT

It's a mere 10-minute ride from the airport to the Town of St George. The taxi fare is about $12. Bus Nos 1, 2, 10 and 11 stop in front of the airport terminal on the way to St George ($3), but the bus is only practical if you're traveling very light, as bus rules require that your luggage fits on your lap.

BICYCLE

Bicycles (p154) can be rented from **Eve's Cycles** (☎ 236-0839; 1 Water St).

BOAT

The public ferry (p154) runs a high-speed catamaran service from St George to the Royal Naval Dockyard ($4) and the City of Hamilton ($8) three times a day. The service operates only from mid-April to mid-November. It leaves Hamilton at 9:30am, noon and 2pm, arriving at the Dockyard after 20 minutes and departing 10 minutes later for the one-hour trip to St George. The boat then leaves St George at 11:15am, 1:30pm and 3:45pm, makes the one-hour trip to the Dockyard, and departs from the Dockyard at 12:30pm, 2:30pm and 4:55pm for the quick trip back to Hamilton. It's a great option for cruise ship passengers, providing a quick and convenient way to get between the three main tourist destinations in a fraction of the time it would take by bus.

BUS

No two places have better public bus service (p155) between them than St George and the City of Hamilton, a boon for visitors, since these are the two main sightseeing, dining and shopping destinations. Buses terminate on (and depart from) York St.

Bus Nos 1, 3, 10 and 11 connect St George with the City of Hamilton, a ride that takes about an hour. Service is frequent during the day, with at least one of these buses operating every 15 minutes from 6:45am to 7pm; bus No 11 provides evening service once every hour until 11:45pm (10:45pm on Sunday). Bus No 6 connects St George with St David's (p84).

MINIBUS

The **St George's Mini-Bus Service** (☎ 297-8199 bus, 297-8492 office) operates around St George's Parish somewhat like a taxi service, with routes and drop-off points determined by where the passengers need to go. Hours of operation are 7:30am to midnight Monday to Friday and 9am to midnight Saturday and Sunday. The cost is $3 around the Town of St George and up to $5 to more distant places in the parish.

The buses, which are blue with a yellow minibus sign on top, pull into King's Square every 20 to 30 minutes or so. You can also call to arrange to be picked up anywhere in the greater St George area. As might be expected, the minibuses are busiest on cruise ship days.

MOTOR SCOOTER

Scooter rentals (p157) are available at **Eve's Cycles** (☎ 236-0839; 1 Water St) and at **Oleander Cycles** (☎ 297-0478; 26 York St). Rates, including mandatory charges, range from about $70 for a one-day rental to $140 for a three-day rental.

TAXI

You can find a ride in a taxi (p157) at King's Square.

AROUND ST GEORGE'S ISLAND

There are several worthy sights to explore and attractive beaches to enjoy around St George's Island.

Sights & Activities

FORT ST CATHERINE

At the northeastern tip of St George's Island, the landmark Fort St Catherine has all the expected trappings – a drawbridge, a moat, ramparts, a maze of tunnels and five powerful 18-ton muzzleloader guns. The whole shebang has been made into a **museum** (☎ 297-1920; 15 Coot Pond Rd; adult/child $5/2; ☺ 10am-4pm).

From the ramparts you're overlooking the beach where Sir George Somers and his shipwrecked crew scurried ashore in 1609. Bermuda's first governor, a carpenter by the name of Richard Moore, constructed a primitive timber fortification here a few years later. The fort has since been rebuilt several times, with most of the current concrete structure dating to 1865.

The fort's old powder magazine now contains a collection of period weapons, the artillery storeroom has dioramas depicting colonial scenes and other rooms have displays ranging from an audiovisual presentation on Bermuda's abundant forts to replicas of Britain's crown jewels.

Fort St Catherine is about a mile north of the Town of St George. To get there, turn right on Sapper Lane, north of the Unfinished Church, and continue on Victoria Rd.

INVASION ANXIETY

In colonial times, no place in Bermuda held greater strategic importance than the Narrows, a slender reef channel that snakes for a mile along the northeast coast of St George's Island. It provided the only navigable shipping lane into the Town of St George. Consequently, this stretch of coastline was heavily fortified by British colonists to fend off potential invaders.

The handful of forts that still line the coast opposite the Narrows today offer an interesting glimpse of the invasion anxiety that gripped islanders for more than three centuries. Despite the energy exerted on their defenses, Bermuda has never been the object of a foreign attack.

In actuality, only once in its entire history has Bermuda even had the opportunity to fire its guns in anger, and that was way back in 1614, when two small Spanish ships surveying the new British colony decided to launch a skiff near the entrance of Castle Harbour. The skiff drew immediate fire and the Spaniards beat a quick retreat, marking the first and last of Bermuda's military 'skirmishes.' The incident did, however, serve to prompt the construction of some 50 forts throughout Bermuda in the years that followed.

OTHER FORTIFICATIONS

Two other monuments to the military madness of the day can be found about two miles southeast of Fort St Catherine, along the waterfront Barry Rd. **Alexandra Battery** (admission free; ☼ sunrise-sunset), which was built in the 1870s and extensively remodeled in the early 1900s, has a cannon with a unique cast-iron faceplate that was intended to protect the gunner from return fire (though of course there never was any!). The battery overlooks the site where the marooned English colonists constructed and launched the *Deliverance* in 1610.

Gates Fort Park (admission free; ☼ sunrise-sunset), at the point where Barry Rd changes to Cut Rd, holds a small battery with a couple of cannons and a lookout tower that offers a bird's-eye view of Town Cut, the strategic channel into St George's Harbour.

And as if that weren't enough, the grounds of the former Club Med, a closed hotel on the hillside southwest of Fort St Catherine, encompass the remains of two more forts: **Fort Victoria** and **Fort Albert**, both dating to the 19th century. The four guns at Fort Albert were of the same class as those displayed at Fort St Catherine, and the guns at Fort Victoria weighed in at 23 tons and shot massive 540lb shells. Neither of these forts can be visited, as the grounds remain closed to the public.

BEACHES

If you're up for a swim, there are a couple of beaches on the northern tip of the parish that are within walking distance of the Town of St George.

With the safest swimming on this end of Bermuda, **Tobacco Bay** (cnr Government Hill & Coot Hill Rds) is a little jewel of a beach with clear aqua-blue waters. It doesn't extend endlessly like Bermuda's south-side beaches, but there's certainly enough sand to make the kids happy. The bay's sheltered waters have intriguing pinnacle-like limestone rock formations that add an interesting element above the waterline and attract lots of tropical fish beneath the surface. If you're ready for some underwater sightseeing, this is a fun place to snorkel and you can rent gear at the beachside **pavilion** (☎ 297-2756; snorkel gear per day $20; ☼ 9am-7pm summer only).

Tobacco Bay, incidentally, played a part in the American Revolution, when gunpowder stolen from St George's magazine was loaded here onto small boats that scurried it across the reef to a waiting American ship, which in turn delivered the desperately-needed gunpowder to Washington's armies.

If you want to try something else, **Achilles Bay**, at the western side of Fort St Catherine, has a pleasant cove with a tiny public beach that's also good for swimming and snorkeling. The cove is backed by Blackbeard's Hideout, a bar and restaurant (p82).

St Catherine's Beach, at the south side of Fort St Catherine, is a longer and broader beach but with less-protected waters. Best for sunbathing, St Catherine's was once the private beach of the now-defunct Club Med.

RAILWAY TRAIL & FERRY POINT PARK

The easternmost section of the **Railway Trail** (p34), a 2.75-mile-long stretch, begins west of the Town of St George, off Wellington Lane, and follows the northern coastline to the desolate western tip of St George's Island at **Ferry Point Park**. Near the midway point, the trail connects back to the main vehicle road for about half a mile to loop around oil storage facilities that are off-limits to the public.

Just before Ferry Point, at the south side of picturesque **Whalebone Bay**, you'll find the foundations of a 19th-century gunpowder magazine and the **Martello tower**, a circular stone gun tower with a good 360-degree view. At Ferry Point itself there are two other historic remains – those of an early 17th-century **fort** and concrete footings that stand as the sole remnants of a **trestle** that once provided a rail link to Coney Island.

Nearby **Ferry Island**, which can be reached via a causeway, has more 19th-century fortification ruins that can be explored. Ferry Island, incidentally, takes its name from its former duty as the terminal for the ferry link that once provided the only connection between St George's Island and the rest of Bermuda.

When you're ready to leave, you can backtrack along the Railway Trail or simply return via Ferry Rd.

BERMUDA BIOLOGICAL STATION FOR RESEARCH

Commonly referred to in Bermuda simply as the **BBSR** (☎ 297-1880; www.bbsr.edu; Ferry Rd; ☼ tours 10am Wed), this very prestigious

ST GEORGE'S PARISH

research center was founded in 1903 as a joint venture of Harvard University, New York University and the Bermuda Natural History Society. Today the center provides facilities for resident staff, visiting scientists and university students. BBSR conducts research on the marine sciences, ranging from coral reef ecology to biological oceanography. Some of its work is in forefront environmental fields – the global geoscience program, for example, studies the effects that oceans have on climate in order to better understand global climate changes.

If you'd like to take a closer look, drop by on Wednesday for the free tour of the research station. The tours, which are led by BBSR docents, generally last about an hour and include a visit to the laboratories and research vessels.

BBSR is west of the Swing Bridge that connects St George's and St David's islands and can be reached by taking Biological Station Lane south from Ferry Rd.

Eating

Blackbeard's Hideout (☎ 297-1400; 6 Rose Hill; lunch $9-12, dinner $15-25; ☒ closed Mon) Best thing about this place is its great location overlooking Achilles Bay. There's a bustling indoor bar that's usually packed with regulars and an outdoor patio where you can dine alfresco and enjoy the view. Lunch offers up the usual fare of sandwiches (order the fish) and burgers. At dinner they add on steak and seafood dishes.

Tobacco Bay Beach Pavilion (☎ 297-2756; items $3-6; ☒ 9am-7pm summer only) This simple counter at Tobacco Bay sells burgers, hot dogs and ice cream.

Getting There & Around

The public bus doesn't go east or north of the Town of St George, but the St George's Mini-Bus Service (p80) runs to this area on demand. The cost is $3 to Tobacco Bay or Fort St Catherine and $4 to the Bermuda Biological Station or Ferry Point.

ST DAVID'S ISLAND

So often overlooked, St David's Island offers a glimpse of Bermuda at its least touristed. The village of St David's, tucked into the east of the island, maintains a more timeless, unchanged character than other Bermudian communities. Its pastel buildings are not fancy but they are picturesque in the late afternoon light. The village simply abounds with flowering hibiscus and is a particularly fun place to kick around on a motor scooter.

Until 1934, when the first bridge was built between St David's Island and St George's Island, St David's could only be reached by boat. For the most part, it was an isolation that was cherished by its inhabitants, a substantial number of whom are of Mahican ancestry – the descendants of native North Americans taken from the colonies during British Indian raids in the early 17th century.

In 1941 most of St David's Island was turned over to the US military for the development of a naval air station, and the residents, reluctant to leave St David's, were concentrated at the eastern end of the island.

In 1995 the US military finally left and returned the base lands to the Bermudian government. Large tracts of the former base still serve as Bermuda's airport, and the rest of the land is gradually being converted to civilian use. Some of the former base buildings are gaining a second life as new startup businesses and the old military homes are being renovated into affordable housing for first-time homeowners.

Information

The **St David's Post Office** (☎ 297-0847; 103 St David's Rd) closes over lunchtime from 11:30am to 1pm.

Sights & Activities

Once reserved for military personnel, **Clearwater Beach**, just south of the airport runway, is now a public swimming spot that's popular with island families both for its beach and for its fun children's playground. An adjacent area opposite the beach has been set aside for conservation as the **Cooper's Island Nature Reserve**, its rocky shoreline a favorite with island fishers.

GUNNER POINT

A good way to start an exploration of St David's Island is to drive to the end of the main road to **Gunner Point**, which offers a view of the nearshore islands that separate St David's from St George's.

The westernmost one, **Smith's Island**, is the biggest island in St George's Harbour. The eastern part of Smith's Island, as well as all of the island of **Paget**, which is north of Gunner Point, are government owned and set aside for natural preservation. In the 18th century, Smith's Island was used by whalers for boiling blubber, and Paget Island is best known as the site of the ironclad **Fort Cunningham**, one of the most costly forts ever erected in Bermuda. Unfortunately, the islands aren't readily accessible to visitors who don't have their own boats.

ST DAVID'S BATTERY

A visit to **St David's Battery** (Battery Rd; admission free; ☉ sunrise-sunset), perched on the edge of Bermuda's highest sea cliffs, will reward you with fine coastal views. This abandoned coastal defense station also boasts the Bermuda's most formidable guns, their rusting barrels sitting like silent sentinels above the vast Atlantic. The two largest guns date to the early 1900s, reach 37ft in length and had a shooting range of more than 7 miles.

The cliff face below contains a number of caves; you can glimpse them from the battery but because of the steep drop here they are not accessible. No matter which way you look there are memorable water views, but for the loveliest, walk a few minutes north past the last gun to look down on scenic **Red Hole Bay**. The south side of Red Hole Bay – like St David's Battery – is encompassed within a 25-acre tract known as **Great Head Park**.

The quickest way to get to St David's Battery is to take Battery Rd up past the cricket

SEEING THE LIGHT

On an island that was 'accidentally' discovered by shipwrecked castaways, it comes as no surprise that marine safety has long been a paramount concern. Indeed, shortly after the English established the first settlement in Bermuda in the early 17th century, a handful of simple light beacons were set on prominent hills to help guide approaching ships through Bermuda's tricky reefs.

By the 18th century, increased sea traffic had brought a sharp rise in the frequency of shipwrecks off Bermuda. Alarmed by the situation, the British Navy erected the first lighthouse at the aptly named Wreck Hill, on the westernmost tip of Sandys Parish. An elementary structure that burned tar as its light source, the Wreck Hill Lighthouse overlooked Western Ledge Flats, a site so notorious for claiming ships that mariners nicknamed it 'the graveyard.'

The light's strength proved insufficient, however, and in December 1838 the French frigate L'Herminie, a 300ft vessel with 60 cannons and a crew of nearly 500 men, went down on the reef just 4 miles west of Wreck Hill. In all, some 39 shipwrecks occurred during that decade off the west side of Bermuda. In 1840 the British government responded by appropriating funds to erect Bermuda's first modern lighthouse.

Situated in Southampton Parish atop 245ft Gibbs Hill, the new lighthouse began operation in May 1846. The tower, constructed of cast iron, extended a lofty 117ft from the base to the light. Fired by sperm whale oil that burned from four concentric wicks, the revolving light had the capacity to reach not only the treacherous western shoals, but substantial sections of the northern and southern shoals as well.

In the years that followed, attention shifted to the northeastern side of the island, where Sir George Somers had wrecked the Sea Venture some 250 years earlier and which remained beyond the reach of the Gibbs Hill light. In the 1870s, following a rash of shipwrecks on the reefs north of St George's, Bermuda's second lighthouse, St David's Lighthouse, was built atop a hill at the eastern side of that parish.

This second light filled in the former blind spot. Furthermore, when viewed together, the two lights cast from opposite ends of Bermuda allowed captains to gauge their ship's exact position. In the decades that followed, the frequency of shipwrecks off Bermuda dropped significantly – with many of the more notorious ones occurring in times of mechanical failures at the lighthouses.

Both of Bermuda's 19th-century lighthouses stand largely unchanged, except for the modernization of their light mechanisms. Instead of burning whale oil, they now operate on 1000-watt electric bulbs, which cast beams 40 miles out to sea. Bermuda's lighthouses also serve as landmarks for airplane pilots, who can spot the lights from more than 100 miles away.

grounds from Great Bay Rd. However, if you're on foot, you can also get to the battery by taking the footpath that begins at the signposted section of Great Head Park on Great Bay Rd. The path, shaded by Bermuda olivewood trees and fiddlewood, begins at the back of the parking area. Continue about 200yd until you reach a narrow dirt road, onto which you bear right; when the track splits, bear left. En route you'll get glimpses of St David's Lighthouse, pass more military ruins and catch a few coastal views.

ST DAVID'S LIGHTHOUSE

Perched atop a hill at the southeastern side of St David's, this vintage 1879 red-striped lighthouse (☎ 297-4481; Lighthouse Hill Rd; admission free; ☺ 10am-6pm Mon-Fri) offers a panoramic 360-degree view. To climb the stairs to the top of the 55ft lighthouse, just ask for the key at the adjacent café. Even if it's outside opening hours it's well worth scooting up here, as most of the view can be readily appreciated from the 485ft lighthouse hill.

To get to the lighthouse, take Lighthouse Hill Rd south from Great Bay Rd.

CARTER HOUSE

One of the nation's oldest homes, **Carter House** (☎ 293-5960; Southside Rd; admission by donation; ☺ 10am-4pm Tue-Thu & Sat) was built in the 1640s by descendants of Christopher Carter, a passenger on the shipwrecked *Sea Venture*. Of hardy stock, one descendant who lived in the house died in 1791 at age 114! Because Carter House was on US military base land, it was closed to the public for many years. Now the St David's Island Historical Society has set up a small museum inside, with displays on St David's culture as well as its history. Perhaps most interesting is the classic house itself, which has the original roof, cedar beams, open fireplace and a type of exterior stair walls known as 'welcoming arms.'

Eating

Black Horse Tavern (☎ 297-1991; St David's Rd; lunch $10-18, dinner $15-30; ☺ 11am-10pm Tue-Sun; ☒ ☒) Simply put, this local restaurant serves up the best fish on the island. Not only is the seafood unbeatable but the waterside view of Great Bay, complete with the fishing boats that bring in the catch, is the perfect match. In spite of being out of the way in

quiet St David's, don't expect the place to be undiscovered. The fish chowder is so famous that it's been written up in *Bon Appétit* magazine and the fresh wahoo is absolutely flawless. If they're out of wahoo, order the rockfish. Wherever you are in Bermuda, this place is well worth the drive – though avoid dinner on weekends as they often have to turn people away.

St David's Lighthouse Cafe (☎ 297-4481; Lighthouse Hill Rd; items $2-5; ☺ 10am-6pm Mon-Fri) This friendly little take-out stand adjacent to St David's Lighthouse serves up ice cream, drinks and sandwiches accompanied, of course, by a panoramic view.

Getting There & Around

Bus No 6 connects St George with St David's ($3, 25 minutes, hourly) from 6:15am to 6:15pm on weekdays; on weekends the service starts an hour or two later but is otherwise the same. In addition to the village, the bus goes to St David's Lighthouse, St David's Battery and Gunner Point. For more information on public buses, including passes, see p155.

St George's Mini-Bus Service (p80) runs an on-demand service between St David's and St George for $5.

TUCKER'S TOWN

Tucker's Town, at the southwestern side of Castle Harbour, is one of the most exclusive corners of Bermuda. Much of it is occupied by the members-only Mid Ocean Club, which boasts Bermuda's top-rated golf course. Tucker's Point Club, the site of the former Marriott hotel, is being developed with new multimillion-dollar homes and a posh hotel and spa.

Tucker's Town Rd, which runs along the narrow peninsula east of the Mid Ocean Club, is the crème de la crème, bordered by a few dozen homes belonging to wealthy foreigners, including the American billionaire Ross Perot and the Italian premier Silvio Berlusconi.

From the end of Tucker's Town Rd, you can look across a narrow strait to **Castle Island**, a nature preserve that contains the stone remains of a British fort, one of the earliest fortifications erected in the Western Hemisphere.

Nonsuch Island, to the east, is a bird sanctuary where great efforts are being made to reintroduce the Bermuda petrel, or cahow, one of the most endangered birds in the world. The cahow's exotic predators have been eliminated and efforts are ongoing to restore the island's precontact ecosystem. Not surprisingly, human access to the island is restricted, but the **Bermuda Biological Station** (p81) and the **Bermuda Audubon Society** (☎ 292-1920) occasionally bring groups over; call for information.

Activities

Tucker's Point Golf Club (☎ 298-6900; Tucker's Town; greens fee $185; ☉ sunrise-sunset), a par-71, 6440yd championship course, offers dramatic ocean views and interesting fairways. It's a private club, but reservations are accepted from nonmembers within 48 hours of tee time on a space-available basis.

You'll need an introduction by a member to play at the even more exclusive **Mid Ocean Club** (☎ 293-0330; Tucker's Town; with/without a member $70/200; ☉ sunrise-sunset), a par-71, 6512yd course. Inquire at your hotel if you're interested in getting on these greens.

Getting There & Away

Bus No 1 connects Tucker's Town with both the City of Hamilton ($4.50, 32 minutes) and Bailey's Bay ($3, 15 minutes). The bus goes to the Mid Ocean Club, where it turns around, but goes no further east. The bus operates every 30 minutes from 6:45am to 6:15pm weekdays and 7:45am to 5:45pm Saturday. On Sunday the service is only once an hour from 11am to 5pm. For more information on public buses, including passes, see p155.

Hamilton Parish

HAMILTON PARISH

HIGHLIGHTS

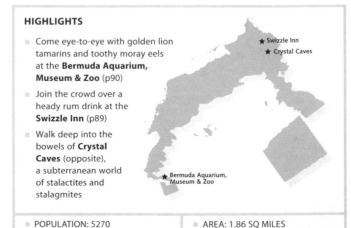

- Come eye-to-eye with golden lion tamarins and toothy moray eels at the **Bermuda Aquarium, Museum & Zoo** (p90)

- Join the crowd over a heady rum drink at the **Swizzle Inn** (p89)

- Walk deep into the bowels of **Crystal Caves** (opposite), a subterranean world of stalactites and stalagmites

★ Swizzle Inn
★ Crystal Caves
★ Bermuda Aquarium, Museum & Zoo

■ POPULATION: 5270 | ■ AREA: 1.86 SQ MILES

Water views abound in this parish, which wraps around scenic Harrington Sound. Bermuda's largest inland body of water, the sound is bordered to the south by Bermuda's most exclusive golf course, to the north by Bailey's Bay and to the west by Flatts Village. Peppered around the rest of the sound are fine upscale homes in enviable settings.

On the surface Harrington Sound has the appearance of a calm lake, but it is in fact a saltwater bay, connected to the sea by a narrow inlet at Flatts. In the village of Flatts, you'll find the island's most-visited sightseeing attraction. Environmentally distinguished and superbly presented, the Bermuda Aquarium, Museum & Zoo should make it onto any itinerary, doubly so for those with kids. The village's quirky railway museum can also be fun.

The parish's second village, Bailey's Bay, is a geographic wonder potholed with grand limestone caves and caverns. Virtually every place in Bailey's Bay seems to center around them. A trail through the village's Blue Hole Park winds along a series of caverns; the Grotto Bay Hotel has two awesome caves right on its grounds; and if you want to see the champion of them all, there's mammoth Crystal Caves which can be visited on a guided tour.

Beaches are few in the parish, but Shelly Bay Park is a popular family spot as the waters are shallow and there is a cool playground and decent snorkeling. Kayaking, sailing and diving are all available at the Grotto Bay Hotel. Or for a uniquely Bermudian underwater adventure, consider a helmet dive with Bermuda Bell Diving in Flatts.

BAILEY'S BAY

Bailey's Bay, the tiny village on the northeastern side of Hamilton Parish, offers an enjoyable little walking trail and an abundance of caves and water-filled grottoes. It also has an attractive beachside resort, a popular pub and one of Bermuda's most traditional restaurants. The village is easy to explore as all of Bailey's Bay's sights – Crystal Caves, Grotto Bay Beach Hotel and Blue Hole Park – are within walking distance of one another.

Information

The postage stamp–sized **Bailey's Bay Post Office** (☎ 293-2305; cnr Blue Hole Hill & Wilkinson Ave) closes for lunch from 11:30am to 1pm.

Sights

CRYSTAL CAVES

The most spectacular of the area's numerous caves is **Crystal Cave** (☎ 293-0640; Crystal Cave Rd; adult/child $12/7; ☽ 9:30am-5:30pm May-Sep, to 4:30pm Oct-Apr), with its thousands of crystal-like stalactites hanging above a greenish-blue pond.

Despite its enormous size, this huge subterranean cavern wasn't even discovered until 1907 when two boys, intent on retrieving a stray cricket ball, dropped a rope through a hole in the ground, shimmied down and found themselves inside.

Today a series of 82 steps leads visitors 120ft below the surface, past stalactites and stalagmites and onto a pontoon walkway spanning the pond that fills the cave floor. The water, which reaches a depth of 55ft, is crystal clear and free of marine life and vegetation.

The tour guide provides commentary on the geological origins of the caves and points out odd formations that resemble profiles, including an amazing likeness of the Manhattan skyline. All in all, it's an enjoyable little excursion that takes about 20 minutes.

If you're absolutely fanatical about caves, there's another one on the property, **Fantasy Cave**, that you can visit for an additional $6, but it's not nearly as interesting as Crystal. The caves are a few minutes' walk from the nearest bus stop on Wilkinson Ave.

HAMILTON PARISH

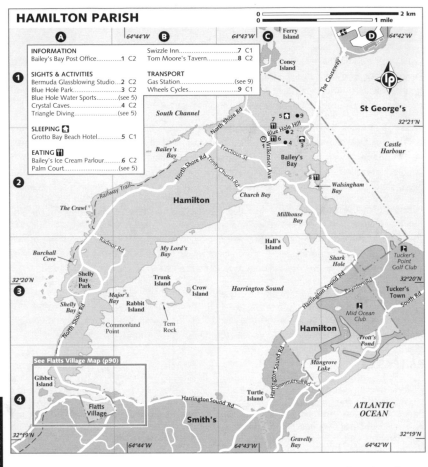

HAMILTON PARISH

INFORMATION	**Swizzle Inn**	...............7 C1
Bailey's Bay Post Office......1 C2	Tom Moore's Tavern	...........8 C2
SIGHTS & ACTIVITIES	**TRANSPORT**	
Bermuda Glassblowing Studio..2 C2	Gas Station	..........(see 9)
Blue Hole Park......................3 C2	Wheels Cycles	...............9 C1
Blue Hole Water Sports..........(see 5)		
Crystal Caves.....................4 C2		
Triangle Diving...................(see 5)		
SLEEPING		
Grotto Bay Beach Hotel.........5 C1		
EATING		
Bailey's Ice Cream Parlour......6 C2		
Palm Court.......................(see 5)		

BLUE HOLE PARK

You'd never realize this **nature reserve** (Blue Hole Hill; admission free; ☼ sunrise–sunset) was there if you hadn't already been told about it. Hidden at the south side of the road just before the causeway, this 12-acre reserve has a veritable treasure trove of limestone caverns and ponds. The main trail passes several very short spur paths that lead to marked sights. It's fun and easy to explore and the whole walk takes only 20 minutes for the roundtrip.

The trail begins along a paved service road at the west side of the reserve parking lot and almost immediately leads to a **bird-viewing platform** overlooking a small pond frequented by ducks and herons. Two minutes further along the trail, a 40ft side path

leads to **Causeway Cave**, a fern-draped open limestone cavern. Get back on the main trail and continue east to a clearing. Bear left here to find a couple of small coastal caves, or bear right to reach a deck overlooking the **Blue Grotto**, a pretty pond-like sunken cave.

BERMUDA GLASSBLOWING STUDIO

This **studio** (☎ 293-2234; 16 Blue Hole Hill; ☼ 10:30am–4:30pm Tue–Sat) is a little glassblowing workshop that produces decorative glassware, including flower vases, serving bowls, paperweights, Christmas tree ornaments and those ever-popular miniature tree frog figurines. The items are sold on site at moderate prices.

From the front of the store you can get a glimpse of the craftspeople blowing glass in the back room; or pay $3 to go back and watch the process up close.

Activities
WATER SPORTS
Triangle Diving (☎ 293-7319; www.triangledriving.com; 11 Blue Hole Hill; 1-/2-tank dives $70/90; ☺ 9am-5pm) at the Grotto Bay Beach Hotel offers a full menu of diving, from night dives to daytime wreck and reef dives. If you're a novice they can take you underwater as well, with a 'Discover Scuba' half-day course ($120) that gives you all the basics followed by an afternoon dive. Snorkelers can go out with divers to wreck and reef dives for $30, or join a tour geared specifically for snorkelers for $45.

Blue Hole Water Sports (☎ 293-2915; 11 Blue Hole Hill; s/d kayaks $15/20; ☺ 9am-5pm) at the Grotto Bay Beach Hotel has a wide range of water sport rentals, including Sunfish sailboats ($25). It is all set up right on the hotel's beach, which has decent snorkeling, and you can rent snorkel sets for $6/$18 per hour/day. If the wind's up, you can also come here to rent windsurfing gear ($25) and windsurf right in front of the hotel. The windsurfing, kayak and sailboat rentals are all by the hour; if you want to go longer, add on $10 for each additional hour.

TENNIS
Grotto Bay Beach Hotel (☎ 293-8333; 11 Blue Hole Hill; per court per hr $12; ☺ 7am-11pm) has four Plexipave cork-based courts open to the public. Grotto Bay offers full wheelchair access to the courts, not only for spectator viewing

---

THE NAME GAME

As you travel around Bermuda you might begin to notice something unusual about people's homes. House numbers are quite scarce, and in their place there's often a decorative nameplate with a single quirky word. Bermudians commonly name, rather than number, their houses. But these aren't common names. If you begin to detect a pattern, but can't quite crack it, here's the scoop: when a couple moves in to a new home, they commonly take the first syllable of each of their names and put them together. So, for instance, Sylvia and Dennis might name their house Sylden, and William and Barbara might christen their home Wilbar.

---

but for wheelchair tennis as well. The courts are lit for night use, racquets can be rented for $4 a day and lessons are available.

Sleeping
Grotto Bay Beach Hotel (☎ 293-8333, in the USA ☎ 800-582-3190, in Canada ☎ 800-463-3190; www .grottobay.com; 11 Blue Hole Hill; winter/summer from $155/270; ✗ ☷ ☲) This place has a lot going for it: the grounds are spacious, there's a sandy beach, and it is a relaxed, smaller resort hotel. It's right on a bus stop, making it convenient to hop on a bus to either the City of Hamilton or the Town of St George. It boasts full resort facilities, including tennis courts, a water-sports center and even a sunken wreck to snorkel. All 201 rooms front the ocean, but ask for one on an upper floor for the best view.

Eating
Swizzle Inn (☎ 293-1854; 3 Blue Hole Hill; lunch $7-15, dinner $10-27; ☺ 11am-1am; ✗) With its motto – 'Swizzle Inn, Stagger Out' – this lively place lays claim to Bermuda's most highly touted rum swizzle. It packs a crowd of tourists and locals alike. In addition to those heady drinks, Swizzle serves up solid pub grub such as shepherd's pie or bangers and mash as well as thick steaks and specialty salads. There's both indoor and patio dining.

Bailey's Ice Cream Parlour (☎ 293-9333; Blue Hole Hill; cones from $2.60, other items $3-7; ☺ 11:30am-6:30pm; ✗ ☷) Opposite the Swizzle Inn, this cheery place serves up all-natural frozen treats and simple salads and sandwiches. Go island-style with the mango-passion sorbet or, for a rich and tangy indulgence, try a scoop of the rum-and-ginger ice cream – both made right on the premises.

Tom Moore's Tavern (☎ 293-8020; Walsingham Rd off Harrington Sound Rd; appetizers $12-19, mains $27-34; ☺ dinner; ✗ ☷) This secluded waterfront tavern, Bermuda's oldest eating house, dates to 1652. A favorite for fine dining, it takes its name from the Irish poet who lived here in 1804. Meals are served in several atmospheric rooms. The award-winning menu is continental with a French accent, filled with the likes of foie gras, quail in puff pastry and rack of lamb. Jackets are suggested.

Palm Court (☎ 293-8333; 11 Blue Hole Hill; appetizers $6-12, mains $20-27; ☺ dinner; ✗ ☷) The Grotto Bay Beach Hotel's dinner restaurant combines an ocean view, tropical decor and island flavors. Appetizers include Bermuda chowder, salads and codfish bites, while the main course focuses on steak and seafood. The catch of the day is always a good bet.

Entertainment

Swizzle Inn (☎ 293-1854; 3 Blue Hole Hill; ⏱ 11am-1am; ✗) This is the place! The bar stays open until 1am every night of the week, and in summer there's music and dancing from 9pm till closing. Wednesday is set aside for karaoke; at other times it's a mix of jazz, folk, country and reggae. There's also billiards, darts and sports on TV.

Getting There & Around

BUS

Both the northern (bus Nos 10 and 11) and the southern (bus Nos 1 and 3) bus routes around Harrington Sound converge at Bailey's Bay, making the village easy to reach on any bus traveling between the City of Hamilton ($4.50, 30 minutes) and the Town of St George ($3, 20 minutes). At least one of these buses operates every 15 minutes from 6:45am to 7pm; bus No 11 provides evening service once an hour until 11:45pm (10:45pm on Sunday). For more information on public buses, including passes, see the Transport (p155) section in the back of the book.

MOTOR SCOOTER

Scooter rentals (p157) are available at **Wheels Cycles** (☎ 293-2378; 17 Blue Hole Hill), at the gas station east of the Grotto Bay Beach Hotel.

FLATTS VILLAGE

The village of Flatts surrounds scenic Flatts Inlet and is home to one of the island's premier attractions – the Bermuda Aquarium, Museum & Zoo.

In times past, Flatts had a reputation as a smugglers' haven, and Gibbet Island, the islet off Flatts, was once used for the execution of islanders accused of witchcraft. Today, Flatts' yacht-filled harbor shows little trace of that more sordid past. The bridge that crosses over the inlet is a good vantage point for views of the harbor and of the rapidly moving tidal waters that rush through the inlet to and from Harrington Sound.

Information

There's an **ATM** (6 North Shore Rd) next to Four Star Pizza and a **post office** (☎ 292-0741; 65 Middle Rd) not too far from the village center.

Sights

BERMUDA AQUARIUM, MUSEUM & ZOO

Bermuda's premier natural attraction, the **Bermuda Aquarium, Museum & Zoo** (BAMZ; ☎ 293-2727; www.bamz.org; 40 North Shore Rd; adult/child $10/5; ⏱ 9am-5pm), wraps three superb sights under a single roof. It's a blast for kids of any age.

It goes a lot deeper than just great visuals, as the BAMZ has won international recognition for its work in species preservation and for its efforts to increase awareness of pressing environmental issues.

Start at the **aquarium** where a dazzling array of tanks, each arranged to show a microcosm

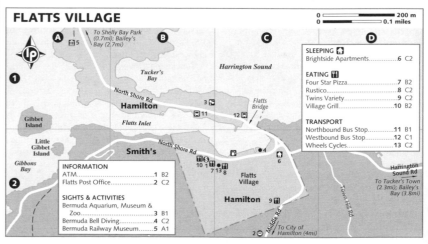

FLATTS VILLAGE

SLEEPING 🏠	
Brightside Apartments..............6 C2	
EATING 🍴	
Four Star Pizza.........................7 B2	
Rustico....................................8 C2	
Twins Variety...........................9 C2	
Village Grill............................10 B2	
TRANSPORT	
Northbound Bus Stop..............11 B1	
Westbound Bus Stop...............12 C1	
Wheels Cycles.........................13 C2	

INFORMATION
ATM...1 B2
Flatts Post Office............................2 C2

SIGHTS & ACTIVITIES
Bermuda Aquarium, Museum &
Zoo..3 B1
Bermuda Bell Diving........................4 C2
Bermuda Railway Museum.............5 A1

OLD RATTLE & SHAKE

During the 1920s, British administrators in Bermuda decided that the island was ripe for a rail system. Locals, who were skeptical of the proposal, gave only tepid support, so the government turned to investors in England to provide the funding.

The complications in executing the project were great. People on land-scarce Bermuda didn't want to give up their property, so the railroad had to be erected largely along the coast, making it less than central. Then there were the engineering challenges: some 33 trestle bridges, half of them over water, had to be constructed along the 21 miles of track. By the time the first train left the station in 1931, the cost of the project had reached a lofty UK£1,000,000, making it one of the most expensive railways, on a per-mile basis, ever built.

The railway never caught on among islanders and quickly became a financial albatross. The reasons were numerous; the placement of the stations wasn't ideal and many people preferred to continue traveling by ferry. Still, most significant of all was the impact of WWII, which introduced the private automobile to Bermudian roads, and also made it difficult for railway operators to obtain spare parts and maintain equipment.

By 1946, Bermuda's little railroad, which by then had been dubbed 'old rattle and shake,' was in such dire straits that the government took it over from its private owners. Passenger counts continued to drop, and on December 31, 1947, the train made its last run.

The engines and cars were packed up and shipped off to British Guiana the next year. After that, most of the track was simply forgotten, though a few miles of it that ran through urban areas were buried to create automobile roads. In 1984 the government set aside the remaining sections of the old railway route for foot and bridle paths, and today the Railway Trail is the most extensive trail in Bermuda, thanks to the follies of the past.

of Bermuda's underwater ecosystem, displays some 200 species of fish and corals. This is an ideal place to identify some of the colorful tropical fish you've seen while snorkeling or taking a glass-bottom boat cruise. Labels on the tanks identify brilliant wrasses, rainbow parrotfish, spotted pufferfish, jazzy trumpetfish and toothy moray eels, among others.

The 140,000-gallon 'North Rock' tank, the aquarium's centerpiece, contains a slice of a reef complete with brilliant corals and circling sharks and barracuda. Another mammoth fish in the tank is the Nassau grouper, which was once common in Bermuda's waters, but now fished to commercial extinction.

The **zoo's** design replicates a natural habitat as closely as possible while bringing visitors up close to the creatures on display. The fantastic 'Islands of the Caribbean,' a netted walk-through exhibit covering one side of the property, is the nearest thing to a cage-free zoo. Enter the double screen doors and find yourself on a winding path with golden lion tamarins scurrying by, a two-toed sloth hanging from a tree above and brilliant scarlet ibis winging about.

Almost as much fun is 'Islands of Australasia,' another walk-through exhibit that brings you eye-to-eye with wallabies, tree kangaroos, a monitor lizard and various nocturnal creatures – though in this one a glass enclosure separates you from the animals.

For those who like the tactile approach, don't miss 'Local Tails,' with its touch pool, and of special interest to young children is the 'Discovery Room' with its hands-on displays and games.

Other oohs and ahhs: catch the flock of rosy flamingos; peek into the alligator pen; and get up close to the Galápagos tortoises. The Bermuda Zoo, incidentally, was the first to breed these giant turtles in captivity and many of the tortoises you see here have offspring in North American and UK zoos.

Although it's hard to compete with all the action elsewhere on the grounds, the renovated **natural history museum** does a fine job of bringing the island's geological origins and diverse ecology alive through interactive displays. Be sure to give it at least a peek.

Allow yourself two to three hours to take in all the sights here. The entire facility, including exhibits and restrooms, is wheelchair accessible.

BERMUDA RAILWAY MUSEUM
Housed in a building that once served as a railway station, this little **museum** (☎ 293-1774;

37 North Shore Rd; admission free, donations appreciated; ☺ 10am-4pm Tue-Fri) has an audio presentation, a collection of period photos and a few other items relating to Bermuda's railroad, but it's largely a curiosity shop with consignment antiques such as old bottles, porcelain, and oil lamps. You can also buy a reprinted map ($5) that shows Bermuda's former rail routes and details the rail's curious history.

The railway museum is a 10-minute walk north of the Bermuda Aquarium, Museum & Zoo, but consider taking the northbound bus (just one stop), which stops in front of both sites, as the busy road is narrow and without sidewalks.

Activities
HIKING
If you're up for a hike, one section of the old **Railway Trail** (p34) starts, not surprisingly, right at the grounds of the Bermuda Railway Museum. You can follow it northeast for 3 miles to the east end of Hamilton Parish, passing the beach at Shelly Bay and scenic coastal areas along Bailey's Bay.

HELMET DIVING
Bermuda Bell Diving (☎ 292-4434; North Shore Rd; dives $60; ☺ departures 10am & 2pm Apr-Nov) offers one of the more unusual water experiences, allowing visitors to don a helmet with an air hose and walk around underwater past shallow coral reefs. You don't even need to know how to swim, as you're actually walking on the sea floor, and not swimming. For someone who has never seen beneath the surface of the water, it's a real thrill.

Sleeping
Brightside Apartments (☎ 292-8410; www.bermuda .com/brightside; 38 North Shore Rd; r $100, 1-/2-bedroom apt from $140/200; ☒ ☒ ☒) Garden-like grounds, picturesque water views of Flatts Inlet and friendly management await at this family-run place. Rates are the same year-round, which makes it a particularly good deal in summer. Select from a basic room with a microwave and refrigerator, or apartment units with full kitchens.

Eating
Rustico (☎ 295-5212; 8 North Shore Rd; lunch $9-14, dinner $12-26; ☺ lunch & dinner; ☒) This reasonably-priced restaurant does it all. It's family-style with Italian decor and a menu to match. The kids can order sandwiches and pizza while hungry adults can opt for hearty steaks and seafood. Plenty of tasty pastas as well.

Village Grill (☎ 296-3634; 4 North Shore Rd; mains $5-15; ☺ 7am-10pm Mon-Sat, to 3pm Sun; ☒) Flatts' only breakfast option, the Village Grill serves up omelettes and pancakes in the morning, and awesome grilled chicken sandwiches, big burgers and old-fashioned codfish cakes at other times.

Four Star Pizza (☎ 292-9111; 6 North Shore Rd; pizza $13-28; ☺ 11am-11pm Mon-Sat, noon-10pm Sun; ☒ ☒) If you just want American-style pizza or some spicy honey-mustard chicken wings, head here. You can eat in, take out or have it delivered.

Twins Variety (☎ 292-4583; 5 Middle Rd; ☺ 8am-7pm Mon-Sat) This is the most convenient place to pick up groceries.

Shopping
Bermuda Aquarium, Museum & Zoo (BAMZ; ☎ 293-2727; www.bamz.org; 40 North Shore Rd; ☺ 9am-5pm) The well-stocked gift shop here is the perfect place to pick up cheery souvenirs while supporting island conservation efforts. Among the many items you'll find are quality environmentally-themed T-shirts, stuffed animals, nature books and waterproof fish ID cards that are handy for snorkeling.

Getting There & Around
BUS
From the City of Hamilton, bus No 3 goes to Flatts via Middle Rd, and bus Nos 10 and 11 run to Flatts via North Shore Rd. Traveling east from Flatts, bus Nos 10 and 11 continue through the north side of Hamilton Parish along the north shore, and Bus No 3 goes along the south side of Harrington Sound. All three buses go on to Bailey's Bay and the Town of St George.

At least one of these buses connects Flatts with both Hamilton ($3, 20 minutes) and St George ($4.50, 30 minutes) every 15 minutes from 6:45am to 7pm; bus No 11 provides evening service once an hour until 11:45pm (10:45pm on Sunday). For more information on public buses, including passes, see p155.

MOTOR SCOOTER
Scooters can be rented at **Wheels Cycles** (☎ 292-0388; 6 North Shore Rd) in the back of Four Star Pizza.

Smith's Parish

HIGHLIGHTS

- Enjoy a leisurely hike at **Spittal Pond** (p95), a mecca for birdwatchers
- Soak up the sun on the lovely pink sands of **John Smith's Bay** (p96)
- Cross the threshold into the colonial past at **Verdmont Museum** (p94)

★ John Smith's Bay

★ Spittal Pond

★ Verdmont Museum

POPULATION: 5658

AREA: 1.78 SQ MILES

SMITH'S PARISH

Smith's may be smallest of the nine parishes but it isn't without its superlatives. Smith's Parish manages to boast Bermuda's largest nature reserve, its safest year-round swimming and its highest point. High is a relative term, of course, so don't expect to see anything towering above the clouds. The Peak, as the hilltop is amusingly called, tops out at just 259ft. To spot the Peak, also known as Town Hill, just look inland toward the middle of the parish – enjoy the sight from a distance as it's on private property and not accessible to the public.

Fret not, the most scenic views in Smith's are not found inland, but from the shoreline: the parish is not only bordered on the north and south by open ocean but also on the northeast by tranquil Harrington Sound.

Although Smith's Parish is primarily residential, it does have some topnotch sightseeing spots. Don't miss Verdmont, the best-preserved historic house in Bermuda, and for birdwatchers or for anyone seeking a peaceful walk in the woods, Spittal Pond is as good as it gets – a haven for migratory shorebirds and waterfowl with a nature trail looping across the reserve.

There are also a couple of smaller green areas in Smith's. For the perfect picnic lunch venue, head to Watch Hill Park, which is spread across seven coastal acres near Albouy's Point, just east of Spittal Pond. The park takes its name from early colonial days when the British, fearful of a Spanish attack, maintained a round-the-clock watch on the cliff here. Winterhaven Nature Reserve, a long narrow strip at the east side of the parish that stretches between the south coast and Harrington Sound, offers a variety of water views. Penhurst Park, on the north shore, encompasses 14 grassy acres with a small dock and horse trails.

The parish has more than pretty seascapes and quiet walks – when you've finished communing with nature, reward yourself with a frosty pint of ale at North Rock Brewing Co, Bermuda's only microbrewery.

Information
ATM (Collectors Hill Apothecary, South Rd; ☾ 24hr)
Collectors Hill Apothecary (☎ 236-4499; South Rd; ☾ 8am-8pm Mon-Sat, 11am-7pm Sun) A full-service pharmacy in the town center.

Sights
VERDMONT MUSEUM
The crown jewel of historic houses under the auspices of the Bermuda National Trust is **Verdmont Museum** (☎ 236-7369; off Collectors Hill nr cnr Sayle Rd; admission $3; ☾ 10am-4pm Tue-Sat), a classic plantation home. This hilltop house, built in 1710 in a four-squared early Georgian style, was once the center of a 55-acre estate.

Amazingly, the place has been virtually unaltered since its construction. The family that occupied it up until 1951, when the trust bought the property, lived at Verdmont without electricity or plumbing. Consequently,

walking through this house is like stepping back in history. It has walls made of Georgia-pine lumber captured through privateering. Portraits of former residents hang from the walls and finely crafted 17th-century furniture fills the rooms. Although some of the items, including Spode pottery and Chinese porcelain, were imported by island traders, most of the furniture was locally made. So much cedar was used within the house that the air is still rich with the scent of the fragrant wood.

You'll notice the house doesn't have a kitchen; instead, a nearby cottage once served as the cookhouse, which was a fairly common arrangement in colonial times as it provided a measure of insurance from accidental kitchen fires. The well-versed trust volunteers that staff Verdmont enjoy providing insightful tidbits on the property.

SMITH'S PARISH

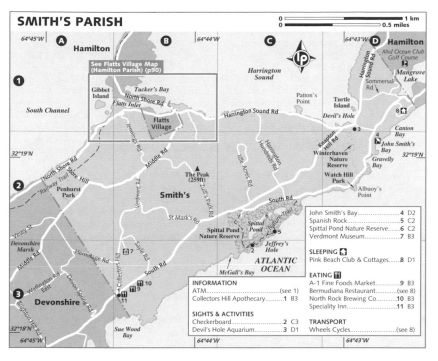

SMITH'S PARISH

INFORMATION
ATM...(see 1)
Collectors Hill Apothecary...........1 B3

SIGHTS & ACTIVITIES
Checkerboard.............................2 C3
Devil's Hole Aquarium................3 D1

John Smith's Bay.......................4 D2
Spanish Rock.............................5 C2
Spittal Pond Nature Reserve.......6 C2
Verdmont Museum......................7 B3

SLEEPING
Pink Beach Club & Cottages......8 D1

EATING
A-1 Fine Foods Market...............9 B3
Bermudiana Restaurant............(see 8)
North Rock Brewing Co...........10 B3
Speciality Inn..........................11 B3

TRANSPORT
Wheels Cycles.........................(see 8)

A special note for birdwatchers: the gardens surrounding the house, planted with flora known to have grown here in the 18th century, attract eastern bluebirds, a colorful native bird with a distinctive blue back and russet-colored breast.

SPITTAL POND NATURE RESERVE

This splendid coastal **nature reserve** (South Rd; admission free; sunrise-sunset), the largest in Bermuda, encompasses some 64 acres. It centers on Spittal Pond, a 9-acre brackish pond that's the island's finest **birdwatching** venue, attracting scores of migratory shorebirds and waterfowl. Once a favored duck-hunting locale, this property is now under the joint protection of the Bermuda National Trust and the government park system, which together maintain a nature trail for birders and hikers. These days the only shooting is done with a camera.

Nature Trail

The inviting mile-long nature trail that runs through the Spittal Pond reserve offers a fine variety of landscapes, with mixed woodlands, salt marshes, ponds and ocean vistas. There are trailheads at both the east and west sides of the property, with parking areas at each side.

It's possible to walk the trail as a loop beginning from either side. As there's no real trail along the northwest side of the pond, you'll have to walk a few minutes along South Rd at the end of the 'loop,' but otherwise you'll be on a footpath the entire way.

Starting at the west-side trailhead, take the middle route when you reach the cattle fence and continue on that path, which leads through a wooded area of mixed vegetation. You'll find the only cactus native to Bermuda, the prickly pear, thriving in open areas here and elsewhere on the trail.

Within 10 minutes, you'll reach a signposted coastal area known as the **Checkerboard**, so named because weathering has worn cross joints into the limestone slab here, leaving a pattern of square-shaped impressions resembling a huge checkerboard. Just after that, a cattle gate leads through the fence as the path continues along the south side of Spittal Pond. The trail passes through a forest of casuarina, an Australian tree that was widely planted throughout Bermuda in the 1950s to replace the groves of native cedars lost to cedar-scale infestation.

The trail then leads into a marshy area with purple sea lavender, tall salt grass and a small freshwater pond favored by mallards and teals. A right fork off the main trail makes a short detour to **Jeffrey's Hole**, a sea cave named for an escaped slave who is said to have stowed away there, and then continues to the site of **Spanish Rock**. The original rock, inscribed with the initials TF and the date 1543, is thought to have been carved by a stranded Spanish or Portuguese mariner.

From Spanish Rock, continue back to the main trail, which offers fine birding vantage points as it passes along the southeast side of Spittal Pond. After reaching the gate, you can either take a short side trail up to the east-side parking area or continue west along the northeast side of the pond until that trail leads up to South Rd.

Birdwatching

If you fancy yourself a birder, grab your binoculars before you head out. In tune with North American bird migration patterns, fall and winter offer the greatest variety of bird life at Spittal Pond.

The earliest arrivals are the shorebirds, which begin appearing in August. The lesser yellowlegs, the most abundant of the two dozen shorebird species that feed at the edge of Spittal Pond, can be recognized by its bright yellow legs, and by the square white rump it flashes when in flight. From the end of September, egrets and herons – including Louisiana herons, which have long slender necks and a wingspan of more than 3ft – can

be spotted at the pond. In October, migratory ducks and coots arrive in force.

Although many of the migrants winter in Bermuda, others merely stop en route to and from the Caribbean, so spring also brings migratory stopovers. In the quieter summer months, Spittal Pond is the domain of resident mallards.

If you want to birdwatch but not hike much, entering the park from the east side will get you to the pond and some good birding vantage points in just minutes.

JOHN SMITH'S BAY

This pretty **beach** (South Rd; admission free), with its broad swath of pink sand, faces east and offers sheltered waters good for swimming and snorkeling. Because the sand slopes gently from the water's edge, it's a popular place for families with children. During the high season there's a lifeguard; it's best to ask about water conditions before heading out into deeper waters, as there are occasional rip currents. Restroom facilities can be found at the south side of the beach, and there's a ramp offering wheelchair access.

John Smith's Bay is right along the side of South Rd. If you happen to pass by at 6am, expect to see the eternally dedicated members of Bermuda's 'Polar Bear Club' taking their daily morning dip.

DEVIL'S HOLE AQUARIUM

Devil's Hole (☎ 293-2072; 92 Harrington Sound Rd; adult/child $10/5; ⏱ 9:30am-4:30pm), at the east side of Smith's Parish, is not really an aquarium per se, but a seawater-filled grotto connected to Harrington Sound by natural tunnels. Visitors can look into the water from a wooden walkway and peer down at stocked sea turtles and tropical fish circling below. For $3,

---

SMALL IS BEAUTIFUL

Smith's is the smallest parish. Here's a short list of some other petite tidbits about Bermuda:

- Bermuda is a compact place – just 21 sq miles in area.
- It's also a narrow land – averaging less than a mile across.
- Even the tallest hill is small – a mere 259ft high.
- It boasts the world's smallest drawbridge, barely the width of a sailboat mast.
- How tiny are those whistling tree frogs? Just 1 inch long.
- Bermuda encourages small local businesses – no Big Macs!
- What to wear to a business meeting? Bermuda shorts, of course!

you can buy a basket of fish food and watch the fellas jump.

Activities
The best hiking and birdwatching in Smith's Parish is at **Spittal Pond** (p95). In addition, one section of the **Railway Trail** (p34), which runs 1.75 miles from Devonshire Parish to Flatts Village, passes through the north side of Smith's Parish. The trail crosses **Penhurst Park** (p94) and offers views of **Gibbet Island**, where in the 17th century people accused of witchcraft were taken to be burned at the stake.

Sleeping
Pink Beach Club & Cottages (☎ 293-1666, in the USA & Canada ☎ 800-355-6161; www.pinkbeach.com; 116 South Rd; units winter/summer $355/420; ✖ ✖ ✖) Two pink-sand beaches and spacious rooms with seaside balconies make this upmarket place a fine choice. Spread across 15 quiet acres on the south shore, the 90 units are in low-rise pink buildings that blend harmoniously with the beach. If you tire of swimming and snorkeling you'll find two tennis courts and a fitness club – or just unwind with a drink in the fireside lounge. Breakfast is included in the price.

Eating
North Rock Brewing Co (☎ 236-6633; 10 South Rd; pub grub $7-20; ✖ lunch & dinner; ✖ ✖) The island's only microbrewery sports a pleasant dark-wood interior and draws some worthy English-style ales. Chug-a-lug as you watch it brew. For $5.25, you can try five different 4oz samples of the frothy final product. Naturally, there's a pub menu to match, with Bermuda fish chowder, steak-and-ale pie, sandwiches and the like.

Bermudiana Restaurant (☎ 293-1666; 116 South Rd; 5-course meal $65; ✖ 7-9pm; ✖ ✖) For formal dining with a superb ocean view, this restaurant at the Pink Beach Club has few rivals. A team of European chefs prepares delicious dishes combining continental and Bermudian cuisines, with a changing menu that concentrates on seasonal delicacies. Jackets are required of men.

Speciality Inn (☎ 236-3133; 4 South Rd; mains $5-16; ✖ 6am-10pm Mon-Sat; ✖ ✖) Good local food and the character of a small-town diner set the tone here. You can get all the usual breakfast offerings as well as sandwiches, salads, burgers and pizza. If you're vegetarian, don't miss the goat's cheese and portabello mushroom sandwich on thick slices of its own homemade bread.

A-1 Fine Foods Market (☎ 236-8763; 6 South Rd; ✖ 8am-10pm Mon-Sat, 1-5pm Sun) This is Smith's largest full-service grocery store.

Getting There & Around
Three main roads run west to east across Smith's Parish: North Shore Rd along the north coast, South Rd along the south coast and Middle Rd through the interior.

BUS
Buses (p155) that run between the City of Hamilton ($3, 20 minutes) and the Town of St George ($4.50, 30 minutes) cross Smith's on all three of the parish's west–east roads.

Bus No 1 takes South Rd, stopping at Collectors Hill, Verdmont Museum, Spittal Pond Nature Reserve and John Smith's Bay. It operates every 30 minutes from 6:45am to 6:15pm weekdays and from 7:45am to 5:45pm Saturday. On Sunday the service is hourly from 11am to 5pm.

Bus No 3 takes Middle Rd to Flatts Village and then takes Harrington Sound Rd, passing Devil's Hole Aquarium as it edges along Harrington Sound. It operates every 30 minutes from 7:15am to 6:15pm weekdays, once hourly from 8:15am to 6:15pm Saturday, and once hourly from 9:15am to 5:30pm Sunday.

Bus Nos 10 and 11 operate along North Shore Rd and provide service about every 15 minutes Monday to Saturday from 6:45am to 7pm and then at least once an hour until 11:45pm. Sunday service runs at least once hourly from 7:45am to 10:45pm.

MOTOR SCOOTER
Scooter rentals (p157) are available at **Wheels Cycles** (☎ 292-0388; 116 South Rd) at Pink Beach Club & Cottages.

Devonshire Parish

CONTENTS

HIGHLIGHTS

- Take a peaceful walk among native and exotic trees at the **Arboretum** (opposite)
- Join the locals for a round of golf at the appropriately-named **Ocean View Golf Course** (p101)
- Throw a good-luck coin into the wishing well at **Palm Grove Garden** (opposite)

★ Ocean View Golf Course

★ Palm Grove Garden

★ Arboretum

■ POPULATION: 7307 ■ AREA: 1.82 SQ MILES

Sitting smack in the center of Bermuda, Devonshire takes its name from an English earl who never set foot in the parish. Most tourists seem to follow suit by bypassing Devonshire. It's a shame, because what Devonshire does have to offer is the real deal – a genuine slice of untouristy Bermuda. So get off the bus or pull over your scooter and take a closer look.

Think gardens, birdwatching, lesser-known historic sights and little parks with water views. Admire the early 18th-century Palmetto House, maintained by the Bermuda National Trust and notable for its interesting architectural features. Or perhaps take a picnic and relax in the green surrounds of Palmetto Park or tiny Robinson Bay Park while admiring the sea views.

If you're feeling a little more active, explore the borders of Devonshire Marsh, keeping a sharp eye out for birdlife. Devonshire Parish also has the closest golf course to the City of Hamilton and is home to a couple of the island's main sports arenas.

Information

The **Devonshire Post Office** (☎ 296-0281; 2 Orange Valley Rd) is fairly central.

Sights

ARBORETUM

This 22-acre **park** (cnr Middle & Montpelier Rds; admission free; ☿ sunrise-sunset), managed by the Department of Agriculture, offers inviting walking paths through a delightful wooded valley.

The arboretum came about in the late 1950s after the property was turned over to the island government by the British War Department. In an attempt to establish a wide selection of trees and shrubs capable of flourishing in Bermuda, horticulturists obtained saplings from countries as far flung as Japan, New Guinea and Canada, in addition to specimens sent by Queen Elizabeth II from the Royal Botanic Gardens in Kew. Today the trees include conifers, palms, fruit and nut trees, and such exotics as rubber trees and black ebony. If you have a fondness for all things green, a more varied place to stroll would be hard to come by.

Enter the grounds at the Montpelier Rd entrance to start off a pleasant 20-minute clockwise walk that takes you through a wildflower meadow of coreopsis, narcissus and endemic Bermudiana flowers. The walk then loops through the arboretum's conifer collection, which includes native Bermuda cedar and Norfolk Island pines; goes past a gazebo framed by large olive trees; and

finally comes to a palm collection, which includes native Bermudian palmettos and Chinese fan palms. The walk ends by looping back to your starting point across a lawn of Bermuda grass.

Bus No 3 stops on Middle Rd directly in front of the arboretum. If you arrive by scooter, there's a parking area at the southeastern side of the arboretum, off Montpelier Rd, near the trailhead.

PALM GROVE GARDEN

Don't miss a stroll through the wonderful **garden** (South Rd opposite Brighton Hill Rd; admission free; ☿ 9am-5pm Mon-Thu) of this private estate. Not only does it have manicured lawns mingling with statues, flowering trees and tropical plants but there's also a handsome moongate and a wishing well. Walk up the hill, beyond the little aviary of exotic parrots and cockatoos, to find the estate's most unique sight. From the hilltop you'll be looking across an amazing reflecting pool shaped as a map of Bermuda, outlined in concrete and given an element of relief with a cover of green turf.

The property is owned by one of Bermuda's more prominent families, the Gibbons, who graciously open the garden to the public four days a week.

DEVONSHIRE BAY PARK

If you're up for a fun little detour, then keep an eye open for **Devonshire Bay Park** (Devonshire Bay Rd; admission free; ☿ sunrise-sunset). To get there, continue on South Rd 300yd east of

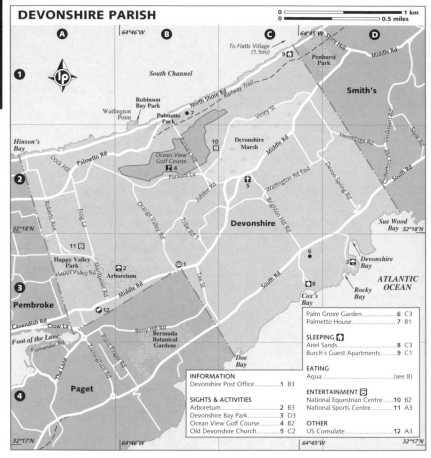

DEVONSHIRE PARISH

INFORMATION
Devonshire Post Office..............1 B3

SIGHTS & ACTIVITIES
Arboretum................................2 B3
Devonshire Bay Park................3 D3
Ocean View Golf Course..........4 B2
Old Devonshire Church............5 C2

Palm Grove Garden..................6 C3
Palmetto House.......................7 B1

SLEEPING
Ariel Sands..............................8 C3
Burch's Guest Apartments........9 C1

EATING
Aqua.................................(see 8)

ENTERTAINMENT
National Equestrian Centre......10 B2
National Sports Centre............11 A3

OTHER
US Consulate...........................12 A3

Palm Grove Garden and then take Devonshire Bay Rd to the end. It's just a couple of minutes' walk from there to the top of a casuarina-shaded hill that was the site of the Devonshire Bay Battery. Built in the 1860s when the US Civil War heightened tensions between the British and the Americans, you can make out the ruined walls, but the main attraction is the fine hilltop coastal view and the sound of the surf crashing in the wild Atlantic below.

The park also has a little cove that's used primarily by fishers to harbor their boats.

PALMETTO HOUSE
The Bermuda National Trust maintains the early 18th-century **Palmetto House** (☎ 236-6483; North Shore Rd), which has a few rooms with antique furnishings but is most interesting for its architectural features: its cruciform shape and welcoming-arm stairs. However, the house is occupied by an elderly couple and therefore has very limited opening hours; call the trust for current visiting information.

PALMETTO PARK
Just west of Palmetto House rest two adjacent parks. The 17-acre **Palmetto Park** (North Shore Rd) is a relatively large green space with water views that's popular with islanders as a weekend picnicking spot. The tiny **Robinson Bay Park**, right at Robinson Bay, has a rocky shoreline but fine views.

DEVONSHIRE MARSH

South of Palmetto House is the Devonshire Marsh, part of which is under the auspices of the Bermuda Audubon Society. Although the brackish marsh doesn't have footpaths, there are good birding possibilities along the narrow roads that border the marsh, particularly along Vesey St.

OLD DEVONSHIRE CHURCH

This old **church** (Middle & Brighton Hill Rds) dates to 1716 but has been rebuilt a few times, most recently following an explosion in 1970. Still, the old church is a Devonshire landmark of sorts and has some 16th-century silver on display.

Activities

HIKING

In addition to the walk through the **Arboretum** (p99), if you're up for a hike, a section of the **Railway Trail** (p34) runs through the north side of Devonshire. It starts at the back side of Palmetto Park and continues east 1.75 miles to the village of Flatts, passing Palmetto House en route and taking in coastal and inland views.

GOLF

With enough challenges to keep things interesting, **Ocean View Golf Course** (☎ 295-9093; reservations 234-4653; Barkers Hill; greens fee $40-65; ✲ sunrise-sunset), a par-35, 2940yd course, can be played either as nine or 18 holes. Come after 3pm for the best rates and don't worry if you didn't bring clubs, as full sets can be rented for $25.

Sleeping

Ariel Sands (☎ 236-1010, in the USA ☎ 800-468-6610; www.arielsands.com; 34 South Rd; r winter/summer $180/290; ✲ ✲) It takes its name from the magical spirit in Shakespeare's *Tempest* but takes its fame from its connection to actor Michael Douglas. Douglas is a part owner, along with his mother who manages the place. Don't expect any Hollywood hype – instead, this cottage-style hotel on a private white-sand beach exudes tranquility. A spa, an ocean-view hot tub and beachside massages will make you feel like a star even if you don't see one. Breakfast is included.

Burch's Guest Apartments (☎ 292-5746, in the USA ☎ 800-637-4116; bermudatourism.com/apt_sm3.html; 110 North Shore Rd; s/d $75/95; ✲) On the parish's north shore, this affordable 10-unit place comes fully equipped, including kitchen facilities, and sports a little garden with ocean views. It's in a residential area that's not central to restaurants or other tourist facilities, but there's a nearby bus stop.

Eating

Aqua (☎ 236-2332; Ariel Sands Beach Club, 34 South Rd; appetizers $8-17, mains $23-40; ✲ lunch & dinner; ✲) Sit on the patio overlooking the beach and delight in one of the most romantic settings on the island. The menu is a creative fusion

---

THE DOUGLAS CONNECTION

Of several celebrities that maintain ties with Bermuda, Michael Douglas is hands-down the most famous. So, what exactly is the actor's connection to the island?

Michael's mother, Diana Dill, is from an old Bermudian family that hails back to early colonial times. She took up acting when she was young and left the island to pursue her career. Diana met Michael's father, the legendary Kirk Douglas, and in 1943 they married and started a family. The couple divorced in 1951, when Michael was 6 years old, and he was raised by his mom, with most of his youth spent in Connecticut. Summers, however, were spent in Bermuda until Michael moved to California to attend college.

Diana eventually resettled in Bermuda and became the manager of the exclusive Ariel Sands resort, which the Dill clan has owned since its opening in 1954. In more recent years, Michael himself has become an investor in the resort and lends a hand with publicity.

In 2001 Michael and his superstar wife, Catherine Zeta-Jones, bought a period mansion in Warwick and now claim the island as home. They are raising their two children in Bermuda, just a few parishes away from grandma's hotel. Commonly seen shopping in Hamilton and dining out around the island, they receive a few more 'good days' than the average person, but seldom draw a crowd, as Bermudians pride themselves on respecting other people's privacy. And there are no pesky paparazzi on the island, which is one of the reasons the couple decided to settle here.

of European and Asian influences that ranges from kabuki shrimp with mango, bamboo shoots and scallions to rack of lamb in lavender sauce. French-accented desserts and well-chosen wines round it out perfectly.

Entertainment

In the summer season, **Aqua** (☎ 236-2332; Ariel Sands Beach Club, 34 South Rd; 🕙 9-11pm Wed-Fri & Sun; 🞩) has after-dinner lounge music, typically a pianist and vocalist.

SPECTATOR SPORTS

The **National Sports Centre** (☎ 295-8085; 50 Frog Lane), a state-of-the-art multipurpose sports stadium, serves as a main venue for soccer, cricket and rugby matches, and occasionally sees some international action. Check the newspapers for current schedules.

The **National Equestrian Centre** (☎ 234-0485; www.bef.bm; Vesey St) is the site of periodic harness racing and dressage shows.

Getting There & Around

Devonshire Parish is crossed by three main roads that run west to east: South Rd along the south coast, North Shore Rd on the north coast and Middle Rd through the interior.

Buses (p155) that run between the City of Hamilton ($3, 10 minutes) and the Town of St George ($4.50, 40 minutes) cross Devonshire on all three of these west–east roads. Bus No 1 operates along South Rd past Palm Grove Garden and Devonshire Bay. Bus No 3 operates along Middle Rd past the Arboretum and Old Devonshire Church. Bus Nos 10 and 11 go along North Shore Rd past Palmetto Park and Palmetto House.

Paget Parish

PAGET PARISH

HIGHLIGHTS

- Stroll the **Bermuda Botanical Gardens** (p104), where you'll find all those plants abloom around the island gathered in one eye-pleasing place

- Join the locals for a day of frolicking and swimming at spectacular **Elbow Beach** (p106)

- Walk on water at **Paget Marsh** (p106), where, beneath a boardwalk, birds teem in the last indigenous ecosystem of its type

★ Bermuda Botanical Gardens

★ Paget Marsh

Elbow Beach ★

- POPULATION: 5088
- AREA: 1.95 SQ MILES

Paget has two distinct faces. The north side, across the harbor from the City of Hamilton, is quiet, scenic and lined with valuable homes. This is where the established families that run the city's most successful shops and law firms live. The south side, on the other hand, takes life a bit less seriously – it's where city folk flock for a day at the beach or a dinner out.

Most of the parish's action centers around the wonderful Elbow Beach, which is a spectacular spot and the first of a string of gorgeous pink-sand beaches that extend along Bermuda's southwest shore. Along the south shore you'll find a collection of the parish's fancy beach resorts, upscale inns and restaurants – some of which rank right up there among the island's finest. For all these reasons, this is the part of Paget Parish that draws in the lion's share of tourists.

However, if being close to the beach isn't a high priority for you, then there are also some delightful little places to stay along the north shore. The guesthouses and inns there are cozy spots that reflect their neighborhood charm, and considering what you get for your money, the prices are a bargain. And virtually every place on the north side is within walking distance of a ferry stop, so it's just a few minutes across the water to the City of Hamilton.

Nature lovers may be surprised to find that this central and bustling parish lays claim to a couple of Bermuda's top nature sites. Paget Marsh, in the center of the parish, is a rare haven for birds and native flora, and the Bermuda Botanical Gardens, on the east side of the parish, is amazingly extensive. While visiting the gardens be sure to stroll over to the Masterworks Museum of Bermuda Art; with its evocative setting and growing collection, it's a terrific little art museum. There are a couple of historic buildings to visit as well, but if you really want to bask in history you can't do better than to join the dinner crowd at the centuries-old Fourways Inn.

Information

ATM (Rural Hill Plaza, South Rd)
King Edward VII Memorial Hospital (☎ 911 for emergencies, 236-2345 for nonemergencies; 7 Point Finger Rd) Bermuda's general hospital; just south of Berry Hill Rd.
Paget Pharmacy (☎ 236-2681; Rural Hill Plaza, South Rd; ☒ 8am-8pm Mon-Sat, 10am-6pm Sun) Full-service pharmacy.
Paget Post Office (☎ 236-7429; 108 Middle Rd) Near the intersection with South Rd.

Sights

BERMUDA BOTANICAL GARDENS

Bermuda's ultimate walk in the park, the 36-acre **botanical gardens** (☎ 236-4201; 169 South Rd; admission free; ☒ sunrise-sunset) are a perfect place to enjoy the island's varied flora. Originally opened in 1898, these delightful gardens encompass everything from formal plantings of roses and perennials to lofty trees and a little aviary.

If you enter from the main gate on Berry Hill Rd, you'll immediately pass a cacti collection that features native prickly pear along with aloes and other succulents that tolerate Bermuda's humid climate.

Just 100 yards south of the gate is the **visitor center** (☎ 236-5291; ☒ 10am-3:30pm Mon-Fri), where you can get a free brochure with a garden map and site descriptions. The center also sells snacks and has restrooms.

Some of the park's highlights include a palm garden with native palmetto trees, a section of endemic plants, a ficus collection with spreading banyan trees, greenhouses with exotic orchids and bromeliads, and an orchard that includes Bermuda's oldest avocado tree. Don't miss the sensory garden, originally created with the blind in mind, where a bubbling fountain is surrounded by some of the garden's most fragrant plants.

All in all, it's a delightful place to stroll. Give the gardens at least an hour. If you want to linger longer, you'll find benches where you can meditate on the cool green sights and distant ocean view. Because the plants are labeled, you can identify much of what the gardens have to offer on your own, but if you want to dig a little deeper

the visitor center offers free **guided tours** at 10:30am Tuesday, Wednesday and Friday.

While you are here, don't miss **Camden** (p107) and the **Masterworks Museum of Bermuda Art** (p106), also on the grounds.

The gardens are bordered by South and Berry Hill Rds. If you take a bus from Hamilton, the easiest way to get there is to get off

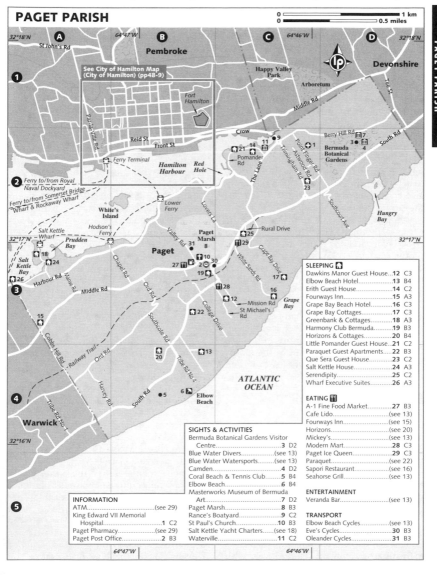

PAGET PARISH

SLEEPING
Dawkins Manor Guest House...**12** C3
Elbow Beach Hotel...............**13** B4
Erith Guest House................**14** C2
Fourways Inn.....................**15** A3
Grape Bay Beach Hotel.........**16** C3
Grape Bay Cottages.............**17** C3
Greenbank & Cottages.........**18** A3
Harmony Club Bermuda........**19** B3
Horizons & Cottages...........**20** B4
Little Pomander Guest House...**21** C2
Paraquet Guest Apartments....**22** B3
Que Sera Guest House..........**23** C2
Salt Kettle House................**24** A3
Serendipity......................**25** C2
Wharf Executive Suites.........**26** A3

EATING
A-1 Fine Food Market...........**27** B3
Cafe Lido........................(see 13)
Fourways Inn..................(see 15)
Horizons.......................(see 20)
Mickey's.......................(see 13)
Modern Mart....................**28** C3
Paget Ice Queen................**29** C3
Paraquet.......................(see 22)
Sapori Restaurant..............(see 16)
Seahorse Grill..................(see 13)

ENTERTAINMENT
Veranda Bar....................(see 13)

TRANSPORT
Elbow Beach Cycles.............(see 13)
Eve's Cycles.....................**30** B3
Oleander Cycles.................**31** B3

SIGHTS & ACTIVITIES
Bermuda Botanical Gardens Visitor
  Centre...........................**3** D2
Blue Water Divers...............(see 13)
Blue Water Watersports.........(see 13)
Camden............................**4** D2
Coral Beach & Tennis Club......**5** B4
Elbow Beach......................**6** B4
Masterworks Museum of Bermuda
  Art..............................**7** D2
Paget Marsh.......................**8** B3
Rance's Boatyard..................**9** C2
St Paul's Church.................**10** B3
Salt Kettle Yacht Charters......(see 18)
Waterville.......................**11** C2

INFORMATION
ATM.............................(see 29)
King Edward VII Memorial
  Hospital.........................**1** C2
Paget Pharmacy..................(see 29)
Paget Post Office.................**2** B3

DOUBLE FANTASY

In 1980, while John Lennon was in Bermuda working on compositions for an upcoming album, he took a break to stroll through the Bermuda Botanical Gardens. Here he spotted a beautiful freesia in bloom and bent down to take a closer look. The flower was labeled 'Double Fantasy.' When Lennon stood up, he reportedly smiled and jotted down the flower's name – he had found the perfect title for his new album.

Double Fantasy, Lennon's final album, was released shortly before his death, in 1980. After the origin of the album's title surfaced, Lennon fans made efforts to seek out the little flower, and for years the staff at the botanical gardens stayed busy replacing the flower's identifying label, which kept disappearing.

The park eventually decided to deal with the souvenir issue by printing T-shirts with a 'Double Fantasy' flower design and selling them at the visitor center gift shop.

---

at King Edward VII Memorial Hospital on Point Finger Rd. Walk south from the hospital and take the path that begins directly opposite Astwood Rd.

ELBOW BEACH

This glorious stretch of soft pink sand extends for more than half a mile. The Elbow Beach Hotel sits at the east end of the beach and claims that section for its guests, but the rest of the beach is public.

Being the closest noteworthy beach to the City of Hamilton, Elbow Beach attracts a crowd of locals and visitors alike, especially on the weekends. Not only is it a very popular swimming and sunbathing locale, but it's a good beach for jogging and strolling as well. The west side of the beach is backed by interesting limestone cliffs that provide habitat for sea grape trees and birds.

Public access to Elbow Beach is at the end of Tribe Rd No 4, which begins at a sharp curve on South Rd, just west of the Elbow Beach Hotel. Elbow Beach has shower and toilet facilities.

MASTERWORKS MUSEUM OF BERMUDA ART

If you love art or historic buildings, don't miss this quality **museum** (☎ 236-2950; Berry Hill Rd; admission free; ☉ 10am-6pm), with its beautiful setting and fine collection. Opened in 2004, it's inside a 250-year-old building that used to be an arrowroot factory. The Masterworks Foundation has preserved some of the historic vats and the press where this starchy cooking substance was once made and spread the art exhibits around the antique factory works. The building, renovated to the tune of $5 million, is quite lovely, with

thick-beamed ceilings and fine views of the surrounding gardens.

The gallery has two sides, one of which exhibits contemporary artists, most of whom have connections with Bermuda and explore island themes in their work. If you see something that catches your fancy in this gallery you can actually purchase it, with the proceeds going directly to the artist.

The Rose Garden Gallery exhibits the main Masterworks collection, which includes more than 1,000 works of art, several by world-renowned artists who were inspired during stays in Bermuda. With the help of wealthy patrons, including Prince Charles, the foundation has managed to repatriate Bermuda-themed paintings by such legendary artists as Georgia O'Keeffe and Winslow Homer.

To get to the museum take the northwest entrance into the Bermuda Botanical Gardens, which is off Berry Hill Rd. The museum is just behind Camden House.

PAGET MARSH

Just minutes from busy South Rd, this unique **marsh** (Lovers Lane; admission free; ☉ sunrise-sunset) stands like a little wetland oasis untouched by all the development beyond its soggy borders. Set aside as a 25-acre nature reserve, Paget Marsh is a birder's delight and an amazing place to visit.

Since colonial times the inhospitable swampy conditions here have kept humans at bay. The marsh was inaccessible until 2000, when the Bermuda National Trust and the Bermuda Audubon Society, who jointly maintained the reserve, constructed a boardwalk across the wetland. Dubbed Dennis' Walk, the boardwalk takes you right through the center of the marsh, past scurrying lizards, beneath a canopy of palms and into the least-disturbed natural area in Bermuda. You walk right through the last virgin forest of two native trees, the Bermuda palmetto and the Bermuda cedar. In addition, Paget Marsh contains the full range of Bermudian marsh habitat, including a mangrove swamp thick with red mangrove trees, readily identified by their hanging prop roots.

The marsh provides a habitat for a number of species of birds. Yellow-crowned night herons like to perch on the boardwalk rails, and belted kingfishers, great egrets, yellowlegs, rails and sandpipers also make their home in the wetland. The mangroves attract nearly two dozen species of wintering warblers, the most common being the myrtle warbler, which feeds on the wax myrtle berries found here.

The trailhead for Dennis' Walk begins at the west side of Lovers Lane, diagonally opposite a dry cleaners' shop; the bus stop is just a few yards west of the cleaners. The whole walk takes only about 15 minutes but give yourself more time than that to thoroughly enjoy your surroundings.

CAMDEN
The official residence of Bermuda's premier, **Camden** (☎ 236-5732; Berry Hill Rd; admission free; ☽ noon-2pm Tue & Fri) graces the northeast corner of the Bermuda Botanical Gardens. This elegant plantation house was built in the early 18th century, though its handsome latticed verandas were later additions. One of Bermuda's most prestigious families, the Tuckers, lived in the house in the 19th century.

In more recent times Camden was turned over to the Bermuda government to be incorporated into the botanical gardens. The house was restored in the 1970s and set aside for the premier, though holders of that office have opted to use it solely for official receptions and not as living quarters.

Camden's gracious interior reflects its history with antique furnishings, Waterford crystal chandeliers, gilt mirrors and portraits of former premiers. The interior liberally incorporates native Bermuda cedar, most notably in the elegant staircase and wall paneling but also in much of the period furniture.

You don't have to wait for a formal invitation to peek inside – just stop by in the early afternoon on Tuesday or Friday, when Camden opens its doors to the general public.

WATERVILLE
Built around 1725, **Waterville** (☎ 236-6483; www .bnt.bm; cnr The Lane & Pomander Rd; admission free; ☽ 9am-5pm Mon-Fri), with traditional salmon walls and a gleaming white roof, is one of the oldest buildings in Bermuda. Quite aptly, it's now the headquarters of the Bermuda National Trust, which maintains historic buildings around the island.

Waterville, at Hamilton Harbour, was built by John Trimingham II, the grandson of an early Bermudian governor, and stayed in the Trimingham family for seven generations, until 1990. Over the years it was used as living quarters, a cargo storehouse for the family's shipping fleet and a guesthouse (authors EB White and James Thurber were two of the better-known guests).

These days, in addition to housing the Bermuda National Trust's administrative offices, Waterville contains a room of antique furnishings, including Staffordshire figurines, china and period portraits. There's a lovely little rose garden along the west side of the building and a 300-year-old tamarind tree out front. The tree, once the largest in Bermuda, took a near-leveling hit from Hurricane Fabian, but its stout trunk, now just a few feet high, is sprouting new shoots – proving history doesn't die easily around here.

Activities
BOATING
Blue Water Watersports (☎ 232-2909; 60 South Rd; Sunfish sailboats/kayaks per 4hr $65/50; ☽ 9am-6pm) at Elbow Beach Hotel rents everything from aqua cycles ($40) to small sailboats. Consider taking one of their daily guided kayak tours ($48) that go out to the reef for snorkeling over coral gardens and a 200-year-old sunken ship.

If you have a small group and are up for a sail, **Rance's Boatyard** (☎ 292-1843; Crow Lane; per 4hr $90; ☽ 9am-5pm) has a 16ft Cape Cod Gemini sailboat that holds six people.

DIVING
Blue Water Divers (☎ 232-2909; 60 South Rd; 1-/2-tank dive $55/75; ☽ 9am-6pm) at Elbow Beach Hotel is a reputable diving operation that serves

divers at all levels, including introductory dives over a shallow reef ($95).

HIKING

For delightful short walks, you can stroll **Paget Marsh**, the **Bermuda Botanical Gardens** and **Elbow Beach**. For a longer outing, a two-mile section of the **Railway Trail** (p34) crosses Paget. Going from west to east, the Railway Trail runs between Middle Rd and South Rd until Paget village and from there continues south of South Rd. Along the trail you'll get glimpses of old Bermudian estates, Paget Marsh and bountiful vegetable gardens where carrots and cabbages grow.

TENNIS

Elbow Beach Hotel (☎ 236-3535; 60 South Rd; per court per hr $12; ☺ 8am-9pm) and **Horizons & Cottages** (☎ 236-0048; 33 South Rd; per court per hr $10; ☺ 7am-9pm) both have tennis courts open to the public.

Sleeping
SOUTH SHORE

There are two hotels right on the beach; most of the other south shore accommodations listed below are about a 10-minute walk from the water.

Grape Bay Beach Hotel (☎ 236-2023, in the USA ☎ 800-548-0547; www.grapebay.com; 55 White Sands Rd; r winter/summer from $145/205; ☒ 🖳 🕿) This intimate little hotel enjoys a quiet beachfront location on the south end of Grape Bay. The accommodations are on par with places charging twice the price. Completely redone after Hurricane Fabian slammed into it, the three dozen rooms have a cheery tropical decor; and it's well worth the extra $20 to add on an oceanview balcony. Facilities include a cozy lounge with a fireplace and a romantic Asian-influenced restaurant.

A CHELSEA EVENING

Bermuda's romantic inns have aroused the passions of many a starry-eyed couple. According to reliable sources, former American First Daughter Chelsea Clinton was conceived during a relaxing vacation taken by Bill and Hillary in 1979 at the Horizons & Cottages resort in Paget. Apparently those four-poster beds and glowing fireplaces really set the mood.

Elbow Beach Hotel (☎ 236-3535, in the USA ☎ 800-344-3526; www.mandarinoriental.com/hotel/534000001.asp; 60 South Rd; r winter/summer from $290/455; ☒ 🕿 🖳 🕿) Dating back nearly a hundred years, this grand resort spread over 50 landscaped acres enjoys a prime location along the glistening sands of Elbow Beach. The accommodations, ranging from rooms in the classic main building to beachside cottages, have been thoroughly renovated and are part of the exclusive Mandarin Oriental chain. The rooms are cushy with all the comforts, right down to terry bathrobes and slippers. In addition to the beach, you'll find health club facilities, tennis courts, a pub and a couple of seaside restaurants.

Horizons & Cottages (☎ 236-0048; www.horizonscottages.com; 33 South Rd; r winter/summer from $265/360; 🕿 🕿) A fireplaced lounge, traditional afternoon tea and four-poster beds characterize this genteel cottage colony atop a 25-acre estate. Nine guestrooms are in the atmospheric main house, while the rest are in a dozen attractive cottages scattered across the grounds. Facilities include a nine-hole golf course, three tennis courts and an excellent restaurant; Elbow Beach is within walking distance. The hotel is a member of the Relais et Chateaux chain. Breakfast is included.

Serendipity (☎ 236-1192; ajcorday@northrock.bm; 6 Rural Drive; studio winter/summer $90/100; ☒ 🕿 🕿) You'll feel like part of the family staying in the duplex cottage at the side of Judy and Albert Corday's home. Although it's all in one room, each unit has everything a visitor is likely to need, including a phone and a kitchen. One unit is furnished with two twin beds that can be made up as a king bed; the other unit has a queen bed and a sleep sofa. The location, set back slightly from South Rd, makes for a quiet stay. It is a bit further from the water than other Paget accommodations, but if you hop the bus Elbow Beach is just a few stops away.

Harmony Club Bermuda (☎ 236-3500, in the USA ☎ 888-427-6664; www.harmonyclub.com; 109 South Rd; r winter/summer $320/378; 🕿 🖳 🕿) There's an enjoyable sense of exclusivity at Bermuda's only all-inclusive hotel. The stylish rooms are in a cluster of low-rise buildings of traditional Bermudian design. Rates include everything – accommodations, three squares and even unlimited drinks at the open bar. The grounds have tennis courts, a putting green and a sauna.

Dawkins Manor Guest House (☎ 236-7419; dawkinsmanorhotel@ibl.bm; 29 St Michael's Rd; r winter/summer $90/140, apt winter/summer $110/175; ☒ ☷ ☑) You'll find a cozy family environment here with guests gathering in the lounge at night to share stories. Whether you opt for just a room or one of the one-bedroom apartments, all eight units have the amenities you'd expect in a pricier place, such as TVs and phones. Some of the units have their own private entrance. A grocery store is within easy walking distance.

Grape Bay Cottages (☎ 295-7017; www.bermuda.com; Grape Bay Dr; cottage winter/summer $210/315; ☷) If you're looking for privacy within earshot of the surf, consider one of these two self-contained cottages perched just above the beach at Grape Bay. Ideal for a small family, each has two bedrooms, a kitchen and a fireplace, and can accommodate four people.

Paraquet Guest Apartments (☎ 236-5842; www.paraquetapartments.com; 72 South Rd; s/d from $120/150; ☷) These apartments, behind a neighborhood eatery, are a bit utilitarian but fully modern. They are also roomy and each is equipped with a coffeemaker and refrigerator. If you expect to be preparing your own meals pay the extra $10 to get an apartment with a full kitchen.

NORTH SHORE

Salt Kettle House (☎ 236-0407; 10 Salt Kettle Rd; s/d winter $80/90, summer $85/110, cottages $100-260; ☷) So friendly and refreshingly informal, this nine-room guesthouse has a prime location right on the water between Prudden and Salt Kettle Bays. It's a delightfully homey scene, whether you're chatting over breakfast with fellow guests or lazing in the seaside hammock. Rooms vary, but all have access to kitchen facilities and interesting nooks and crannies. A favorite in the historic main house is the tower room, which has fantastic water views in both directions. The Salt Kettle ferry stop is just a few minutes' walk away. Breakfast is included in the price.

Wharf Executive Suites (☎ 232-5700; www.wharfexecutivesuites.com; 11 Harbour Rd; s/d ste winter from $205/220, summer from $220/235; ☷ ☐) Catering to business travelers, this all-suites hotel masterfully blends luxury and modern conveniences. The spacious units have king beds, kitchen facilities, desks with high-speed Internet connections and balconies that are literally on the harbor, just a stone's

throw from the ferry stop to Hamilton. Each unit also has voice mail, a printer and a fax machine with a dedicated phone number. Forget your laptop? There's a spare loaner at the front desk. Breakfast is included.

Little Pomander Guest House (☎ 236-7635; www.littlepomander.com; 16 Pomander Rd; r winter/summer $90/130; ☷) A lovely waterfront home overlooking Hamilton Harbour, this guesthouse has high standards and tasteful decor. Each of the five guestrooms has its own personality and a different bed setup so no matter how you're traveling there's something to suit you. The rooms have TVs, microwave ovens and refrigerators. Breakfast is included. The lawn in the rear, which has lounge chairs and a barbecue grill, makes a perfect spot to watch boats sail around the harbor.

Fourways Inn (☎ 236-6517, in the USA ☎ 800-962-7654; www.fourwaysinn.com; 1 Middle Rd; r/ste $260/390; ☷ ☑) Although this place is most famous for its superb restaurant, it also has a handful of delightful rooms and suites in the garden out back. Each has a king-size bed, minibar, kitchenette and little extras such as bathrobes and fresh-cut flowers. The suites add on a spacious living room as well. Mouthwatering pastries from the inn's bakery adorn the breakfast table; breakfast goodies are included in the price.

Erith Guest House (☎ 252-1827; erith@therock.bm; 15 Pomander Rd; r winter/summer $140/150; ☷ ☐ ☑) This beautiful old Bermudian home, which is surrounded by palms and borders the harbor, has been renovated into a guesthouse. The rooms are spiffy, with a queen or king bed, a microwave and a refrigerator; for an extra $15 you can get a room with cooking facilities. Breakfast is included in the room price. Despite its classic appearance, everything is fully modern inside, right down to the Ethernet Internet access, and there's a hot tub.

Greenbank & Cottages (☎ 236-3615; www.greenbankbermuda.com; 17 Salt Kettle Rd; r winter/summer 110/130, cottages $150/$180; ☒ ☷) Like neighboring Salt Kettle House, this place consists of a period Bermuda home and a handful of waterside cottages. Most of the units have kitchens and water views and all are quite pleasant for the money. The property has a private dock – so if you fancy doing a little sailing from the backyard you're in the right place. Otherwise, the Salt Kettle ferry dock is a minute's walk away.

PAGET PARISH

Que Sera Guest House (☎ 236-1998; quesera@ibl .bm; 28 Astwood Rd; unit $85; 🕸 🐾) Affordable prices and a central location near the botanical gardens are just part of the appeal of these two studio units at the side of the home of Richard and Harriett Grimes. Each unit has all the expected amenities from TV to kitchen and is furnished with two twin beds that can be made into a king bed. Guests have access to a pleasant little pool and a barbecue grill.

Eating

The south side of the parish has some excellent places to eat, some with fine water views, others with traditional charm. If you're staying on the north side of the island, there are no restaurants or even grocery stores up there – most people hop the ferry and go over to the City of Hamilton to dine.

RESTAURANTS

Fourways Inn (☎ 236-6517; 1 Middle Rd; lunch $10-16, dinner $18-36; 🕙 lunch & dinner; 🕸 🐾) Great style and terrific food characterize this top-rated fine-dining restaurant. Occupying a 1727 manor house, the setting is formal with a menu that offers both rich traditional dishes and lighter contemporary fare. At lunch there are creative sandwiches, spinach and goat's cheese salads and the like but dinner is the real prize. And it's not necessary to break the bank to dine here: come before 7pm for the three-course early evening meal ($35), which always allows several choices for each course.

Sapori Restaurant (☎ 236-7201; 55 White Sands Rd; sushi $6-13, pizza $12-15, mains $18-28; 🕙 lunch & dinner) Poolside alfresco dining and a romantic ocean view set the tone at this eclectic little restaurant at the Grape Bay Beach Hotel. They do a little bit of everything – Thai, Japanese, Italian and Bermudian – and amazingly they do it all well. The sushi is excellent, the thin-crust pizzas make a nice lunch, and the Thai coconut fish curry tantalizes the tastebuds. Everything from the sea is fresh and locally caught.

Horizons (☎ 236-0048; 33 South Rd; fixed-price dinner $55; 🕙 dinner; 🐾) At the Horizons & Cottages resort, this formal fine-dining restaurant offers a traditional Bermudian setting, a hilltop ocean view and good service and food. The multicourse, fixed-price menu changes daily, but you can typically choose from two soups, three appetizers and five main dishes, with offerings such as lobster ravioli or pan-roasted lamb with tomato chutney. Men are required to wear a jacket and tie.

Mickey's (☎ 236-9107; Elbow Beach Hotel, 60 South Rd; lunch $14-24, dinner $18-30; 🕙 11:45am-10:45pm, closed in winter) Right on Elbow Beach, you can dig your toes into the sand as you dine on the beachfront patio. Lunch features sandwiches and a few hot catch-of-the-day-type dishes, while dinner ranges from pastas to steaks. Mickey's is also the perfect spot to linger over a sunset cocktail.

Seahorse Grill (☎ 236-3535; 60 South Rd; appetizers $10-18, mains $22-40; 🕙 dinner; 🕸 🐾) This fine-dining restaurant, in the main building of the Elbow Beach Hotel, creatively blends island flavors with contemporary styles. Shark hash summer rolls, oven-roasted rockfish and lobster thermidor are specialties. For dessert, don't miss the black rum tiramisu.

Cafe Lido (☎ 236-9884; Elbow Beach Hotel; 60 South Rd; appetizers $12-18, mains $18-32; 🕙 dinner; 🕸 🐾) For a romantic beachside dinner this place is hard to beat, at least in terms of the setting. Service and food could be more consistent, but if you come during the week when it's less busy it's a safer bet. The menu has a Mediterranean accent with the likes of smoked salmon penne, rack of lamb and grilled vegetables with blackened shrimp.

Paraquet (☎ 236-9742; South Rd; breakfast & lunch $8-15, dinner $15-25; 🕙 8am-midnight; 🕸 🐾) Sit at the counter and rub elbows with the locals at this neighborhood diner just a short walk from the Elbow Beach Hotel. It serves up three squares a day, seven days a week, with all the usual egg dishes at breakfast, sandwiches and soups at lunch, and hearty meat dishes at dinner. They also sell a few simple pastries and homemade bread for take-out.

Paget Ice Queen (☎ 236-3136; Rural Hill Plaza, South Rd; items $3-7; 🕙 10am-5am; 🕸 🐾) If you've got the munchies in the wee hours, or virtually any time of the day, head here for ice cream, fried chicken and the like.

GROCERIES

Modern Mart (☎ 236-6161; 104 South Rd; 🕙 8am-10pm Mon-Sat, 1-5pm Sun) This mid-size grocery store has a decent wine section and a small deli that sells baked chicken and a few other take-out foods.

A-1 Fine Food Market (☎ 236-0351; Middle Rd near Valley Rd; ☾ 8am-10pm Mon-Sat, 1-5pm Sun) Another modern grocery store.

Entertainment

Veranda Bar (☎ 236-3535; Elbow Beach Hotel, 60 South Rd; ☾ 5pm-midnight) Paget's night scene is centered at the Elbow Beach Hotel. The Veranda, in the hotel's main wing, has entertainment nightly, typically keyboards and vocals during the week, a jazz band on Saturday and steel pan on Sunday. It attracts a well-dressed mixed crowd of locals and visitors.

Mickey's (☎ 236-9107; Elbow Beach Hotel, 60 South Rd; ☾ 11:45am-10:45pm, closed in winter) Sip a cool rum swizzle with the salt spray drifting by.

Getting There & Around

Paget Parish is crossed from west to east by three main roads: Harbour Rd along the north shore, Middle Rd in the central area and South Rd along the south shore.

There's no bus service along Harbour Rd, but that area is connected to the City of Hamilton by public ferry and sections of it are within walking distance of Middle Rd bus stops.

BICYCLE

Bicycles can be rented at **Eve's Cycles** (☎ 236-6247; 114 Middle Rd) and at **Elbow Beach Cycles** (☎ 236-9237; 60 South Rd).

BOAT

The Pink Route of the public ferry (p154) connects the north side of Paget with the City of Hamilton, making a 20-minute roundtrip loop from Hamilton that stops at Lower Ferry, Hodson's Ferry and Salt Kettle Wharf along the way. An exception is in the evening and on Sunday, when some sailings skip the Lower Ferry stop.

In addition, some of the ferries, mainly those that operate from 9am to 4pm, but also a few in the evenings, continue on to Warwick, stopping at Darrell's Wharf and Belmont Wharf before returning to Hamilton. On the ferries that serve both Paget and Warwick, the whole trip from Hamilton via all five stops takes only 36 minutes, so you're never long on the ferry and the ride is scenic as it weaves through the harbor islands.

The cost between any two points on this route is $2.50 one way. The boats, which run from 7:15am to 9:45pm, leave Hamilton about once every 30 minutes. On Saturday the first ferry leaves Hamilton at 8:15am. On Sunday and holidays the ferry operates about once an hour from 10am to 7pm.

BUS

The two main bus routes through the parish are No 8, which runs from Hamilton to the Royal Naval Dockyard via Middle Rd, and bus No 7, which runs between the same two points but via South Rd. Both buses operate once every 15 minutes during the day Monday to Saturday and about once every 30 minutes in the evening and on Sunday. The last No 7 bus leaves Hamilton at 9:15pm (6pm Sunday), and the last No 8 bus departs at 11:45pm (10:45pm Sunday). The once-hourly bus No 1 and the frequent bus No 2 run to parts of the parish but stop short of the western extent of it.

From the City of Hamilton you can take bus No 1, 2 or 7 to get to the hospital ($3, 10 minutes) or the adjacent botanical gardens. Bus No 2, 7 and 8 stop at Paget village ($3, 14 minutes) and nearby Paget Marsh. To get to Elbow Beach ($3, 17 minutes) catch Bus No 2 or 7. For more information on public buses, including passes, see p155.

MOTOR SCOOTER

Scooter rentals are available at **Elbow Beach Cycles** (☎ 236-9237; 60 South Rd) at the Elbow Beach Hotel. Scooters can also be rented in Paget village at **Eve's Cycles** (☎ 236-6247; 114 Middle Rd) and at **Oleander Cycles** (☎ 236-5235; Valley Rd), north of St Paul's Church.

PAGET PARISH

Warwick Parish

WARWICK PARISH

HIGHLIGHTS

- Take a leisurely walk on the dazzling sands of **Warwick Long Bay** (opposite)
- Enjoy **horseback riding** (p115) along the scenic south shore
- Spot Bermuda's only 'wild' flamingo on the edge of **Warwick Pond Nature Reserve** (opposite)

★ Warwick Pond
Nature Reserve

★ Warwick
Long Bay

★ Horseback
Riding

- POPULATION: 8587
- AREA: 2.12 SQ MILES

Beautiful beaches and a central location are just part of Warwick's appeal. No place in all of Bermuda is more than an hour away from it and the bus service in the parish is among the most extensive and frequent in Bermuda. All of that also makes it an ideal place to call home and, not surprisingly, Warwick is the second most populated parish in Bermuda.

But it's not just locals who have taken a fancy to the parish. Movie stars, from silent-film actor Charlie Chaplin to thriller-movie star Michael Douglas, have landed in Warwick as well. Chaplin opted for the quiet windswept south shore, while Douglas lives in a 200-year-old mansion overlooking the north shore.

The north side of the parish enjoys fine water views of the islands in the sound, and it's sprinkled with fine period homes. But it's the south side that visitors flock to. It lays claim to those lovely pink-sand beaches on the cover of tourist brochures. Collectively they offer beachgoers a delightful range of options, from the quiet little coves at Astwood Park, Jobson Cove and Chaplin Bay to the long, splendid stretch of open shoreline at Warwick Long Bay.

Although you don't need to stay in Warwick Parish to use the beaches, all served by the South Rd bus route, Warwick has some choice accommodation options. Instead of major resorts there are inviting guesthouses and apartment-style places. This is an area best suited for visitors who want to prepare their own meals. Restaurant choices are limited, but most accommodations are equipped with kitchens.

WARWICK PARISH

Information

Warwick Laundromat (☎ 236-5403; 15 Ten Pin Cres; ⊗ 7am-9pm Mon-Fri, 6am-9pm Sat & Sun) Off Middle Rd just east of the bowling alley.

Warwick Post Office (☎ 236-4071; 70 Middle Rd) On the corner of Khyber Pass.

White's Pharmacy (☎ 238-1050; 22 Middle Rd; ⊗ 8am-9pm Mon-Sat, 1-5pm Sun) At White's Supermarket.

Sights

WARWICK LONG BAY

This splendid **beach** (South Rd), with its confetti of pink sand speckled with bits of white coral, extends unbroken for half a mile. It's a real beauty. Because it's open to the ocean, it often has more surf action than other beaches in the area and can be a good place for bodysurfing. It's also a fine choice for those who enjoy long beach strolls. When it's calm there's decent snorkeling on the reef, which is about 75 yards from the beach.

If you arrive at the east side of Warwick Long Bay, you'll find several short footpaths that lead from the parking area down to the beach. Better, however, is the entrance at the west end of Warwick Long Bay, as the walkway from the parking lot leads west to a rocky outcropping that separates the expansive beach from a run of smaller coves and bays.

Jobson Cove, just minutes from the west-side parking lot, is a delightful little cove with a small white-sand beach that's nearly encircled by shoreline rocks. Because of its protected waters, Jobson Cove is popular with families that have young children. Next is Stonehole Bay, which has a wider beach and bright turquoise waters, followed by the adjacent Chaplin Bay, which has inviting double coves and is broader still. All are connected to one another by a footpath forming part of the South Shore Park Trail (p122), which extends from Warwick Long Bay along the shoreline into Southampton Parish all the way to Horseshoe Bay.

WARWICK POND NATURE RESERVE

Bermuda's second-largest freshwater pond is the centerpiece of a 9-acre **nature reserve** (cnr Middle Rd & Tribe Rd No 3; admission free; ⊗ sunrise-sunset) teeming with birds.

WARWICK PARISH

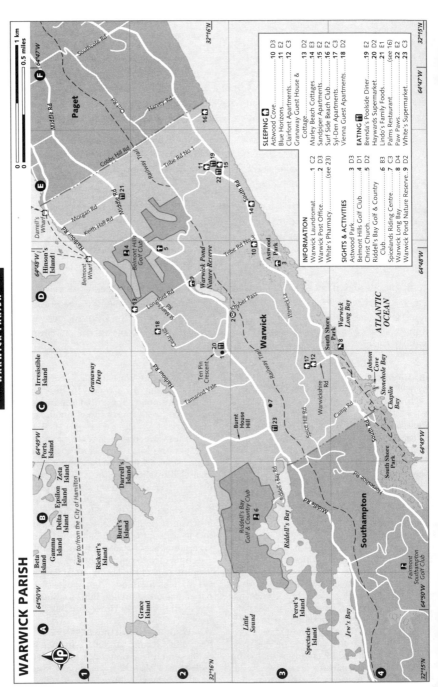

A footpath skirts the south side of the pond, beginning off Tribe Rd No 3, weaving in and out of a woods of fragrant allspice trees and cedars. Beware of poison ivy along the route. The trees here abound with birds, providing shelter for the Bermuda white-eyed vireo and more than a dozen species of migratory wood warblers.

Warwick Pond is one of the best places on the island for spotting migratory shorebirds. In winter herons, rails and grebes stalk fish along the pond's rim. Since the pond is reliant upon rainwater, extensive mudflats form when the water level drops in the drier summer months; at that time, Warwick Pond attract scores of sandpipers and black-necked stilts.

Keep an eye out for moorhens, a chicken-like rail with a red beak that can be spotted here all year round, and for Flo, a flashy pink flamingo who's escaped so many times from the Bermuda Zoo that she's officially been liberated and now resides quite prominently on the pond's northern edge.

One of the reasons Warwick Pond is so thick with birdlife is that ponds were filled in to control mosquitoes elsewhere on the island. Realizing the environmental significance of Warwick Pond, it was spared a similar fate and became a preserve under the jurisdiction of the Bermuda National Trust in 1988. But if you forget to bring mosquito repellent you'll soon understand why folks in a less enlightened time acted so hastily to rid themselves of these wetlands.

ASTWOOD PARK

One of the most popular spots in Bermuda for outdoor weddings, the 23-acre **Astwood Park** (South Rd, opposite Tribe Rd No 3) has panoramic ocean views, a little cove and a grassy picnic area on a coastal knoll.

The pretty little beach here is a bit rocky, but when it's calm the nearshore rocks and reef provide good snorkeling for confident swimmers. The scenic cliffs at the east side of the park are a favorite area for local shore fishers, and in summer white-tailed tropic birds, known on the island as longtails, nest in the rockface. If you're here in spring or fall, from the cliffs, migratory birds can be seen among the stand of casuarina trees inland, as well as at the western extent of the park, where native palmetto trees and Bermuda cedars have been reintroduced.

SECOND THOUGHTS

The area that now forms Astwood Park was once earmarked to become the site of a new oceanfront resort. To make room for the development, South Rd, which dipped down to the coast at Astwood, had to first be rerouted north. After the roadwork was completed, islanders began to have second thoughts about giving up such a fine fishing spot for another tourist resort, and in 1984 the government jumped in and negotiated the purchase of the property from the would-be developers. Today, instead of leading visitors down to a mega-hotel, the faded asphalt of the old South Rd is the entryway into an unspoiled public park.

CHRIST CHURCH

This historic **church** (☎ 236-0400; Middle Rd) opposite the Belmont Hills Golf Club dates back to 1719, making it one of the oldest Presbyterian churches in the Western Hemisphere. The interior has stained-glass windows and a period pulpit. Equally intriguing is the churchyard, where you'll find historical gravestones with poignant epitaphs which provide insights into the lives of Bermuda's early inhabitants. Once an independent congregation, the church is now part of the Presbyterian Church of Scotland.

Activities
GOLF
Belmont Hills Golf Club (☎ 236-6400; 97 Middle Rd; weekdays/weekends $100/120; ☼ sunrise-sunset), a par-70, 5769yd course, has Bermuda's toughest opener and is a beauty that will suit players up for a challenge.

Riddell's Bay Golf & Country Club (☎ 238-1060; 26 Riddell's Bay Rd; $145; ☼ sunrise-sunset), a par-70, 5713yd course, offers snug fairways and narrow greens that will keep golfers tightly focused.

HORSEBACK RIDING
Spicelands Riding Centre (☎ 238-8212; Middle Rd, Warwick; $60; ☼ 7, 10 & 11:30am, also 4 & 6pm May-Sep) offers delightful one-hour guided rides along scenic south shore beaches. All rides are at a walking pace so it's well suited for novices – the only requirement is that riders be at least 12 years old.

HIKING

A section of the **Railway Trail** (p34) traces the length of Warwick Parish two miles from west to east, running between Middle Rd and South Rd. En route it passes on the south side of Warwick Pond Nature Reserve and the Belmont Hills Golf Club.

Sleeping

Clairfont Apartments (☎ 238-0149; www.clairfontapartments.com; 6 Warwickshire Rd; studio/1-bedroom apt $130/150; ☒ ☒) Beautiful roomy apartments, a cheery resident manager and just a 10-minute walk to the beach combine to make this a clear winner. For what you get this is one of the best deals on the island, but book well in advance as there's a steady stream of return guests. Each of the eight units is a bit different but all have full kitchens and little extras including DVD players and Internet access (if you bring your own computer). The corner units are particularly roomy and one even has a fireplace.

Vienna Guest Apartments (☎ 236-3300; www.bermuda1.com; 63 Cedar Hill; apt winter/summer from $110/130; ☒ ☒ ☒) This place is so hospitable that it's a bit like staying with your favorite uncle. Leopold Küchler, who doubles as the Austrian honorary consul, welcomes all international visitors and provides little extras like taking you to pick up groceries on your first night. The six apartments each have a full kitchen, a bedroom with both a queen bed and a single bed, and a living room with a sofa bed. It's in a quiet upscale neighborhood, a bit off the beaten track but on a bus route.

Surf Side Beach Club (☎ 236-7100, in the USA ☎ 800-553-9990; www.surfside.bm; 90 South Rd; r winter/summer from $150/275, with kitchen $195/325; ☒ ☒ ☒) Large, well-appointed units and a quiet setting with a private beach await at this small resort on the southeastern edge of Warwick Parish. The rooms, many with dazzling balconies perched above the ocean, are twice the size of a typical hotel room. The suites are even larger and, considering the parish's limited dining options, are the best way to go as they have full kitchens. The beach offers good swimming and the facilities include a sauna, hot tub and spa.

Granaway Guest House & Cottage (☎ 236-3747; www.granaway.com; 1 Longford Rd; r winter/summer from $100/130, cottage $150-220; ☒) Treat yourself to ocean views out the front and a lovely poolside garden at the rear in this classic manor house built in 1734. Opt for one of the five atmospheric guestrooms in the main house or splurge on the cottage, which has hand-painted Italian tiles, a full kitchen and a fireplace – and yes, it dates to colonial times as well. Breakfast is included with the guestrooms.

Sandpiper Apartments (☎ 236-7093, in the USA ☎ 800-637-4116; www.bermuda.com/sandpiper/index.htm; 10 South Rd; apt winter/summer from $100/140; ☒ ☒) This small apartment complex, at the east side of Warwick Parish, offers 14 pleasant units, each with full kitchens, two double beds and a single sofa bed. There are also a couple of larger units that have separate living rooms and can sleep up to four people for $50 more. The only drawback is that it's not close to a beach, although it is convenient for the bus.

Syl-Den Apartments (☎ 238-1834, in the USA ☎ 800-637-4116; syl@bsbp.bm; 8 Warwickshire Rd; apt $110-160; ☒ ☒) Adjacent to Clairfont Apartments, the five units in this place aren't as cushy as their neighbor's, but they make a fine alternative choice. Each is modern and comfortably furnished, with all the essentials including phones and full kitchens. There's a pool and sundeck, and the beach at Warwick Long Bay is within walking distance.

Blue Horizons (☎ 236-6350, in the USA ☎ 800-637-4116; blu@bspl.bm; 93 South Rd; s/d $80/100, apt $150-270; ☒ ☒) This little family-run place, painted ocean blue, has five comfortable units ranging from a straightforward room suitable for a couple to apartments that can accommodate a small family. Rates are the same year-round, making it particularly good value in

---

O'NEILL'S INTERLUDE

Famed American playwright Eugene O'Neill had a house on Harbour Rd in Warwick for a time, and it was here that he wrote *Mourning Becomes Electra*, *Lazarus Laughed*, *Strange Interlude* and *The Great God Brown*. O'Neill's daughter Oona, who married silent-film actor Charlie Chaplin, was born in Bermuda in 1925.

For a good read that details the author's life on the island, pick up a copy of the biography *Eugene O'Neill & Family; the Bermuda Interlude*, by Joy Bluck Waters, whose family lives in the house O'Neill once owned.

the summer. Although it's on busy South Rd, the house is set back far enough to be beyond the sound of traffic.

Marley Beach Cottages (☎ 236-1143, in the USA ☎ 800-637-4116; marleybeach@therock.bm; South Rd; apt winter/summer from $130/210; ✗ ▣) Fall asleep at night to the sound of the surf at these bluffside units scenically set above a private sandy beach. The unit interiors are simple and a bit worn, but the grounds are beautiful and the staff is as hospitable as they come. All units have kitchens and there's a heated whirlpool perfect for stargazing.

Astwood Cove (☎ 236-0984, in the USA ☎ 800-637-4116; www.astwoodcove.com; 49 South Rd; studio winter/summer from $110/150; ✗ ▣) This place sports a fine location opposite Astwood Park and 20 studios equipped with everything you'll need right down to the wine glasses. Other perks include verandas, barbecue grills, a sauna and a coin laundry. Plop down an extra $10 and get yourself a 2nd-story unit with a cathedral ceiling and water view.

Eating
RESTAURANTS
Paw Paws (☎ 236-7459; 87 South Rd; lunch $10-15, dinner $16-26; ✹ 11am-10pm; ✗) This cheery pub-like restaurant serves up good food and provides the parish's only moderately-priced option. Lunch, served until 5pm, features fresh salads, sandwiches with fries and a couple of simple hot dishes. At dinner there are steaks, pastas and the like, but go for one of the house specials: shark steak in Creole sauce or 'Paw Montespan' – a baked green papaya (paw paw) dish with ground beef, cheese and tomato.

Palms Restaurant (☎ 236-7100; Surf Side Beach Club, 90 South Rd; breakfast & lunch $7-16, dinner $27-37; ✹ breakfast, lunch & dinner; ✗ ✗) Poolside and with an ocean view, the Palms catches the south shore mood. The only hotel restaurant in Warwick, the Palms serves three meals a day, with breakfast options from cereal to eggs Benedict, and lunch the expected menu of salads and light fare. At dinner the chef shines with innovative flair – to spice up the night, try the tequila-seared tiger prawns or the coconut curry rockfish.

Brenda's Poolside Diner (☎ 236-7807; 93 South Rd; snacks $5-8; ✹ lunch) Roadside in front of Blue Horizons, this simple snack bar has hot dogs, burgers, fries and other simple eats.

GROCERIES
The most central grocery store in the parish is **Haywards Supermarket** (☎ 232-3995; 49 Middle Rd; ✹ 7am-7pm Mon-Sat), which also sells hot take-out items around lunchtime. The other options are **White's Supermarket** (☎ 238-1050; 22 Middle Rd; ✹ 8am-9pm Mon-Sat, 1-5pm Sun), at the west side of the parish, and **Lindo's Family Foods** (☎ 236-1344; 128 Middle Rd; ✹ 8am-7pm Mon-Sat), at the east side of the parish.

Getting There & Around
Warwick is crossed from east to west by three main roads: Harbour Rd on the north shore, Middle Rd through the interior and South Rd along the south shore. There's no bus service on Harbour Rd, but there is public ferry service to the City of Hamilton from the northeast side of the parish.

BOAT
The Pink Route of the public ferry (p154) connects the City of Hamilton with Warwick, making a 30-minute roundtrip loop from Hamilton that stops at Darrell's Wharf, near the intersection of Harbour and Cobbs Hill Rds, and at Belmont Wharf, near the Belmont Hills Golf Club.

The first ferry leaves Hamilton at 7:15am and takes 15 minutes to reach Belmont Wharf, another five minutes to reach Darrell's Wharf and another 10 minutes from there back to Hamilton. The ferries run on weekdays about once every half-hour, with the last ferry leaving Hamilton at 8:20pm. On Saturdays the schedule is similar except that the first ferry out of Hamilton is at 8:15am. On Sunday the service is less frequent and operates from 10am to 7pm.

In addition, during the middle of the day most Warwick ferries on the Pink Route also stop at the Paget wharfs of Lower Ferry, Hodson's Ferry and Salt Kettle. The fare between any two points on the Pink Route is $2.50.

BUS
Bus No 8 travels along Middle Rd to Warwick Pond and the village center, while bus No 7 travels along South Rd to Astwood Park and Warwick Long Beach; both of the routes connect Warwick with the Royal Naval Dockyard ($4.50, 35 minutes) to the west and the City of Hamilton ($3, 25 minutes) to the east. Both buses operate once

every 15 minutes during the day Monday to Saturday and about once every 30 minutes in the evening and on Sunday.

Bus No 7 operates weekdays from around 7am to 10pm (last bus out of Hamilton is at 9:15pm; last bus from the Dockyard is at 10:20pm), from 8am to 10pm Saturday and 9:30am to 6pm Sunday. Bus No 8 operates from 6:45am to around midnight Monday to Saturday and 8am to 11pm Sunday. For more information on public buses, including passes, see p155.

Southampton Parish

SOUTHAMPTON PARISH

HIGHLIGHTS

- Spend a day at the beach on the unrivaled pink sands of **Horseshoe Bay** (p120)
- Play a challenging round at the stunning **Port Royal Golf Course** (p123)
- Relax over tea and scones at the **Gibbs Hill Lighthouse Tea Room** (p125)

★ Port Royal Golf Course

Gibbs Hill Lighthouse Tea Room ★

★ Horseshoe Bay

■ POPULATION: 6117	■ AREA: 2.16 SQ MILES

If you had to sum up the crowning characteristic of Southampton Parish in one word, it's a cinch – beaches. Fantastic beaches – whether your preference is sunbathing, swimming or snorkeling, there's a beach in the parish to suit everyone's seaside requirements. Little wonder there are more hotel rooms in Southampton than in any other parish on the whole island. What's more, the recreational choices don't stop at the water's edge. Southampton boasts golfing opportunities for players of every level from miniature golf to championship greens. The range of accommodations will suit any taste as well, with quiet cottages and pampering small hotels contrasted against big oceanfront resorts. Some accommodations are located so close to the water that you can just mosey on out of your room and step right on to the beach, while others are built around the edges of golfing greens.

Southampton Parish, sometimes referred to as the western elbow of Bermuda, is bordered by Little Sound to the north and the Atlantic to the south. Because the land is so long and thin, with a width that tapers to a mere one-third of a mile at its narrowest point, wherever you are in the parish you're just minutes from the water. The north side of the parish is residential with a rocky shoreline; all those gorgeous pink-sand beaches and picture-postcard bays and coves run along the south coast. If you're up for a hike, a gem of a trail connects the south shore beaches, offering dramatic scenery to the hiker en route.

To take in a panoramic vista of both the north and south shores in one fell swoop, climb to the top of the historic Gibbs Hill Lighthouse. While you're there, enjoy some tea in one of Bermuda's most atmospheric settings, the lighthouse tea room. Seaside dining while you breathe the scent of the salt air is another treat to be savored in Southampton Parish.

Information

The **post office** (☎ 238-0253; cnr Church & Middle Rds) is in the center of the parish and there are Bank of Butterfield ATMs at the Fairmont Southampton (101 South Rd) and the Marketplace grocery store (Middle Rd).

Sights

GIBBS HILL LIGHTHOUSE

The parish's predominant landmark, this handsome **lighthouse** (☎ 238-8069; 68 St Anne's Rd; admission $2.50; ☒ 9am-4:30pm), towering 117ft above Gibbs Hill, is the tallest cast-iron lighthouse in the world.

Hoping to stem a rash of shipwrecks along Bermuda's treacherous western shoals, the British erected the lighthouse in 1846. The lens, which consists of concentric prisms, weighs 2¾ tons and is capable of generating a half-million candlepower. Using just a 1000-watt electric bulb, it produces a beam that can be seen up to 40 miles out to sea.

Climb the eight flights of stairs to the top – some 185 steps in all – and you'll be rewarded with a panoramic 360° view of the entire West End of Bermuda. On the way up the stairs, you'll encounter some interesting shipwreck-related displays, a fine excuse to stop and catch your breath.

On the same grounds, opposite the driveway into the lighthouse, is a lookout that's been known as the **Queen's View** ever since Queen Elizabeth II paused there in 1953 to admire the scenery; a plaque duly notes the event.

The Gibbs Hill Lighthouse is just off Lighthouse Rd, which begins west of the Henry VIII restaurant on South Rd. If you don't have a scooter, it takes only about 10 minutes to walk up to it.

A delightful way to top off a visit is to have lunch or afternoon tea at the atmospheric **tea room** (p125) on the ground level of the lighthouse.

HORSESHOE BAY

With its turquoise waters lapping onto pink sands, **Horseshoe Bay** (South Rd) is as gorgeous

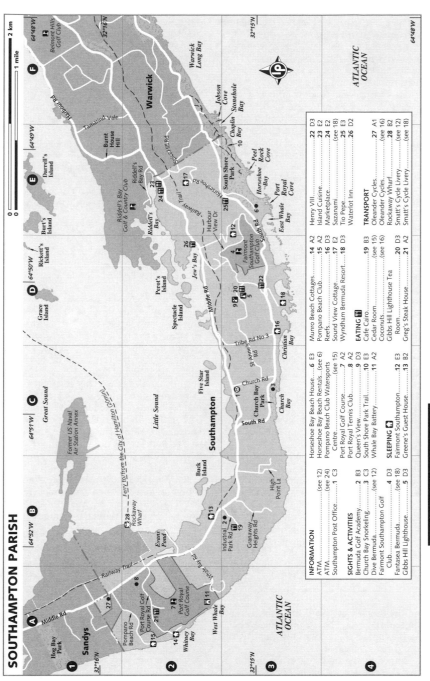

SOUTHAMPTON PARISH

INFORMATION

ATM	(see 12)
ATM	(see 24)
Southampton Post Office	1 C3

SIGHTS & ACTIVITIES

Bermuda Golf Academy	2 B3
Church Bay Snorkeling	3 C3
Dive Bermuda	(see 12)
Fairmont Southampton Golf Club	4 D3
Fantasea Bermuda	(see 18)
Gibbs Hill Lighthouse	5 D3
Horseshoe Bay Beach House	6 E3
Horseshoe Bay Beach Rentals	(see 6)
Pompano Beach Club Watersports Centre	(see 15)
Port Royal Golf Course	7 A2
Port Royal Tennis Club	8 A2
Queen's View	9 D3
South Shore Park Trail	10 E3
Whale Bay Battery	11 A2

SLEEPING

Fairmont Southampton	12 E3
Greene's Guest House	13 B2
Munro Beach Cottages	14 A2
Pompano Beach Club	15 A2
Reefs	16 D3
Sound View Cottage	17 E2
Wyndham Bermuda Resort	18 D3

EATING

Cafe Cairo	19 B3
Cedar Room	(see 15)
Coconuts	(see 16)
Gibbs Hill Lighthouse Tea Room	20 D3
Greg's Steak House	21 A2
Henry VIII	22 D3
Island Cuisine	23 E2
Marketplace	24 E2
Sazanami	(see 18)
Tio Pepe	25 E3
Waterlot Inn	26 D2

TRANSPORT

Oleander Cycles	27 A1
Oleander Cycles	(see 16)
Rockaway Wharf	28 B2
Smatt's Cycle Livery	(see 12)
Smatt's Cycle Livery	(see 18)

as it gets. Once you set eyes on it, you'll understand why this is the most popular beach in Bermuda. It's also the only beach in the area with full facilities and lifeguards. Not surprisingly, both locals and tourists flock here on a hot summer's day, but because it has such a wide crescent of sand there's always plenty of room to spread your towel.

Rocky outcroppings mark both ends of this horseshoe-shaped bay. Just beyond the outcropping at the west end of the beach you'll find the tiny **Port Royal Cove**, whose clear and typically calm waters make for protected swimming and snorkeling.

All of the facilities sit at the west end of the beach, along with an ample parking lot. The **Horseshoe Bay Beach House** (admission free; 🕑 8am-8pm Apr-Oct) has changing rooms with toilets and private shower stalls. Adjacent to the beach house is **Horseshoe Bay Beach Rentals** (☎ 238-2651; 94 South Rd; rental items per day $5-10; 🕑 9:30am-5pm Apr-Oct), a concession that rents beach chairs, towels, body boards, umbrellas and locker space. Next to the concession stand, and with the same opening hours, is a little café that sells hot dogs, burgers, sandwiches and ice cream.

The main entrance to Horseshoe Bay is on South Rd, opposite Tio Pepe restaurant, where you'll also find a bus stop.

CHURCH BAY PARK
It may not be as grand as popular Horseshoe Bay, but this attractive **beach** (South Rd) has its own appeal, including some of Bermuda's best snorkeling.

The reef comes in relatively close to the shore here, making Church Bay's snorkel sites easy to reach. You can find fish almost as soon as you enter the water, but for the best underwater scenery swim out to the reef, which is approximately 100yd from the beach. There you'll find lots of colorful tropical fish, including large parrotfish that feed on algae growing on the coral. In the process of chomping at the coral, the parrotfish actually create some of the sand that eventually accumulates on the beach.

A concessionaire (opposite) sets up right on the beach from April to October, renting snorkel gear, beach umbrellas, chairs and lounges, selling cold soda and cheerily dishing out snorkeling tips.

Although the main sights are found in the water, there's a bit of history here as well. In early colonial times a coastal fort stood at the east side of the bay; if you walk up onto the knoll above the beach you'll find a plaque marking the spot where the fort was erected in 1612.

SOUTH SHORE PARK TRAIL
If you do just one long beach walk, make it this one. The **South Shore Park Trail** is an absolute beauty of a hike that takes you past a run of hidden coves sandwiched between the island's two most glorious beaches, **Warwick Long Bay** (p113) and **Horseshoe Bay** (p120). Picturesque views abound along the way as the undulating trail winds up to coastal cliffs and then back down to lovely little beaches. Bring a bathing suit!

You can walk in either direction, but if you start at Horseshoe Bay and head east, you'll keep the midday sun at your back. The walk goes from one end to the other of **South Shore Park**, a 1.5-mile-long coastal park established to protect Bermuda's finest stretch of undeveloped beaches.

The trail is easy to follow. At Horseshoe Bay, just walk along the beach and when you reach the end you'll find a path jutting up the cliffside that marks the east end of the bay. At the top you'll be rewarded with a fine view of turquoise seas lapping at pink sands below. This cliff is the first in a series of outcroppings of craggy rocks that form the nine secluded coves and small bays dotting the shoreline between the two bookend beaches. The first one you come to, **Peel Rock Cove**, is just a five-minute walk beyond Horseshoe Bay and has an inviting little beach.

After Peel Rock Cove, continue along the shoreline and the path will wind you up to scenic clifftops and back down to the water's edge. In about 20 minutes you'll

---

KEEP YOUR TOP ON

It's tempting, so tempting…those glorious expanses of glistening sand, those hidden private coves, all look as if they're inviting you to fling off your cares and bare your skin to the sun.

Yet, no. Not only is nudity illegal on Bermudian beaches, so is topless sunbathing for women. You'll just have to get rid of those tan lines someplace else.

reach **Chaplin Bay**, a sandy beach that once belonged to the family of movie star Charlie Chaplin. The path continues through flowering beach morning glory and oleander into Warwick Parish, past a fine beach at **Stonehole Bay** and little **Jobson Cove** before bringing you to Warwick Long Bay.

WEST WHALE BAY
Off the main tourist beat, **West Whale Bay** (end of Whale Bay Rd) offers a little sandy cove in a quiet, natural setting. And if you want to pack a lunch, you'll find a couple of picnic tables on the hillside above the beach.

The remains of a small fort, **Whale Bay Battery**, can be explored by making a mere three-minute walk up the hill to the northwest. The fortification, overlooking the Port Royal Golf Course, offers a panoramic view of the endless turquoise and cobalt waters of the Atlantic.

The gun battery was built in 1876 to defend Hog Fish Cut, a channel through the reefs leading to the Royal Naval Dockyard. The battery's original cannons weighed 12 tons and provided a hefty defense against potential raids on the Dockyard. Whale Bay Battery was recommissioned during WWII to serve as a lookout for German boats. Now abandoned, its guns are gone but you can still rummage through the former ammunition magazines and barracks.

Activities
SNORKELING
The west side's best easy-access snorkeling spot is Church Bay, where the nearshore reef harbors a variety of colorful tropical fish and you can rent quality snorkel gear right on the beach from **Church Bay Snorkeling** (☎ 799-5657; snorkel gear per day $15; ☖ 10am-5pm Mon-Sat May-Oct).

Both Dive Bermuda and Fantasea Bermuda dive shops (below) allow snorkelers to go out with their dive boat when their divers are diving shallow reefs. Snorkelers pay $40 to $50, gear included.

DIVING
Fantasea Bermuda (☎ 238-1833; 6 Sonesta Dr; 1-/2-tank dive $65/84; ☖ 9am-5pm) at the Wyndham Bermuda Resort has numerous dive options. For people who have never dived before, these folks make it easy with their 'Discover Scuba' course ($100) for begin-

ners, which includes an hour-long introductory lesson at the hotel pool and then goes out to dive on a 25ft reef – all you need is a bathing suit. For experienced divers there's everything from wreck dives to night dives.

Dive Bermuda (☎ 238-2332; 101 South Rd; 1-/2-tank dive $70/100; ☖ 9am-5pm) at the Fairmont Southampton also offers a full range of professionally run dives.

GOLF
Championship **Port Royal Golf Course** (☎ 234-0974; automated reservation system ☎ 234-4653; 5 Middle Rd; greens fee $132; ☖ sunrise-sunset) offers dramatic views and demanding greens. The course, par 71, 6561yd, was designed by Robert Trent Jones.

A better choice for beginning golfers, **Fairmont Southampton Golf Club** (☎ 239-6952; Fairmont Southampton, 101 South Rd; greens fee $70; ☖ sunrise-sunset) is shorter and has players concentrating on close shots more than power strokes. This par-54, 2684yd course is no slouch in the scenery department either, with lakes, hills and ocean views.

Just want to hit, hit, hit? The **Bermuda Golf Academy** (☎ 238-8800; Industrial Park Rd; basket of balls at driving range $5, mini-golf $8; ☖ 9am-10pm) has a 320yd driving range, 40 practice bays, target greens and a charming 18-hole miniature golf course.

BOATING
Pompano Beach Club Watersports Centre (☎ 234-0222; 36 Pompano Beach Rd; boats per hr $15-35; ☖ 9am-5pm May-Oct) at the Pompano Beach resort rents a wide range of boats including sailboats, kayaks, paddleboats and glass-bottom boats.

Fantasea Bermuda (☎ 238-1833; 6 Sonesta Dr; pedal boat per hr $20, 2-person kayak per hr $30; ☖ 9am-5pm) at the Wyndham Bermuda Resort rents self-propelled boats for paddling around.

HIKING
In addition to the coastal **South Shore Park Trail** (opposite), a section of the **Railway Trail** (p34) runs clear through Southampton Parish, connecting with neighboring Sandys Parish to the northwest and Warwick Parish to the east. The Railway Trail parallels Middle Rd most of the way, offering views of Southampton's less-touristed north shore and Little Sound.

SOUTHAMPTON PARISH

LOST IN THE TRIANGLE

Few terms conjure up images of the paranormal the way that 'Bermuda Triangle' does.

The name is given to a triangular section of the Atlantic Ocean that's bound by Bermuda to the north, Florida to the west and Puerto Rico to the south. It's thought that as many as 100 ships and planes have vanished in the triangle. The mysterious disappearances in this zone, which is also known as the Devil's Triangle, date back to the mid-19th century. It wasn't until the 1970s, however, when a popular interest in UFOs and other unexplained phenomena arose, that the disappearances drew international attention and the term Bermuda Triangle came into common use.

What makes the triangle unusual is that not only are the disappearances quite substantial for an area of this size, but many of the vessels have gone down without so much as emitting a distress signal – and with no subsequent trace of the craft ever appearing. In other cases ships have reappeared intact months after disappearing, but with no trace of the crew ever found.

The largest single disappearance in the Bermuda Triangle was that of the infamous Flight 19, a group of five US Navy torpedo bombers that flew out of Florida on a routine flight in December 1945 and vanished; a search plane sent in their wake also disappeared.

Various theories have been advanced to explain the disappearances, ranging from atmospheric disturbances and erratic magnetic forces to time warps and extraterrestrial kidnappings. Others just write most of it off as coincidence and the usual combination of mechanical failure, bad weather and human error.

However you look at it, the Bermuda Triangle gives those with a rich imagination plenty to work with.

TENNIS

The **Port Royal Tennis Club** (☎ 238-9070; 5 Middle Rd; per court per hr $10; ☼ 8am-8pm), near the golf course, has four Plexipave courts, and the **Fairmont Southampton** (☼ 239-6950; 101 South Rd; per court per day $15; ☼ 8am-9pm) resort has 11. Both have lights for night play.

Sleeping

Fairmont Southampton (☎ 238-8000, in the USA & Canada ☎ 800-441-1414; www.fairmont.com/southampton; 101 South Rd; r winter/summer from $219/419; ✕ ✖ ✍) Bermuda's largest and most upscale resort exudes elegance. Despite its size it's an unhurried place with a quiet hilltop location amidst an 18-hole golf course. Other facilities include a spa, a fitness center, tennis courts and several restaurants. The rooms have waterview balconies and some pleasant touches like velour bathrobes. Although the hotel is about a half-mile inland, its own private white-sand beach – and anywhere else on the 100-acre grounds – can be reached by a complimentary shuttle. The resort is a member of the Fairmont chain.

Pompano Beach Club (☎ 234-0222, in the USA & Canada ☎ 800-343-4155; www.pompanobeachclub.com; 36 Pompano Beach Rd; r winter/summer from $280/375; ✖ ✍) Friendly staff, striking ocean views and comfy rooms await at this small upmarket hotel. The rooms are spread in a scattering of two-story buildings along a coastal cliff at the north side of the Port Royal Golf Course. It's all very quiet and low-key, making it an ideal getaway choice. Facilities include clay tennis courts and a fitness room. There's a small beach with shallow waters that are good for snorkeling. The rooms have rattan furnishings, king-size beds and oceanview balconies. Breakfast is included.

Wyndham Bermuda Resort (☎ 238-8122, in the USA ☎ 800-996-3426; www.wyndham.com; 6 Sonesta Dr; r winter/summer from $275/320; ✕ ✖ ✍) Perched on a rocky outcrop that separates twin bays, this resort boasts two beautiful beaches. In an effort to attract more families it's dedicated one sandy area to the kids, adding some neat water slides and pools just inland of the beach. The resort took a beating (it lost a whole wing!) during Hurricane Fabian – so virtually everything has been rebuilt. With its long curving design, nearly every room here enjoys a fine water view. Tennis courts, a health spa and a fitness center round out the facilities.

Reefs (☎ 238-0222, in the USA & Canada ☎ 800-742-2008; www.thereefs.com; 56 South Rd; r winter/summer from $185/365; ✖ ✍) This pampering upscale hotel has a handsome private beach at Christian Bay just west of the Wyndham Bermuda Resort. There are 73 attractive rooms in a series of terraced hillside buildings. Most sport waterview balconies and all have cheery tropical decor. The grounds have two tennis courts, a fitness center and a good seaside restaurant. Breakfast is included. Swimming, snorkeling and diving are possible from the beach.

Munro Beach Cottages (☎ 234-1175, in the USA ☎ 800-637-4116; www.munrobeach.com; 2 Port Royal Golf Course Rd; apt winter/summer from $130/230; ✗ ☒) The perfect choice for golfers, this quiet complex looks out on the Port Royal Golf Course in one direction and the ocean in the other. The place is composed of nine duplex units spread in an arc along low seacliffs. The units are modern, with full kitchens, oceanfront patios and all the expected amenities. A path leads down to a small, private beach at Whitney Bay, and tennis is available nearby.

Sound View Cottage (☎ 238-0064; 9 Bowe Lane; apt $85; ✗ ☒ ☒) Enjoy a hilltop view of the Great Sound from one of these three apartments in a residential neighborhood midway between Middle Rd and South Shore Park. Each of the compact units has a kitchenette and there's a poolside patio with a barbecue. All in all, it's good budget value. It's open from April through October only.

Greene's Guest House (☎ 238-0834; greenes guesthouse@yahoo.com; 71 Middle Rd; s/d $110/130; ☒ ☒) Set back away from the road, this friendly family-run guesthouse has six comfortable rooms appointed with little extras like refrigerators, coffeemakers and VCRs. Breakfast is included. Join your fellow guests in the cheery lounge at night. The only drawback is that the location, at the north side of the parish, isn't close to the south shore's sandy beaches, though it is on a bus route.

Eating

Gibbs Hill Lighthouse Tea Room (☎ 238-8679; Gibbs Hill Lighthouse, 68 St Anne's Rd; ⊕ 9am-4:45pm; ✗ ☒) When was the last time you ate at a lighthouse? This cozy spot combines a lovely setting and view with a casual air and an English-style menu. While away the afternoon over a pot of hot tea and some luscious scones served warm with butter

and jam. In the morning you can also get egg breakfasts and after 11:30am some old-fashioned lunches like codfish croquettes with salad.

Cedar Room (☎ 234-0222; Pompano Beach Club, Pompano Beach Rd; breakfast & lunch $10-15, dinner $52; ⊕ breakfast, lunch & dinner; ✗ ☒) Wrap-around picture windows looking across an azure ocean, good food and attentive service make for a winning combination. Lunch is casual fare, including tasty fish chowder, creative sandwiches and Greek salads. Dinner is a more upscale affair featuring a five-course prix fixe meal, with several choices for each course. The menu changes daily but dinner mains typically include fresh seafood, a beef dish and a gourmet country-style offering like grilled quail.

Henry VIII (☎ 238-1977; 56 South Rd; lunch $12-20, dinner $20-40; ⊕ lunch & dinner; ✗ ☒) Southampton's best-known restaurant plays up a convivial Olde English ambiance, all burgundy and dark wood, with waitresses in Tudor-style dress. Lunch features sandwiches and pub grub like steak-and-kidney pie, but most everybody comes here for dinner. The cornerstone for big meat-eaters is the Angus prime rib with Yorkshire pudding, but in addition to beef dishes there's lighter fare such as curried vegetable strudel or poached salmon. The adjoining pub features English lagers on tap. All in all a bit pricey, but a fun night out.

Coconuts (☎ 238-0222; The Reefs, 56 South Rd; lunch $9-16, 4-course dinner $64; ⊕ noon-4pm & 7-9:30pm) Dine to the sound of the surf at this romantic beachside restaurant that features a menu with Caribbean and Cajun accents. At lunch choose between the likes of jerked chicken sandwiches, Cajun quesadillas and curried salads. At dinner there's a prix fixe menu that changes daily but dangles such temptations as coconut-crusted tiger shrimp in mango dipping sauce.

Island Cuisine (☎ 238-3287; 235 Middle Rd; breakfast $6-10, sandwiches $4-6, dinner $11-15; ⊕ 6am-10pm Mon-Sat, 6am-1pm Sun; ☒) Don't be put off by the bland exterior – this place serves up good hearty breakfasts and real homestyle local food. You can get pancakes and various egg dishes any time of the day. Meals of fried chicken or fish, dished up with peas and rice, provide a solid, affordable dinner option. On Sundays the thing to order is the traditional codfish-and-potatoes breakfast.

Greg's Steak House (☎ 234-6092; 5 Port Royal Dr; lunch $10-18, dinner $22-40; ✆ lunch 11:30am-5pm, dinner 6:30-10pm; ✗ ✖) Bermuda's best steak restaurant graces the greens at Port Royal Golf Course. Greg's 16oz Angus beef T-bone is legendary but if you're looking for something on a more reasonable scale the filet mignon is as tender as they come. There are also lamb and fish options, but everyone comes up here at dinner for the steaks. Lunch features the more typical light golf-club fare of sandwiches and salads.

Tio Pepe (☎ 238-1897; 117 South Rd; lunch $10-20, dinner $15-34; ✆ 11am-10pm; ✗ ✖) If you've worked up an appetite after a day at the beach, this homestyle Italian restaurant opposite Horseshoe Bay has crispy pizza and good pastas. At dinner it adds on steaks and tempting specials like lobster ravioli in a light cream sauce. You can dine outside at umbrella-shaded tables or indoors in air-con comfort.

Waterlot Inn (☎ 239-6967; Middle Rd; appetizers $12-24, mains $26-40; ✆ dinner; ✖) Within the walls of a 320-year-old dockside inn, this dinner restaurant is a throwback to an earlier era. The cuisine blends Mediterranean and Bermudian fare, with everything from fresh seafood to rack of lamb and dry-aged steaks. The wine list is award winning and the service is polished. Affiliated with the Fairmont Southampton, Waterlot is the resort's most formal choice and tends to appeal to an older crowd; cigar smoking is allowed and jackets and ties are suggested.

Sazanami (☎ 239-3322; 6 Sonesta Dr; à la carte sushi $3-10, mains $15-30; ✆ dinner; ✗ ✖) The most interesting of the Wyndham Bermuda Resort's several restaurants, Sazanami offers authentic Japanese fare and dramatic ocean views. For the most fun, sit at the revolving sushi bar and choose whatever catches your eye. You can also dine at tables and enjoy everything from sashimi to tempura dinners.

Cafe Cairo (☎ 238-1831; 10 Industrial Park Rd; lunch $9-15, dinner $12-35; ✆ 11am-10pm; ✖) Walking through the door is a bit like stepping into a Bedouin tent. Carpets on the floor, low-slung cushions in place of chairs and candle lighting set the tone at this Middle Eastern restaurant. The menu runs the gamut from wrap sandwiches and burgers to moussaka and *shish tawook* with hummus. On weekends there's a grand buffet spread ($35) at dinner.

Marketplace (☎ 238-1993; Middle Rd; ✆ 7am-10pm Mon-Sat, 1-5pm Sun) If you need groceries, get 'em here.

Entertainment

Henry VIII (☎ 238-1977; 56 South Rd) Here you'll find a frolicking pub atmosphere and entertainment almost nightly. Usually it's a keyboardist, with the music going until 1am, but on Sunday night it rocks with a DJ and dancing until 3am.

Getting There & Around

The two main roads through Southampton are Middle Rd, which runs along Little Sound, and South Rd, which runs past the beaches and hotels on the south shore.

BICYCLE

Bicycle rentals are available from **Oleander Cycles** (☎ 234-0629; Middle Rd), just north of the Port Royal Golf Course.

BOAT

In an effort to relieve vehicle congestion on the roads, the government has instituted a high-speed commuter ferry service (p154) between Southampton and the City of Hamilton. Not surprisingly, the schedule is busiest during commuter hours, from 7am to 9am and 5pm to 7pm Monday to Friday, when sailings take place every 30 minutes.

The ferry – called the Rockaway Express, or the Green Route – takes just 20 minutes and costs $4 one way. On Saturday there are half a dozen sailings between 8am and 5:30pm from Hamilton and 8:25am and 6pm from Rockaway. There is no service on Sunday.

BUS

Middle Rd is served by bus No 8 and South Rd is served by bus No 7. The service along either route runs once every 15 minutes during the day and about once every 30 minutes in the evening and on Sunday. It takes about 30 minutes to reach either the Royal Naval Dockyard ($4.50) or the City of Hamilton ($3). If you're going to Hamilton for dinner, keep in mind that the last No 7 bus leaves Hamilton at 9:15pm (6pm Sunday), and the last No 8 bus departs at 11:45pm (10:45pm Sunday).

South Rd merges with Middle Rd about midway in the parish at a spot called Barnes

Corner. Note that a number of buses terminate at Barnes Corner, so if you're going any further west, make sure you take a bus that's marked 'Dockyard' or 'Somerset.' Things are simple if you're heading east, as all No 7 and 8 buses terminate in the City of Hamilton.

For more information on public buses, including passes, see p155.

MOTOR SCOOTER

Scooter rentals are available at two branches of **Oleander Cycles** (☎ 234-0629; Middle Rd): just north of the Port Royal Golf Course, and at the **Reefs** (☎ 234-5235; 56 South Rd). Scooters can also be rented from **Smatt's Cycle Livery** (☎ 295-1180; 101 South Rd) at the Fairmont Southampton and at **Wyndham Bermuda Resort** (☎ 238-7900; 6 Sonesta Dr).

SOUTHAMPTON PARISH

Sandys Parish

HIGHLIGHTS

- Explore the **Royal Naval Dockyard** (p134) with its craft shops, galleries and superb maritime museum

- Take a peek at the **world's smallest drawbridge** (opposite), in Somerset Village

- Walk around the extensive grounds of **Scaur Hill Fort Park** (p131)

★ Royal Naval Dockyard

★ Scaur Hill Fort Park

★ Somerset Bridge

■ POPULATION: 7275   ■ AREA: 1.82 SQ MILES

SANDYS PARISH

If Bermuda has a hinterland, then it's certainly Sandys (pronounced 'sands'). This western-most parish, also known as the West End, is made up of five islands connected by bridges.

Sandys has a multi-faceted history born of rich soil and a powerful motherland. It is some-times referred to as 'up the country' because of its rural roots, and many old-time Bermudians can trace their ancestry back to the family farmsteads that once dotted the parish.

The main village of Somerset derives its name from Sir George Somers, whose shipwrecked crew were the first settlers to Bermuda – this, it is said, was 'Somers seat.' Somers was just the first of many admirals to leave a mark on the parish. Two hundred years after Somers' death, the British Royal Navy arrived in force and began staking its claim.

The parish's main sightseeing attractions include, on one hand, nature preserves with quiet trails that wind through farms and woodlands and, on the other hand, mighty impres-sive forts. None is more impressive than the 75-acre Royal Naval Dockyard, an immense com-plex with munitions storehouses, cannon-topped bastions and a moat-encircled fortress.

Sandys' northernmost islands – Watford Island, Boaz Island, Ireland Island South and Ireland Island North – were all once occupied by the Royal Navy. Today, naval cemeteries flank the road leading out of Somerset to the Royal Naval Dockyard.

Ireland Island North, the outermost part of Sandys, was entirely the navy's. Its HMS *Malabar* naval base closed in 1995, ending the Royal Navy's centuries-old presence in Bermuda.

The Royal Naval Dockyard was also decommissioned but it's not sleeping. This collection of 19th-century buildings, along with the former military dockyard and fort, has been turned into one of Bermuda's foremost visitor destinations, with its own cruise ship dock, small marina, snorkel park, maritime museum, shopping center, craft galleries and restaurants.

SOMERSET & AROUND

Somerset, the largest of the islands in Sandys Parish, sits serenely between the beach re-sorts in Southampton Parish to its south and the tourist-driven Royal Naval Dock-yard to the north.

The heart of Somerset Island is the sleepy **Somerset Village**, which is virtually untouched by tourism and can be an interesting place to poke around in if you want to get off the beaten track. The village is fronted by Man-grove Bay and has a couple of waterview restaurants that can make for a scenic meal break.

The entry to Somerset Island is across the world's smallest drawbridge. **Somerset Bridge**, built in the 17th century, has a mere 30-inch span. It's amazing to watch in action. It opens just wide enough to allow the mast of a sailboat to pass through as the boat sails, ever so gently, between the Great Sound and Ely's Harbour. Obviously, the sailor needs to have a good command and steady hand!

Somerset Island has many other sights as well, the most prominent being Scaur Hill Fort Park, an old fort with superb views and lots of nooks and crannies to explore.

Orientation

The main road through Sandys is Middle Rd, which changes its name to Somerset Rd as it crosses Somerset Bridge, to Mangrove Bay Rd as it passes the village of Somerset, and to Malabar Rd as it continues toward the Royal Naval Dockyard. There's a gas station at Robinson's Marina.

Information
EMERGENCY
Police station (☎ 234-1010; 3 Somerset Rd)

SANDYS PARISH

0 ————— 1 km
0 ————— 0.5 miles

See Royal Naval
Dockyard Map (p135)

Dockyard
Wharf

Ireland
Island
North

Pender Rd

Ferry to/from the
Town of St George (1hr);
Ferry to/from City
of Hamilton (30min)

ATLANTIC
OCEAN

Ireland
Island
South

The
Lagoon

15min

Boaz
Island

Boaz
Island
Wharf

Malabar Rd

Outer
Island

Inner
Island

Middle
Island

Mangrove
Bay

Watford
Island

Watford Bridge
Wharf

Mangrove
Bay Rd

15min

Daniel's
Island

Daniel's
Head

Long Bay

Cambridge Rd

Somerset
Village

Sandys

10min

West Side Rd

Somerset
Island

Broome St

Scotts Hill Rd

Sound View Rd

Front Street Rd

Cavello
Bay Wharf

ATLANTIC
OCEAN

Heydon's
Bay

Morgan's
Island

Heydon
Trust
Estate

Somerset Rd

Great
Sound

Hawkins
Island

Bethell's
Island

Scaur Hill
Fort Park

15min

32°17'N

Ely's
Harbour

The Scaur

Wreck
Hill
(140ft)

Whale
Island

Railway Trail

Somerset Bridge
Wharf

Ferry to/from the City of Hamilton (30min)

Somerset Bridge

Wreck Rd

Middle Rd

Railway Trail

Grace
Island

Former US Naval
Air Station Annex

Hog Bay
Park

Port Royal
Golf Course

Rockaway
Wharf

Ferry to/from the City of Hamilton (20min)

Little
Sound

Southampton

LAUNDRY
Sandys Laundromat (☎ 238-9455; 48 Somerset Rd; ⊙ 7:30am-8pm Mon-Sat, to 5pm Sun)

MEDICAL SERVICES
Somerset Pharmacy (☎ 234-2484; 49 Mangrove Bay Rd, Somerset Village; ⊙ 8am-8pm Mon-Sat, 10am-6pm Sun)

MONEY
Bank of Butterfield (☎ 234-0048; Mangrove Bay Rd, Somerset Village; ⊙ 9am-3:30pm Mon-Thu, to 4:30pm Fri)

POST
Mangrove Bay Post Office (☎ 234-0423; 3 Somerset Rd, Somerset Village)
Somerset Bridge Post Office (☎ 234-0220; 1 Middle Rd) This smaller post office, at the south side of Somerset Bridge, closes for lunch from 11:30am to 1pm.

Sights
SCAUR HILL FORT PARK
The most ambitious out of Bermuda's many forts, **Scaur Hill** (☎ 234-0908; Middle Rd; admission free; ⊙ 10am-4:30pm) stands as a monument to the tensions that existed between the British and the Americans in the mid-19th century. During the US Civil War the British had backed the defeated Confederacy, so despite the fact that the victorious North emerged from the war in such a battle-weary condition, the British were worried about a possible retaliatory US invasion of Bermuda.

Britain, with its colonial ties in Canada and possessions in the West Indies, looked upon Bermuda as the forward citadel of its naval power in the New World. Consequently, in 1865 the British allocated a hefty sum for fortifying Bermuda, and in 1868 work began on Scaur Hill Fort, the largest of several such projects.

Scaur Hill Fort was built at the south side of Somerset Island, on the crest of its highest hill, with the express purpose of protecting the Royal Naval Dockyard from a land invasion. For the same reason, a deep ditch was dug from Ely's Harbour in the west to Great Harbour in the east, effectively slicing Somerset Island in two. Ramparts were built along the elevated northern side of the ditch, where platforms were installed for use by infantry men who – theoretically, at least – could mow down invading soldiers as they leaped into the ditch from the south.

So extensive was the design of the fort that it took the better part of two decades to complete the work. By the time it was finished it was obsolete, but, considering Bermuda's history of nonexistent military confrontations, that seemed to be beside the point.

In an interesting twist of fate, American troops finally did come to occupy Scaur Hill Fort, albeit by British invitation, when the 52nd Coast Artillery Battalion of the US Army took up station at the fort during WWII.

The fort was originally equipped with a pair of hefty rifled muzzleloader cannons mounted on the Moncrieff 'disappearing' carriages that recoiled out of sight for reloading after firing; 5-ton counterweights then raised the carriages back to position.

Visitors are able to explore the old parade grounds, march along the ditch, view the stone galleries with their cannon and rifle windows, and peer into the concrete emplacements that held the disappearing cannons. However, true to their names, the big guns themselves have disappeared from the site.

One other plus in visiting the fort is the amazing views. On a clear day you can see both ends of Bermuda from the Dockyard in the west to St George's in the east. Bring a lunch and enjoy it on one of the hillside benches while soaking up the scene.

HOG BAY PARK
If you enjoy exploring old house sites and that sort of thing, **Hog Bay Park** (Middle Rd; admission free; ⊙ sunrise-sunset) can be an interesting place to wander through. This unique 38-acre park has been patched together from abandoned farms purchased from three adjoining estates.

All three had kept the land in a natural state, free of any 20th-century development; consequently, the park is a repository of sorts for Bermuda's rural past and holds many relics dating to the early colonial period. In those days, Sandys and nearby Southampton Parish abounded with small farms and Hog Bay Park incorporates an unspoiled slice of that original agricultural land. In the early 1990s, before the property was opened as a public park, researchers came from the College of William and Mary in Williamsburg, Virginia, and uncovered numerous artifacts. They also identified the uses of former sites, such as a kiln used for the production of lime, the remnants of servants' quarters, and the remains of a buttery – a small structure used for cold storage in pre-refrigeration days.

Spread around the property are fallow tobacco and cassava fields, several abandoned cottages and stands of native trees. The path begins at the roadside parking area at the northeast corner of the park and can be followed all the way down to the bay, where hikers will be rewarded with fine coastal views.

HEYDON TRUST ESTATE

The large **Heydon estate** (Heydon Dr; admission free; sunrise-sunset), north of Scaur Hill Fort, is the biggest tract of undeveloped open space in Sandys Parish. The trust that owns the property generously opens the 43 acres to the public.

The centerpiece of the estate is a lovely little **chapel** perched on the hillside. Thought to have been built by an early colonist as a homestead cottage, this simple limestone building dates to at least 1616. Take a look behind the altar and you can still see the home's original oven.

Inspired by its peaceful setting, an interdenominational Christian organization uses the cottage as a chapel for informal sunrise and afternoon prayer services. Unless a service is taking place, visitors are free to take a look inside. Opposite the chapel you'll find a lookout point with an impressive vista of the Great Sound. Look straight out to get a bird's-eye view of Tucker's Peninsula, which once served as home to the US Naval Air Station Annex.

In addition to the views and tranquility, during the spring and autumn migratory seasons the wooded areas of Heydon Trust Estate are good spots for birdwatching.

The road into the property begins opposite the Willowbank hotel on Middle Rd and leads east about 500yd, where it makes a loop around the chapel.

SOMERSET LONG BAY

Sandys simply isn't endowed with the glorious beaches found in neighboring parishes to the south. The main public bathing spot at **Somerset Long Bay Park** (Cambridge Rd; admission free; sunrise-sunset) has a sandy beach with shallow waters that are best suited for

children. The park, at the northwest side of Somerset Island, has toilets and picnic facilities.

Nature lovers will find the adjacent **Somerset Long Bay Nature Reserve** (Cambridge Rd; admission free; sunrise-sunset) well worth a stroll. This reclaimed wetland habitat owned by the Bermuda Audubon Society serves as a prime nesting site for resident waterfowl and attracts migratory birds. A trail through tall grasses at the southwest side of Somerset Long Bay Park leads into the sanctuary. Just a two-minute walk along that trail will bring you to a duck-viewing area, where you can spot redbreasted mergansers in winter and gallinule year-round. At various times of the year, you might also see migratory herons, egrets, warblers and kingfishers, as well as resident catbirds and cardinals.

SPRINGFIELD & THE GILBERT NATURE RESERVE

This combined **historic site and nature reserve** (236-6483; 29 Somerset Rd; admission free; sunrise-sunset) at the south side of Somerset Village once comprised a small plantation. The manor house, known as Springfield, dates to the 1740s and has been a holding of the Bermuda National Trust since 1967. Today Springfield houses a community center.

The adjacent 5-acre property, the Gilbert Nature Reserve, was purchased by the Trust in 1973 to protect its rural character from potential development. The reserve is crossed with short footpaths that begin at the southwest side of the parking lot and connect the property to the Railway Trail. The paths start in thick brush and wind past wooded sections of native cedar and palmetto trees that are thick with warblers and other woodland birds.

Activities

DIVING

Blue Water Divers (234-1034; Robinson's Marina; 1-/2-tank dive $55/75; 8am-6pm) is a reputable dive operation that also offers snorkel tours ($40).

For a fun diversion – and you don't even have to be a swimmer – sign up with **Greg Hartley's Under Sea Adventure** (234-2861; Watford Bridge; adult/child $58/44; departures 10am & 1:30pm Apr-Nov) helmet dive operation and take a walk on the ocean floor.

CUP FEVER

For two days in midsummer, in even-numbered years, Somerset becomes the center of the universe for absolutely everyone in Bermuda.

Thousands of people flock to the otherwise-sleepy village for Cup Match, filling the streets leading up to the Somerset Cricket Club, all of which sport apt names: Bat 'n' Ball Lane, Grandstand Lane and Cricket Lane. Bet-starved Bermudians crowd the Crown 'n Anchor gaming tables for the only public gambling allowed on the island all year. Food booths dish up steaming plates of conch stew, mussel pie and fried fish, and Somerset fans adorn themselves in their team's colors of light and dark blue. Their opponents, who come from St George's, can be identified by their garb of dark blue and red colors.

Don't fret if you can't grasp the lingo. What's a square leg, you wonder? A silly mid off? A sticky wicket? Just ask and Bermudians will gladly fill you in. Cricket fever is infectious…

BOATING

Somerset Bridge Water Sports (☎ 234-0914; Robinson's Marina; kayak/canoe/motorboat per 4hr $40/50/120; ☺ 9am-5pm) handles water-related gear, with everything from snorkel sets ($6) to fishing gear ($15) and boat rentals.

HIKING

A 2.3-mile stretch of the **Railway Trail** (p34) runs from Southampton Parish to Somerset Village. The section on Somerset Island is open to both hikers and scooters and is a scenic stretch, with views of the Great Sound along the way. En route, the Railway Trail passes the eastern sides of Scaur Hill Fort Park, the Heydon Trust Estate and the Gilbert Nature Reserve, offering hikers some nice diversions.

WATERSKIING

Bermuda Waterski Centre (☎ 234-3354; Robinson's Marina; per hr $120; ☺ 8am-7:30pm May-Sep) offers slalom, trick skis, tubes and knee boards.

TENNIS

Willowbank Hotel (☎ 234-1616; 126 Somerset Rd; per court per hr $8; ☺ 8am-6pm) has two Plexipave tennis courts open to the public for a fee and free for hotel guests. Lessons and tennis equipment rental are available.

Sleeping

Cambridge Beaches (☎ 234-0331, in the USA ☎ 800-468-7300; www.cambridgebeaches.com; 30 King's Point Rd; r winter/summer from $305/370; ☒ ☒) Bask in the sun on your choice of five private beaches at this exclusive hideaway resort spread along a 25-acre peninsula at the northernmost point of Somerset Island. It's got it all – elegant rooms, breakfast included and pampering facilities that include a health spa, indoor and outdoor pools, tennis courts and a marina with a complimentary ferry to Hamilton. Most anything else you can imagine from kayaking to deep sea fishing is available and guests receive a temporary membership to all Bermuda golf courses.

Willowbank (☎ 234-1616, in the USA ☎ 800-752-8493, in Canada ☎ 800-463-8444; www.willowbank.bm; 126 Somerset Rd; r winter/summer from $135/170; ☒ ☒ ☒) A wholesome family setting is offered at this nondenominational Christian hotel on the beach southwest of Somerset Village. Accommodations, which are in low-rise buildings spread around the 6-acre grounds, are straightforward but comfortable. The whole place is alcohol free; breakfast and dinner are included in the price. There are some religious services, mainly a morning Bible study and evening hymn sessions, but they are optional. The grounds have two tennis courts, a shuffleboard and a playground.

Eating

Salt Rock Grill (☎ 234-4502; 27 Mangrove Bay Rd; lunch $8-15, dinner $14-32; ☺ noon-4pm & 6-10pm; ☒ ☒) Sit on the terrace and enjoy superb grilled fare while watching the sun set over Mangrove Bay. Everything about this place is a class act. The menu is creative – try the barbecued wahoo club sandwich for lunch. Dinner specialties include Dijon rack of lamb and fresh local seafood like spiny lobster thermidor and char-grilled tuna. Every Sunday until 4pm one of Bermuda's very finest codfish breakfasts ($14) is also on offer. And if you want a dessert to remember, try the cognac pumpkin cheesecake!

New Traditions (☎ 234-3770; 2 Middle Rd; breakfast & lunch $4-10, dinner $9-20; ☺ 6am-9pm Mon-Sat; ☒)

Come here for the tasty codfish-cake sandwiches served up with a smile in a quintessentially local atmosphere. When it's available, the spicy bean soup makes a perfect accompaniment. Everything here is home-style, made from scratch. Breakfast includes the usual pancake and egg dishes, and at dinner there are steaks and hearty seafood meals.

Somerset Country Squire (☎ 234-0105; 10 Mangrove Bay Rd; lunch $8-14, dinner $15-28; ☯ 11:30am-4pm & 6:30-10pm; ✖) A cozy pub atmosphere and well-prepared local seafood are the catch at this old Somerset village favorite. At lunch the menu revolves around traditional pub fare with sandwiches, chowder and steak-and-kidney pie. At dinner, the broiled Bermuda rockfish and sirloin steak take center stage. In summer, you can opt to sit at the outdoor patio that overlooks Mangrove Bay.

Dean's Bakery (☎ 234-2918; 17 Somerset Rd; items $1-4; ☯ 6:30am-6pm Mon-Sat) If you're looking for quick eats, search out this small bakery west of the police station in the center of the village. Dean's bakes up a mean apple turnover and inexpensive sandwiches and meat pies.

Marketplace (☎ 234-0626; 48 Somerset Rd; ☯ 7am-10pm Mon-Sat, 1-5pm Sun) Somerset's grocery store is opposite Springfield and the Gilbert Nature Reserve.

Entertainment

Salt Rock Grill (☎ 234-4502; 27 Mangrove Bay Rd) On weekends this restaurant turns into the hottest nightspot at this end of the island. On Friday and Saturday evenings the place caters to diners, with a pianist playing golden oldies. When the clock strikes 10pm, the tables are cleared and a DJ and dancers take to the floor until 3am. On Sundays from 8pm to midnight an R&B band performs.

Getting There & Around

BOAT

The Blue Route of the public ferry (p154) provides service between the City of Hamilton and Sandys Parish. Some of the trips are nonstop from Hamilton to the Royal Naval Dockyard, but five to seven of the runs each day make intermediate stops at Somerset Bridge, Cavello Bay, Watford Bridge and Boaz Island. The order of the stops varies with the sailing – so it can take as little as 30 minutes to get to Somerset from Hamilton or as long as 1¼ hours, depending on which boat you catch.

On weekdays, the first ferry departs Hamilton at 6:25am, the last at 6:15pm (9:45pm in summer); the first boat from Somerset Bridge is at 7:40am on weekdays, the last at 7:30pm (10:20pm in summer). The schedule is lighter on weekends. The one-way fare between any two points on the Blue Route is $4.

BUS

Bus Nos 7 and 8 operate along the main road through Sandys. When you're boarding in the City of Hamilton, take note of the destination marked on the front of the bus, as some of these buses only go as far as Barnes Corner in Southampton Parish; others stop in Somerset Village, and still others go on to the Royal Naval Dockyard. The service between Hamilton and Somerset Village ($4.50, 55 minutes) runs once every 15 minutes during the day and about once every 30 minutes in the evening, with the last bus in either direction at around 11:45pm (10:45pm Sunday).

For more information on public buses, including passes, see p155).

ROYAL NAVAL DOCKYARD

This fascinating place is like no other in Bermuda. Once dubbed the 'Gibraltar of the West,' this immense former naval base has something for everyone.

The Dockyard's handsome old stone buildings that once served the mighty Royal Navy now buzz with vacationing tourists. The former Keep has been turned into a maritime museum. The Cooperage, where barrels were made, is now the site of an atmospheric pub, a movie theater and a craft market. The handsome twin-towered naval administration building on the waterfront has been turned into a shopping center, called the Clocktower Mall.

You could easily while away a full day here. Most people visit the Royal Naval Dockyard to have lunch at one of the restaurants and browse for souvenirs. But there's much more to do than that. The Bermuda Maritime Museum is the island's most extensive history museum and well worth a couple of hours of your time. And strolling about the rest of the Dockyard

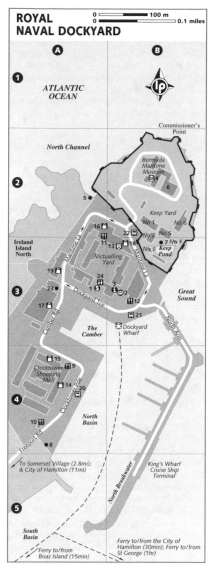

ROYAL NAVAL DOCKYARD

History

After the American Revolution in 1776, the British, who were no longer able to use ports in the former American colonies, needed a new naval base that had the capacity to repair warships and serve as a midway station between Nova Scotia and the British West Indies.

Bermuda fit the bill. The Royal Navy selected Ireland Island at Bermuda's western tip, which provided a natural deepwater cove, a huge sheltered anchorage and commanding land and sea views of all approaches. Military engineers drew up surveys and construction began in 1810.

It was a huge undertaking. Most of the back-breaking work was carried out by British convicts quartered in 'prison ships' – old, permanently docked hulks with unspeakably crowded conditions and wretched sanitation. Outbreaks of disease, including yellow fever, claimed hundreds of prisoners. In all, nearly 10,000 convicts were sent to Bermuda between 1814 and 1863 to work on the Dockyard and related projects.

with its curious buildings and fine water views can be an experience in itself.

Not all the sights are on land. Don a mask and explore the underwater world at the Bermuda Snorkel Park or swim with dolphins in the Keep Pond, a stone-lined pool once used to unload ammunition from warships and now home to Dolphin Quest.

SANDYS PARISH

The main elements of the Georgian-style, limestone-block Dockyard fort were completed in the 1820s, but construction on other buildings, including many of the magazines, continued until the 1860s.

One of the Dockyard's first military operations took place while the fort was still being built: during the War of 1812, a British fleet set sail from here in August 1814 on the infamous raid that sacked and burned Washington, DC. In the years that followed, the Dockyard not only kept tabs on American activities in the Atlantic, but also on French privateers in the West Indies.

In the 20th century, the Royal Naval Dockyard served as a North Atlantic base during WWI and WWII and was used briefly by NATO during the postwar period. Still, with the collapse of the British Empire, activities at the Dockyard base tapered off. Strapped for cash, the British Admiralty decided it no longer needed the remote outpost and in the 1960s the Royal Naval Dockyard was closed. Subsequently, the property was turned over to the Bermuda government for civilian use. In 1975 Queen Elizabeth II herself came to showcase the Dockyard's new life by inaugurating the opening of the Bermuda Maritime Museum within the walls of the old fortress.

Information

For tourist brochures and information pop in to the **Visitors Service Bureau** (☎ 234-3824; Dockyard Tce; ☉ 9am-5pm Sun-Fri, to 8:30pm some cruise ship days), where you can also buy phone cards, bus tokens and transportation passes. There's a small **post office** (☎ 234-0220; ☉ 10am-3pm Tue-Thu, to noon Fri) adjacent to the tourist office and a Bank of Bermuda ATM just west of the tourist office. You'll find pay phones around the Dockyard, including at the cruise ship terminal and Clocktower Mall. For Internet access, **Freeport Cybercafé** (☎ 234-1692; 1 Freeport Rd; per 30min $6; ☉ 11:30am-10pm) is a lounge with six computers inside Freeport Seafood Restaurant.

Sights & Activities
BERMUDA MARITIME MUSEUM

Don't miss a visit to the **Bermuda Maritime Museum** (☎ 234-1418; Maritime Lane; adult/child $10/5; ☉ 9:30am-4:30pm). With massive bastions this 6-acre fortress on the tip of the Dockyard known as the Keep is the real deal. And

keep it has; it's virtually unchanged since its construction in the 19th century. Indeed, to enter the gate of the Keep today you must still walk across the old moat footbridge.

More than anything, this place was an arsenal and the exhibits are in ordnance buildings. Their vaulted brick ceilings were once stacked high with munitions; these days each building contains a themed exhibit.

Building No 1, known as the **Queen's Exhibition Hall**, has exhibits on whaling and navigation with handcrafted model ships of the *Deliverance* and Bermudian-built schooners. A mighty 5000 barrels of gunpowder were once stored here. Notice the floors – they're layered in bitumen. This was done to prevent sparking when the gunpowder barrels were rolled across the floor. As a little insurance in the event that bitumen alone didn't handle the situation, the limestone walls were constructed a full 4ft thick to minimize damage from a potential explosion.

Out the back is the former **Shifting House** (Building No 2), erected in 1837 to temporarily store munitions unloaded from ships. Today it houses a fascinating collection of artifacts recovered from shipwrecks, including pieces of pewter and pottery from the *Sea Venture,* as well as gold coins, bars and jewelry recovered from 16th-century Spanish shipwrecks.

Building No 3 showcases a collection of Bermuda bills and coins, including specimens of the island's unique hog money, while **Building No 4** displays period maps and paraphernalia from early explorers. The **Forster Cooper Building** (Building No 5) is a former cooperage that made the all-essential barrels that stored everything from ale to gunpowder.

The **Boatloft** (Building No 6) pays tribute to the island's maritime heritage. The prize here is the collection of handcrafted Bermuda dinghies, 14ft boats made of Bermuda cedar and driven by oversized sails.

When you're done browsing the buildings in the yard, walk through the gate to the upper grounds. The path leads onto the lofty **fortress walls** that are still dotted with old cannons and offer panoramic views of the surrounding seas. On the highest point on the museum's grounds, you'll find the **Commissioner's House**. This grand old building, sporting a unique cast iron and limestone construction, was build by convicts in 1823 to house the Dockyard commissioner. Its rooms hold heritage displays that explore the backgrounds and contributions of Bermudians.

BERMUDA SNORKEL PARK
Jump into a bathing suit and explore the undersea world at the **Bermuda Snorkel Park** (☎ 234-6989; Maritime Lane; admission free, snorkel rental per day $20, kayak rental per hr $25; ☺ 9am-6pm May-Oct). The park's shallow lagoon is fronted with a nearshore reef that's home to several varieties of tropical fish, including bright butterfly fish, turquoise wrasses and large coral-chopping parrotfish. But they're not the whole show. The park sits beneath towering fortress walls and the water contains a handful of colonial-era cannons that were apparently shoved over the ramparts when they proved defective.

The attendant can give you the skinny on where to look for cannons, and if you're heading here from elsewhere on the island, call ahead to inquire about water conditions. The wind sometimes picks up here, making the water choppy even when it's calm elsewhere around Bermuda. When you've finished snorkeling there's a sandy beach where you can soak up some rays, as well as showers and changing rooms.

DOLPHIN QUEST
Ever dreamed of swimming with dolphins? **Dolphin Quest** (☎ 234-4464; www.dolphinquest.org; Bermuda Maritime Museum, Maritime Lane; 30/60 min programs $150/275; ☺ 9:30am-4:30pm) fulfils the fantasy, operating out of a pool in the Keep Yard at the Bermuda Maritime Museum. The pool the dolphins swim in is connected to the ocean by a sluice gate, which allows the water to circulate while keeping the dolphins from beating their tails back out to sea. These guys are actually quite domesticated and relate well with people, and a couple of them were born right here in the pool. Call ahead for reservations if you'd like to join Flipper for a swim. Participants must be at least eight years old and be good swimmers.

OTHER WATER SPORTS
Windjammer Watersports (☎ 234-0250; Freeport Rd; half-day kayak rental s/d $50/55; ☺ 9am-5pm) does a little bit of everything related to the water. Half-day rentals include Sunfish sailboats ($60), windsurfing gear ($55), motorboats ($115) and fishing gear ($15).

TRAIN TOUR
The **Bermuda Train Company** (☎ 236-5972; adult/child $27/14) offers a 90-minute guided tour in summer around the Dockyard and Somerset Village on its 'miniature motorized train.' Tours are usually twice daily, at 9:30am and 1pm, but depend on cruise ship passenger demand.

Eating
Frog & Onion (☎ 234-2900; Cooperage Bldg, Maritime Lane; lunch $10-18, dinner $14-29; ☺ 11:30am-midnight, closed Mon in winter; ⚅) This pub-restaurant takes its spirit and its name from its two owners, one French and one Bermudian. Burgers and pub grub shore up lunch, while dinner adds on heavy-hitters like steak and grilled tuna. You might notice a pattern as you read the menu – the items are named after Old English pubs; choose from 'Tumbledown Dick' (salmon and crab cake), 'Bishop's Head' (curried chicken) and 'Snooty Fox' (vegetarian linguine). Truly a pub lover's pub!

Beethoven's (☎ 234-5009; Clocktower Mall; breakfast $4-12, lunch $7-15, dinner $17-30; ☺ 9am-9:30pm; ⚅ ⚅) With two Swiss chefs running the kitchen, you can bet on reliably good continental cuisine at this chic restaurant. Look for fine pastries and indulgent Belgian waffles for breakfast, sumptuous salads at lunch and robust dinner offerings such as braised duck à l'orange and Angus steak in wine sauce. In the evening, when candlelight sets the tone, it's easily the most romantic choice in the Dockyard.

Pirate's Landing (☎ 234-5151; 6 Dockyard Tce; lunch $8-15, dinner $10-20; ☺ 11:30am-10pm; ⚅) Set at the end of the cruise ship dock, people really do jump off the ship and land here, though presumably few are pirates. Because of its outdoor tables and water view, on sunny days this place really packs in a crowd. The mainstay of sandwiches and burger fare pairs well with a frosty beer and convivial chatter. At dinner the Landing offers more substantial meat and pasta meals – nothing fancy but all reasonably priced.

Freeport Seafood Restaurant (☎ 234-1692; 1 Freeport Rd; mains $7-20; ☺ 11:30am-10pm; ⚅) It might seem surprising in the tourist-driven Dockyard to find a solidly local eatery. But here it is, in a quieter corner opposite the south side of the Clocktower Mall. Freeport makes a good fish sandwich and respectable pizza, pasta and curry dishes. But the real find here is the takeout counter, where you'll find freshly baked pastries and an unbelievable curry pie ($4).

Entertainment

Frog & Onion (☎ 234-2900; Cooperage Bldg, Maritime Lane; ⏲ 11:30am-midnight, closed Mon in winter; ✦) This pub and restaurant is the main place for nighttime activity in the Dockyard, whether you want to shoot pool, have a drink or dance. The place livens up on nights the cruise ships are in dock, with a DJ spinning tunes from 10pm to 3am. In winter it's a quieter scene, but on weekends there's sometimes live music.

Neptune Cinema (☎ 234-2923; Cooperage Bldg, Maritime Lane) This theater opposite the Frog & Onion shows first-run Hollywood movies.

Shopping

The Royal Naval Dockyard has two distinct shopping areas. If you're looking for handicrafts and other Bermuda-made items, the Cooperage area is the place to head. If you want to do more serious shopping for fashionable clothing, fragrances, jewelry and the like, stop off at the Clocktower Mall, which essentially has a sampling of some of the high-end shops found in Hamilton.

COOPERAGE AREA

Dockyard Glassworks & Bermuda Rum Cake Company (☎ 234-4216; Maritime Lane) A fun place, whether you're shopping or not. Watch glassblowers at work, sample island-made rum cakes and, if tempted, take home the final products. The yummy rum cakes are made with black seal rum and spiced up with your choice of ginger, coconut or chocolate. The glass ranges from inexpensive tree frog figurines to cool wind chimes and large vases.

Bermuda Arts Centre (☎ 234-2809; Maritime Lane) Come to this gallery shop to buy quality works by local artists in a variety of media including woodwork, paintings, jewelry, batiks and prints. Several artists have permanent studios in the center, including internationally known Chesley Trott, who sculpts with fragrant native Bermuda cedar.

Bermuda Clayworks (☎ 234-5116; Camber Rd) You can watch as potters create decorative din-

nerware with island-themed designs, such as dolphins and cottages. Or try your hand yourself. Visitors can paint a dish, mug or other piece of pottery and have it glazed and fired before leaving the island.

Bermuda Craft Market (☎ 234-3208; Maritime Lane) Craft booths of varying quality are set up here, most with locally made handicrafts such as candles, dolls, jewelry, handprinted T-shirts and similar items that could make good souvenirs.

CLOCKTOWER MALL

Among the many shops and galleries in the mall are branches of two of Bermuda's leading department stores.

AS Cooper & Sons (☎ 234-4156) Everything from designer clothing and perfumes to Wedgwood porcelain and Waterford crystal.

A Taste of Trims (☎ 296-1290) Sells the island's best polo shirts and Bermuda shorts, plus a few souvenir items such as gourmet jams and jellies.

Makin Waves (☎ 234-5319) This shop specializes in beach items such as bathing suits, sunglasses, sun hats, T-shirts and sandals.

Michael Swan Gallery (☎ 234-3128) Features the work of Bermuda artist Michael Swan, with some nice pastel prints of Bermuda scenes.

Dockyard Linens (☎ 234-3871) For a little bit of Bermuda with an English accent, take a look at the bun warmers and tea towels here, most decorated with Bermuda flower prints.

ER Aubrey Jewellers (☎ 234-4577) Offers a large selection of earrings, bracelets, pendants and other jewelry.

Crisson (☎ 234-2223) Best known for its selection of fine watches, ranging from

---

THE TIDES OF TIME

At first glance it might seem redundant that the Clocktower Mall, which once served as an administration building for the Royal Navy, has two separate 100ft-high clocktowers. If you look closer, you'll notice that the clocks on the two towers read differently – but that's by design, not error. As with everything else in the Dockyard, the clocks had a practical purpose related to the sea: one was installed to show the actual time, the other to indicate the time of high tide.

high-end brands like Rolex and Omega to some moderately priced Seiko and Casio watches.

Getting There & Around

The ferry between Hamilton and the Royal Naval Dockyard makes an interesting alternative to the bus, offering different views along the way; you might want to take the boat one way and the bus the other.

BOAT

The Dockyard is served by three lines of the public ferry (p154). Speediest is the Orange Route, which stops at the Dockyard in each direction on its run between the City of Hamilton ($4) and the Town of St George ($4). The thrice-daily service operates in summer only, leaving Hamilton at 9:30am, noon and 2pm, arriving at the Dockyard in 20 minutes and departing 10 minutes later for the one-hour trip to St George. The boat then leaves St George at 11:15am, 1:30pm and 3:45pm, makes the one-hour trip to the Dockyard, and departs from the Dockyard at 12:30pm, 2:30pm and 4:55pm for the 20-minute trip back to Hamilton.

The Blue Route runs between Hamilton and the Dockyard at least 16 times a day on weekdays and a dozen times on weekends, with services more frequent in the summer. The first boat from Hamilton leaves at 6:25am on weekdays, 9am on weekends. The last boat leaves the Dockyard at 6:35pm on weekdays and Saturdays (10:50pm in summer) and at 5:30pm on Sundays. It costs $4 and takes between 30 and 75 minutes, depending on whether you catch a nonstop Hamilton–Dockyard boat or one that stops elsewhere in Sandys Parish en route (p134).

In addition, the Green Route (p126) between Hamilton and Southampton, the Rockaway Express, goes on to the Dockyard ($4) from Southampton at 4:30pm every day except Sunday.

BUS

Bus No 7, which travels via the south shore, leaves the Royal Naval Dockyard for the City of Hamilton ($4.50, 1 hour) at 20 and 50 minutes past the hour, and bus No 8, which travels to Hamilton via Middle Rd, leaves the Dockyard at five and 35 minutes past the hour. On weekdays, buses operate on this schedule from 6:35am to 6:35pm, after which there are a few staggered night buses, the last leaving the Dockyard at 11:50pm. On Sunday the schedule is slightly lighter and there's no bus service from the Dockyard after 6:35pm.

From the City of Hamilton the Dockyard-bound buses begin at 6:45am on weekdays and 9:30am Sundays, with the last bus leaving at 10:45pm daily. If you pick up a No 7 or 8 bus in Hamilton, make sure that it reads 'Dockyard,' as not all buses continue that far.

For more information on public buses, including passes, see p155.

MOTOR SCOOTER

Scooter rentals (p157) are available from **Oleander Cycles** (☎ 234-2764; Maritime Lane) at the west side of the Royal Naval Dockyard.

Directory

CONTENTS

ACCOMMODATIONS

Accommodation options in Bermuda range from small guesthouses to big beachside resorts. There are plenty of delightful options to choose from but don't expect any bargains. Bermuda doesn't offer truly cheap accommodations – no youth hostels, no family campgrounds and no economy-chain motels.

Rates that fall below $125 a night are considered budget. If you're looking in the mid-range, expect to pay between $125 and $275. Top-end places start around $275. You can find attractive places in all price ranges; even the ones that fall into the budget category have nicely equipped rooms and sometimes a pool to boot. What you get as you spend more are fancier digs, private beaches and more pampering.

Throughout this book, we give published rates which the industry refers to as rack rates. Some of the resort hotels, which are affiliated with international chains, occasionally offer discounts from their rack rates on their websites, but deals at smaller places are few and far between. One way to cut down your accommodations bill is to come in the winter season, from November to March, when many places offer lower winter rates.

PRACTICALITIES

- **Electricity** Plug in to Bermuda's 110V, 60Hz electric current using a flat, two-pronged plug – the same as in the USA. Some hotels have adapters for electric shavers.

- **Newspapers** Keep up with Bermudian current affairs and local entertainment with the *Royal Gazette* newspaper, published daily except Sunday, or the twice-weekly *Bermuda Sun*.

- **Magazines** As soon as you arrive at the airport or dock, pick up *This Week in Bermuda* and *Preview Bermuda,* free magazines packed with useful visitor information.

- **TV** Bermudian cable TV is loaded with US programming plus BBC World. Tune in to ZBM (channel 3) at 7pm for local news, and channel 4 for ongoing Bermuda weather updates.

- **Radio** FM 89 and FM 106.1 have rock and contemporary music and AM 1160 broadcasts the BBC World Service and local public affairs.

- **Video Systems** If you're buying videos to take home, be aware Bermuda uses the NTSC system – the same as in the USA and Canada, but incompatible with the PAL system used in Europe and Australia.

- **Weights & Measures** Bermuda has gone partly metric (such as for speed limits) but retains the imperial system of measurement for many uses (temperatures are reported in Fahrenheit; weights are measured in pounds).

Bermuda's tourist industry likes to divide accommodations into several categories, based on a place's predominant character. Keep in mind that these groupings are somewhat imprecise and categories often overlap a bit. A room in a small hotel or a cottage colony may have the same cooking facilities that you'd find in an apartment, for instance.

In addition to the places listed in this book, which operate as full-time businesses and accept direct reservations, there are private families that occasionally rent out rooms and apartments solely via a booking service. To peruse these and make reservations go online to **Bermuda Rentals** (www.bermudarentals.com).

B&Bs & Guesthouses

Many of these places are in lovely period homes, often overlooking gardens or sporting water views. They might have just a couple of rooms in a family home or be larger places with several wings. What they have in common is an intimate setting in which you get to know the host. In most cases, breakfast is included in the rate and you share the table with fellow guests. Sometimes there's a group kitchen where guests can prepare other meals.

Apartments

Hugely popular, tourist apartments provide not only a place to stay but also full cooking facilities. As a rule they pack the most space for the buck and are also economical because they save you from having to dine out for every meal. Considering that the average hotel charges a good $10 per person for breakfast, being able to prepare your own coffee and toast can represent a tidy saving!

Cottage Colonies

Now this is where things start to get fancy. The term 'cottage colony' is generally used in Bermuda with more upmarket places that offer units inside individual cottages, or in small clusters of buildings, each of which contain a few units. The 'cottages' sometimes have limited cooking facilities and invariably have a genteel setting with landscaped grounds, water views, afternoon teas and the like. All very private and pampering.

Small Hotels

Small hotels are by and large just that: smaller places, typically around 50 rooms, that usually have a restaurant, lounge and swimming pool but don't necessarily offer the extensive array of services found at the large resort hotels. These range from unpretentious family-oriented places to some of the island's more prestigious and intimate spots.

Resort Hotels

Bermuda has five resort hotels: the Elbow Beach Hotel, the Grotto Bay Beach Hotel, the Fairmont Hamilton Princess, the Fairmont Southampton and the Wyndham Bermuda Resort. Together they provide about half of all the guest rooms in Bermuda. Each has all the amenities you'd expect in an upmarket resort – restaurants, swimming pools, room service, activities and the like.

Camping

Although you may see Bermudians setting up tents, foreign visitors cannot camp in Bermuda. The only exception is for organized groups, who may apply for permits to camp at group sites run by the government on nearshore islands. Information on group camping is available from the **Ministry of Youth, Sport and Recreation** (☎ 297-7619).

ACTIVITIES

Bermuda offers plenty for active visitors. Essentially, the best time of the year for most things to do in the water, including swimming, snorkeling and diving, is during the summer season of April to October. Golf and tennis are good year round, though the most pleasant weather for a vigorous outdoor workout is during the cooler winter season. Golfers will find information at **Bermuda Golf Association** (www.bermudagolf.org). Tennis players can log on to **Bermuda Lawn Tennis Association** (☎ 296-0834; www.blta.bm). For more information on all sorts of outdoor fun, see p34.

BUSINESS HOURS

Business offices are typically open 9am to 5pm Monday to Friday. Shops are generally open 9am to 5pm Monday to Saturday, though there are exceptions – for example, grocery stores have longer hours and Sunday openings, and tourist-geared shops catering to cruise shop passengers often stay open into the evening when ships are in port.

Most restaurants and cafés serve lunch from around 11:30am to 2:30pm, and dinner from 6pm to 10pm. Bars tend to keep much later hours, and are typically open to at least 1am, with even longer hours on weekends.

CHILDREN

Although Bermudians are family oriented, Bermuda can pose some challenges to travelers with children. For instance, families who are accustomed to renting a car and piling all the kids inside will be dismayed to learn Bermuda has no car rentals. Large resort hotels don't place restrictions on children, but many other hotels and guesthouses tend to be formal and gear their activities solely to adults.

On the plus side, apartment-style accommodations that are well-suited for families are readily available in Bermuda, and most have a swimming pool that kids can splash around in. All places except fine-dining restaurants welcome families with young kids. In addition to beaches and swimming pools, there are snorkeling tours, miniature golf (p123), a wonderful aquarium and zoo (p90), and plenty of cool forts to explore.

Travelers with babies will readily find baby food, formula and disposable diapers at local supermarkets, although prices will be higher than at home. Some hotels can provide cribs and high chairs; if not, they can be rented from the **Bermuda Red Cross** (☎ 236-8777) at the King Edward VII Memorial Hospital in Paget.

For those vacationing with children, Lonely Planet's *Travel with Children* has lots of valuable tips and interesting anecdotal stories.

CLIMATE CHART

Bermuda being a small place, the weather's the same throughout the island. For information on the best time to visit, see p9.

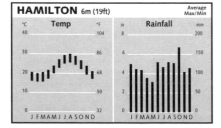

HAMILTON 6m (19ft)	Average Max/Min
Temp	Rainfall

J F M A M J J A S O N D   J F M A M J J A S O N D

CUSTOMS

Visitors to Bermuda may bring in duty-free 200 cigarettes, 50 cigars, 0.5kg of tobacco, 1L of liquor and 1L of wine as well as clothing, sports equipment, cameras etc intended for personal use. Each visitor is also entitled to a $30 gift allowance.

Because of the high price of imported food, it's not uncommon for return visitors staying in places with kitchens to bring in frozen steaks and other meat. Visitors are allowed to bring in up to 50lb of meat and other food items for their own consumption, though these are subject to a 22% duty.

Bermuda restricts or prohibits the importation of animals, plants, fresh fruits and vegetables, firearms, spear guns and drugs. For more information about customs laws, contact the **Customs House** (☎ 295-4816; www.customs.gov.bm).

DANGERS & ANNOYANCES
Crime

Although Bermuda is relatively safe, it has its fair share of crime and drug abuse problems just like any other place. Violent crime has been on the increase in recent years, and tourists are occasionally targeted for muggings. Travelers should use the standard precautions they would use anywhere when walking alone at night, especially in areas that are not well lit. Women carrying handbags should keep them close to their bodies to prevent purse snatchings. One local mugging offense is the drive-by in which a thief rides by on a motorbike and snatches the purse of a pedestrian from behind.

Still, the most common problem encountered by visitors is motor scooter theft, which is at epidemic proportions in Bermuda. It's so great a problem that it's virtually impossible to get theft insurance on scooters anymore. Some of the bikes end up in 'chop shops' where they are stripped for parts, although others just end up being taken for a joyride before being dumped over a cliff. If you rent a scooter, you can cut down on the odds of having it stolen by locking it every time you stop and by parking in well-lit public places.

Land Dangers

There are no poisonous snakes or other such dangerous creatures lurking in Bermuda. Hikers, however, should be aware that poison ivy is abundant on interior trails. Wear socks and long pants as a precaution. Mosquitoes can also get pesky, particularly around marsh areas.

Ocean Dangers

RIP TIDES

If you're not familiar with water conditions, ask a local. It's best not to swim alone in any unfamiliar place.

Chief among the ocean dangers are rip currents, fast-flowing currents of water moving from shallow nearshore areas out to sea. They are most common in conditions of high surf, forming when water from incoming waves builds up near the shore. Essentially the waves are coming in faster than they can flow back out. The water then runs along the shoreline until it finds an escape route out to sea, usually through a channel or out along a point. Swimmers caught up in the current can be ripped out to deeper water. Although rip currents can be powerful, they usually dissipate 50yd to 100yd offshore. Anyone caught in one should either go with the flow until it loses power or swim parallel to shore to slip out of it. Trying to swim against a rip current can exhaust the strongest of swimmers.

JELLYFISH

Always take a peek into the water before you plunge in to make sure it's not jellyfish territory. These gelatinous creatures, with saclike bodies and stinging tentacles, are sometimes found in Bermuda. The sting of a jellyfish varies from mild to severe, depending on the variety. Unless you have an allergic reaction to their venom, the stings are generally not dangerous.

The Portuguese man-of-war is by far the worst type to encounter. Its body consists of a translucent, bluish, bladder-like float, which generally grows to be about 5in long, though its tentacles can extend many feet. In the waters off Bermuda, the Portuguese man-of-war is most prevalent from March through July. A man-of-war sting is very painful, similar to a bad bee sting except that you're likely to get stung more than once from clusters of long tentacles containing hundreds of stinging cells. Even touching a Portuguese man-of-war a few hours after it's washed up on shore can result in burning stings.

DISABLED TRAVELERS

Unlike in the UK, Bermuda has no laws requiring businesses to make adjustments to their property to accommodate the physically disabled. So, not surprisingly, access varies greatly.

For wheelchair users, Bermuda's larger resort hotels generally have the greatest accessibility with elevators, wider doorways and the like. Some smaller places also have wheelchair-accessible guestrooms and common areas, but others don't, so visitors with special needs should make their requirements known at the time of booking.

Wheelchair access on public transport is limited. Public buses do not have hydraulic lifts and are unable to accommodate wheelchairs at all. Public ferries are readily accessible only from the three largest ports – the City of Hamilton, Town of St George and Royal Naval Dockyard – which have ramps. Taxi companies have wheelchair-accessible vans but they are in limited supply and sometimes require booking the day before.

Travelers with special needs should log on to the website of the **Bermuda Physically Handicapped Association** (www.bermuda-online.org /BPHA.htm), which is chock-full of information, including specifics to how to handle the ins and outs of getting around Bermuda.

DISCOUNT CARDS

If you're a member of the National Trust in Australia, Barbados, Britain or another Commonwealth country, you'll get free entry into Bermuda National Trust sites by showing your membership card.

EMBASSIES & CONSULATES
Bermudian Embassies & Consulates

As a dependency of the UK, all of Bermuda's diplomatic representation is handled by British embassies and consulates around the world. British embassies are listed at www.fco.gov.uk and include the following:

Australia (☎ 02-6270-6666; British High Commission, Commonwealth Ave, Yarralumla, Canberra, ACT 2600)

Canada (☎ 613-237-1530; British High Commission, 80 Elgin St, Ottawa K1P 5K7)

France (☎ 01 44 51 31 00; British Embassy, 35 rue du Faubourg St Honoré, 75383 Paris Cedex 08)

Germany (☎ 30 20457 0; British Embassy, Wilhelmstrasse 70, 10117 Berlin)

Ireland (☎ 1 205 3700; 29 Merrion Rd, Ballsbridge, Dublin 4)

Netherlands (☎ 070 4270 427; Lange Voorhout 10, 2514 ED The Hague)
New Zealand (☎ 04-924-2888; British High Commission, 44 Hill St, Wellington 1)
USA (☎ 202-588-6500; British Embassy, 3100 Massachusetts Ave NW, Washington, DC 20008)

Embassies & Consulates in Bermuda

Bermuda has no embassies but the USA maintains a **consulate** (Map p100; ☎ 295-1342; Crown Hill, 16 Middle Rd, Devonshire).

In addition, numerous countries have designated individuals as 'honorary consuls' in Bermuda. Keep in mind that these honorary consuls are often businesspeople, not permanent diplomats, and thus the list changes rather frequently. Currently it includes Austria, Belgium, Canada, Denmark, Finland, France, Germany, Ireland, Italy, Jamaica, Luxembourg, Netherlands, Norway, Spain, Sweden and Switzerland. See the blue pages of the Bermuda phone book for honorary consuls' contact details.

FESTIVALS & EVENTS

Bermudians are a festive bunch; visitors can enjoy cultural and sporting events throughout the year. As no event is more than 20 miles away, you're never far from the action. Many events vary with the season. For example, yacht races take place early in the summer before the hurricane season gets underway and golf tournaments are most frequent from fall to spring when the weather is cooler.

Keep in mind that dates can vary a bit each year and the venues are not always the same; check with the **Bermuda Department of Tourism** (www.bermudatourism.com), which maintains updated schedules, for the latest information.

January & February
New Year's Day The first day of the year features performances by costumed troupes of Gombey dancers at various locations around the island.
Bermuda International Race Weekend (www .bermudatracknfield.com) The island's biggest running event includes a marathon, half marathon, 10km race, 10km fitness walk and festivities on the second weekend in January in the City of Hamilton.
Bermuda Regional Bridge Tournament (www .bermudaregional.com) The best time of the year for bridge players is during this nine-day event at the end of January, featuring a variety of bridge tournaments and activities.

Bermuda Festival (www.bermudafestival.com) This seven-week festival of the performing arts brings in international artists for dance, drama, comedy and musical performances at various locations. Eagerly awaited each winter, it runs from early January to late February.

March
Ladies Pro-Am Golf Classic (www.bermudagolf.org) This week-long tournament with teams consisting of one professional and three amateur women golfers is held in early March at the Port Royal Golf Course in Southampton.
Bermuda Amateur Match Play Championship A six-day singles match for golfers, with separate events for men and women, held in mid-March at the Mid Ocean Club.
Bermuda International Film Festival (www.ber mudafilmfest.com) Independent films from around the world are shown at island theaters for a week in mid-March, accompanied by parties, workshops and talks with filmmakers.
Good Friday Kite Festival Show up at Horseshoe Bay in Southampton on Good Friday to experience one of Bermuda's most festive family events – an afternoon of kite flying, competitions, music, children's games and more.
Palm Sunday Walk (www.bnt.bm) The Bermuda National Trust holds a popular guided walk each Palm Sunday; the location changes each year.

April
Good Friday Kite Festival (see March) Sometimes falls in April.
Peppercorn Ceremony With as much pomp as can be mustered while handing over a single seed, the Town of St George reenacts the mid-April ceremony in which the Masonic Lodge pays its annual rent of one peppercorn for use of the Old State House. The ceremony dates to 1816.
Bermuda Annual Exhibition (www.agshowbda.com) One of the most traditional events in Bermuda, this three-day event features exhibits of flowers and livestock, along with equestrian shows and music. It's held in mid-April at the Bermuda Botanical Gardens in Paget.
XL Capital Tennis Classic (www.xlcapitalbermudaopen .bm) Bermuda's top tennis event, held mid-month at the Coral Beach & Tennis Club in Paget, is an ATP challenger tournament for professional tennis players from around the world, including Bermuda resident Patrick Rafter.

May
Royal Bermuda International Race Week (www .rbyc.bm) This event features yachters from Bermuda, the UK and North America competing in various boat categories in the Great Sound.
Open House & Garden Tours The Garden Club of Bermuda hosts several tours of distinctive island homes during the month.

Bermuda Senior Amateur Championships (www
.bermudagolf.org) Men have to be age 55 or older, though
women can be as young as 50, for this three-day stroke play
event held mid-month at Riddell's Bay Golf & Country Club.

TransAt Daytona–Bermuda Race This yacht race is
held in May on odd-numbered years from Ponce de Leon,
Florida, to Bermuda.

Bermuda Day This public holiday on May 24 kicks off the
summer season. It features a half-marathon that begins
in Somerset, a colorful afternoon parade in the City of
Hamilton and fitted dinghy races in St George's Harbour.

Beating Retreat Ceremonies Historic military
reenactments performed by the Bermuda Regiment Band,
complete with bagpipes, take place at various times of
the month in St George's, Hamilton and the Royal Naval
Dockyard.

June

Bermuda Amateur Stroke Play Championships
(www.bermudagolf.org) This golf tournament spans four
days in mid-June at the Port Royal Golf Course in
Southampton with separate events for men and women.

Queen's Birthday This public holiday features a military
parade led by the Bermuda Regiment that marches down
Hamilton's Front St.

Newport–Bermuda Race (www.rbyc.bm) Held in
late June during even-numbered years, this is one of the
world's premier ocean races, starting in Newport, Rhode
Island. The Royal Bermuda Yacht Club coordinates events at
the Bermuda end.

Bermuda 1-2 Single-Handed Race Held in June in
odd-numbered years, this yacht race goes single-handed
from Newport, Rhode Island, to Bermuda, and returns
double-handed to Newport.

Bermuda Ocean Race Held in June in even-numbered
years, this yacht race starts in Annapolis, Maryland, and
ends at St George's Harbour.

Beating Retreat Ceremonies See the event
description under May.

July & August

Bermuda Big Game Classic Fishing Tournament
(www.bermudabiggameclassic.com) The search is on for
the largest blue marlin, tuna and wahoo during five days
in mid-July.

Cup Match Cricket Festival (www.cupmatchbermuda
.com) The most popular event of the year for Bermudians,
this two-day match between West End and East End
cricket teams takes place on Somers Day and Emancipation
Day, both public holidays. It's held in Somerset in even-
numbered years and in St David's on odd-numbered years.
Abounds in local flavor with food booths, music – and, of
course, cricket.

Beating Retreat Ceremonies See the event
description under May.

September

Labour Day Speeches by union leaders and politicians
and a small parade in the City of Hamilton mark this public
holiday on the month's first Monday.

Bermuda Triathlon This swimming, bicycling and
running competition takes place from Albouy's Point in the
City of Hamilton in late September or early October.

Bermuda Mixed Foursomes Championship (www
.bermudagolf.org) This two-day stroke play event is held
mid-month at the Port Royal Golf Course in Southampton.

Beating Retreat Ceremonies See the event
description under May.

October

Bermuda Music Festival (www.bermudamusicfestival
.com) The year's biggest music event spans five days in
mid-October and features jazz, R&B, soul and more, with
international musicians such as Anita Baker and Isaac
Hayes. Includes a series of open-air concerts at the Royal
Naval Dockyard and around the island.

Bermuda Open for Men (www.bermudagolf.org) This
golf tournament held over four days in mid-October at the
Port Royal Golf Course in Southampton is open to pro
golfers and amateurs with a handicap limit of 6 or less.

**King Edward VII Gold Cup International Match
Racing Championship** (www.kingedwardviigoldcup
.com) In late October, Bermudians compete for prize
money with international boaters, including America's Cup
Match contenders.

Bermuda Cat Fanciers Association Cat Show
Pedigree and mixed-breed cats show their fluff at the end
of the month at the No 1 Cruise Ship Terminal on Front St
in the City of Hamilton.

Beating Retreat Ceremonies See the event
description under May.

November

Convening of Parliament This ceremonial event takes
place at Sessions House in the City of Hamilton near the
start of the month.

**Bermuda Four Ball Stroke Play Amateur
Championships** (www.bermudagolf.org) A 72-hole golf
event for men and a separate 54-hole event for women is
held for four days in early November at the Port Royal Golf
Course in Southampton.

Remembrance Day This public holiday on November
11 features a military parade along Front St in the City of
Hamilton and the laying of wreaths at the Cenotaph.

Bermuda Culinary Arts Festival (www.bermuda
culinaryarts.com) Celebrity chefs and other culinary experts
from the USA and Europe present cooking demonstrations,
seminars and wine tastings during this tasty five-day event
held mid-month in the City of Hamilton.

World Rugby Classic (www.worldrugby.bm) Rugby
fever sweeps the island at this nine-day tournament event

featuring eight teams made up of former international rugby players. Held in mid-November at the National Sports Centre in Devonshire.

Bermuda International Dog Show (www.thedog trainingclubofbermuda.com) International exhibitors arrive with their canine best to join Bermuda's showpiece dogs in this weeklong woof-fest. It's held in mid-November at the Bermuda Botanical Gardens in Paget.

December

Bermuda Goodwill Tournament (www.bermudagolf .org) This pro-am golf event for men is held over a week in early December at five different golf courses.

Bermuda Christmas Boat Parade (www.bermuda boatparade.bm) Boaters decorate their vessels with lights and holiday cheer and sail around Hamilton Harbour in this mid-month event, ending with a fireworks display.

Christmas Day Midnight candlelight services are held at many churches on the island.

Boxing Day The day after Christmas sees colorful Gombey dancers taking to the streets all around Bermuda. If you hear the drums, you'll know they're near.

New Year's Eve Celebrations take place at King's Square in the Town of St George with live music, food stalls, midnight fireworks and the 'lowering of the onion.'

FOOD

Bermuda's restaurants run the gamut from casual local eateries to indulgent gourmet cuisine. You can eat your fill at budget spots for $6 to $15, while midrange restaurants run from about $15 to $30. Top-end spots offer dishes from around $30, but don't expect to walk away from a full meal for much less than $60 per person ($80 with wine). See p43 for more details on eating in Bermuda.

GAY & LESBIAN TRAVELERS

Bermuda is certainly not a mecca for gay travelers. A century-old criminal code that outlawed gay sex wasn't removed from the books until 1994, and that was after a fractious debate in parliament. Homophobic attitudes still exist in many quarters and most gay people keep a pretty low profile outside of their personal circle of friends. That closet must be awfully full! Public displays of affection, which are uncommon among Bermudians regardless of sexual orientation, may well draw unwanted attention.

Bermuda doesn't have exclusively gay bars, but Casey's Lounge (p59) and Blue Juice (p59) within the City of Hamilton are gay-friendly places. A useful website is www.gay bermuda.com.

HOLIDAYS

On public holidays, all government offices, most business offices and some shops and restaurants close, and buses and ferries run on a reduced schedule.

Note that when a public holiday falls on a Saturday or Sunday, it is often observed on the following Monday. The following are Bermuda's public holidays:

New Year's Day January 1
Good Friday Friday before Easter (March/April)
Bermuda Day May 24
Queen's Birthday Second Monday in June
Emancipation Day Thursday before first Monday in August
Somers Day The day after Emancipation Day
Labour Day First Monday in September
Remembrance Day November 11
Christmas Day December 25
Boxing Day December 26

INTERNET ACCESS

Getting online isn't a challenge in Bermuda. There are now cybercafés in the three major tourist centers – the City of Hamilton (p49), the Town of St George (p72) and the Royal Naval Dockyard (p136). The cost averages $10 to $12 an hour. Hamilton has the greatest variety and the best facilities for business travelers. Those looking for free access can use the computers at the public library in Hamilton on a space-available basis.

LEGAL MATTERS

For the most part, the police in Bermuda tend to be lenient with tourists and few visitors are likely to have run-ins with the law. For minor traffic violations, such as forgetting to put on your helmet while driving a scooter, you could be stopped by a police officer, but as long as your response is polite, a brief lecture will likely be the end of it.

On the other hand, any infraction of Bermuda's strict drug laws will almost certainly land violators in court, and perhaps in jail as well. The importation or possession of unlawful drugs, including marijuana and other 'soft' drugs, is subject to a fine of up to $10,000 or five years in prison or both.

Customs officers are very strict these days, with luggage-sniffing dogs and the occasional body search. Those on cruise ships are not exempt – police have been known to search cruise ship cabins after a whiff of cannabis has wafted through the air.

GETTING HITCHED, BERMUDA STYLE

Everyone knows Bermuda is a favorite with honeymooners, but it's a thoroughly romantic place to tie the knot as well. And to smooth the way there are both public offices and private wedding consultants set up to manage all the arrangements.

For those who want to take the public route, both the required paperwork and the ceremony can be handled by the **Registrar General's office** (www.registrygeneral.gov.bm) in the City of Hamilton. For a fee of $231, this government agency will put the mandatory 'Notice of Intended Marriage' in local newspapers. Assuming no formal objection is raised to your marriage intention, the marriage certificate is issued after a two-week waiting period. The registry maintains its own cozy little 'Marriage Room' where, for an additional fee of $193, a civil marriage ceremony can be performed.

Should you prefer something more tailored, private wedding consultants can arrange anything from a traditional church wedding to a seaside ceremony, and take care of all the incidentals from a cake and flowers to bagpipe music and a horse and carriage.

For full information on arranging a wedding in Bermuda, download the *Weddings & Honeymoons* brochure by the **Bermuda Department of Tourism's** (www.bermudatourism.com), which includes all the nitty-gritty details and contact addresses you'll need.

When a visitor is arrested, the police will call their consulate, which can usually provide advice on securing a lawyer. The **Legal Aid Society** (☎ 297-7617) can also help visitors obtain the services of a lawyer.

MAPS

The Bermuda Department of Tourism's free *Bermuda Handy Reference Map*, updated annually, should cover everything you'll need for a short visit. It shows major roads and locations of hotels, sightseeing attractions, beaches and the like. Pick one up at the airport or any one of the Visitors Service Bureaus in Bermuda after your arrival.

MONEY
ATMs

The Bank of Bermuda has 24-hour ATMs in nearly two dozen locations – including the airport, Hamilton, St George and Somerset – which will accept Cirrus and Plus system ATM cards and MasterCard and Visa credit cards.

The Bank of Butterfield also has a widely dispersed network of ATMs that accept the same ATM and credit cards as the Bank of Bermuda. Among the places you can find these ATMs are Bank of Butterfield branch offices, Marketplace grocery stores and larger shopping centers.

Cash & Currency

The legal tender is the Bermudian dollar, pegged at a 1:1 ratio with the US dollar. The Bermuda dollar's relationship to the other nations' currencies fluctuates according to their value against the US dollar.

The Bermuda dollar is divided up into 100 cents (¢). Coins come in denominations of 1¢ (penny), 5¢ (nickel), 10¢ (dime), 25¢ (quarter) and one dollar ($). The coins display special Bermudian designs: a hog on the back of the copper penny, an angelfish on the nickel, an Easter lily on the dime, a longtail tropic bird on the quarter and a sailboat on the bronze $1 coin.

Bills come in $2, $5, $10, $20, $50 and $100 denominations.

The best currency to take to Bermuda is the US dollar, as it can be used interchangeably with the Bermudian dollar. If you have US dollars there's no need to even exchange it for Bermudian money – just use it, as it's accepted everywhere at full value.

See p10 for a general idea of costs, and the inside front cover for an exchange rate table.

Credit Cards

Major credit cards, such as Visa and MasterCard, are accepted by most shops and restaurants, and the American Express charge card is accepted by many as well. Hotels and guesthouses are more fickle when it comes to credit cards; the larger resort hotels accept them, but several of the smaller places do not. If you intend to pay off your room bill with a credit card, be sure to inquire at the time of booking your reservation as to whether it will be honored – surprisingly, even some of the high-end places don't accept them.

Exchanging Money

US dollar traveler's checks are widely accepted. Other foreign currencies, including the British pound sterling, will need to be exchanged at a bank.

The Bank of Bermuda, which has branches at the airport as well as near the cruise ship docks in Hamilton and St George, cashes traveler's checks that add up to a total value of US$500 in US dollar, Canadian dollar or British pound denominations, free of service charges. Expect to pay a 1% commission if you cash more than $500 in a single transaction. Although the bank does not accept other foreign traveler's checks, it will exchange cash in most other major currencies.

Tipping

The usual restaurant tip is 15%, which most restaurants automatically add to the bill – if not, you should add the tip yourself. Hotels typically tag a 10% service charge onto your final room bill, which covers gratuities to hotel workers. For taxi drivers, a tip of about 10% is appropriate.

POST

There are post offices in every major village and town in Bermuda. Service is very reliable; airmail posted by 9:30am at the General Post Office in the City of Hamilton leaves the island the same day.

Most hotels will hold mail for their guests. In addition, poste restante mail can be received in your name, c/o General Delivery, General Post Office, 56 Church St, Hamilton HM PM, Bermuda. Items not collected at the GPO in Hamilton within 30 days will be returned to sender.

Postal Rates

To post airmail letters costs 70¢ for the first 10g and 40¢ for each additional 10g when sent to the USA, Canada, Mexico, Central America, Venezuela, Colombia or the Caribbean. Postcards to these same destinations cost 70¢.

The cost is 85/40¢ for the first/additional 10g for letters (80¢ for postcards) to the UK, Europe, North Africa and most of South America.

The cost is 95/50¢ for the first/additional 10g to other destinations (90¢ for postcards) – including Australia, New Zealand, Asia and most of Africa.

Aerograms cost 70¢ to any international destination.

For mail sent within Bermuda for local delivery, the cost is 30¢ for a postcard and 35¢ for a letter of up to 20g.

SHOPPING

Shoppers are going to have fun here. Standout Bermuda-made items include hand-blown glasswork that ranges from miniature tree frogs to extravagant serving bowls and vases. There's also good-quality pottery made in Bermuda, including mugs and dinnerware with island designs.

Jewelers on the island create some attractive earrings, charms and pendants using island motifs, such as Bermuda onions, longtail tropic birds, hog pennies – even scooters.

Bermuda designs show up on numerous other items, including silk-screened T-shirts,

---

LET'S PRETEND THERE'S A BOAT

The Bermuda postal system offers one of the more unusual 'sea mail' services. What is peculiar about it is that ships are not involved in the service, but the mail is instead airlifted from Bermuda to the country of destination.

To make sure people don't overuse the discounted 'sea mail' rates, all surface mail is held in Bermuda until a closing date, which is equivalent to the scheduled date that the imaginary ship would leave Bermuda, plus the additional time – typically three days for mail to the USA, four days for mail to the UK – that it would normally take for a ship to sail between Bermuda and the destination.

Bermudians take it all quite seriously – the closing date for sea mail is displayed in all post offices. If you manage to get something off shortly before the closing date, it can actually be an efficient way to mail things, and the rates are roughly half those of regular airmail.

tea towels, note cards and the like, any of which can make a lightweight memento of your trip. Bermuda inspires many artists who put the island's lovely pastel scenes onto canvas, and these are available in both originals and prints.

If you want a whiff of the island after you leave, Bermuda's Royall Fragrances mixes up four varieties of men's colognes: Royall Bay Rhum, Royall Lyme, Royall Spyce and Royall Muske. Or bring home a taste of the island with Outerbridge's spicy sherry peppers sauce, Bermuda honey or island-made liqueurs and rums.

Bermuda's shops carry an excellent variety of top-name English and European imports. You'll find everything from Swiss watches to French fashions but generally the best selections and prices are found on items imported from the British Isles, like English bone china, Waterford crystal and Scottish tweeds.

Bermuda has no sales tax, so the price you see on everything is what you pay.

TELEPHONE

Bermuda telephone numbers have seven digits – there's only one area code for the whole island and it's not used when making domestic calls. All calls made in Bermuda to another place in Bermuda are local calls and cost 35¢ from a pay phone.

Pay phones, which are readily available in public places, accept both Bermuda and US coins as well as major credit cards.

You can also purchase phonecards, which can be convenient if you're going to be making a lot of calls or are making overseas calls, as you won't need a pocketful of coins. Phonecards in $10, $20 and $50 denominations are sold at tourist offices and shops around the island.

If you're a cellular phone user, the Bermuda Telephone Company's mobile network supports North American Analog (AMPS) and Digital (TDMA) standard service.

International Calls

Bermuda's area code is ☎ 441, which must be added to the seven-digit local number when calling Bermuda from overseas. Bermuda's country code is ☎ 1 and its international access code is ☎ 011, the same as it is in the USA and Canada.

You can call Bermuda direct from the USA, Canada and most Caribbean countries by dialing ☎ 1 + 441 + seven-digit local number. To call Bermuda from anywhere else in the world, dial the international access code for the country you're calling from + 1 + 441 + seven-digit local number. For instance, the UK access code is ☎ 00, so from the UK dial ☎ 00 + 1 + 441 + local number.

From Bermuda, you can call direct to the USA, Canada and most Caribbean countries by dialing ☎ 1 + area code + local number. To call direct to other parts of the world, dial ☎ 011 + country code + area code + local number. For example, the country code for the UK is ☎ 44; hence ☎ 011 + 44 + area code + local number.

TIME

Bermuda is in the Atlantic standard time zone, which is four hours behind GMT/UTC (London) and one hour ahead of eastern standard time (North American east coast).

When it's noon in Bermuda, it's 11am in New York and Toronto, 10am in Chicago, 8am in Los Angeles and Vancouver, 2am in Sydney, midnight in Hong Kong and 4pm in London.

Daylight saving time is in effect in Bermuda from the first Sunday in April to the last Sunday in October.

TOURIST INFORMATION

First stop should be the website of the **Bermuda Department of Tourism** (www.bermudatourism.com), where you can browse all sorts of visitor information.

There are Visitors Service Bureaus in the City of Hamilton (p50), in the Town of St George (p73) and at the Royal Naval Dockyard (p136), where you can pick up stacks of tourist brochures and the skinny on what's happening around the island.

The Bermuda Department of Tourism maintains the following overseas offices, which will mail out packets of tourist information upon request:

Canada (☎ 416-923-9600; 1200 Bay St, Suite 1004, Toronto, Ontario M5R 2A5)

UK (☎ 0 207 202 6364; Bermuda Tourism UK, Notcutt House, 36 Southwark Bridge Rd, London SE1 9EU)

USA Head office (☎ 800-223-6106; 675 Third Ave, 20th Fl, New York, NY 10017); Atlanta office (☎ 404-524-1541;

SMART MOVE

If you're planning to move to Bermuda, here are a few things that might interest you.

- Bring only what you need, as a hefty duty is charged on the importation of household goods (even old ones!).

- A free three-month bus/ferry pass is available to employed newcomers; pick up an application at the ferry terminal.

- If you need to open an account at a local bank you may need a reference from your home bank, so it's a good idea to bring one along to smooth the way.

- A superb source of information for newcomers is the *New Resident in Bermuda* magazine.

- A good online classified-ad resource for apartments for rent is www.bermuda.e-moo.com.

- If you intend to drive you'll have to get a new driver's license – foreign licenses aren't valid in Bermuda.

---

245 Peachtree Center Ave NE, Suite 803, Atlanta, GA 30303); Boston office (☎ 617-422-5892; 184 High St, 4th Fl, Boston, MA 02110)

VISAS

Visas are not required of citizens of most countries, including the USA, Canada, the UK, Australia, New Zealand and Western European countries.

Visas are required of citizens from most countries in North Africa, the Middle East and the former Soviet Union as well as from Albania, Bosnia and Herzegovina, Bulgaria, Cambodia, China, Croatia, Cuba, Haiti, Mongolia, Nigeria, North Korea, Pakistan, Romania, Slovakia, Slovenia, Sri Lanka and Vietnam. Visitors from these countries can obtain a visa from a British embassy or a consulate abroad.

Immigration authorities at the Bermuda International Airport will determine your permitted length of stay. They commonly grant a stay of up to 21 days. Extensions can be applied for at the **Immigration Headquarters** (Map pp48-9; ☎ 295-5151; 30 Parliament St, City of Hamilton).

WOMEN TRAVELERS

Women travelers are no more likely to encounter problems in Bermuda than they are elsewhere, but the usual common-sense precautions apply when it comes to potentially dangerous situations like walking alone at night, accepting rides from strangers etc. Also, keep in mind that skimpy clothing is the norm only on the beach in Bermuda, and it could elicit unwanted attention anywhere else.

WORK

People wishing to enter Bermuda for the purpose of employment are required to obtain a work permit in advance from Bermuda's immigration authorities. Because employers on the island are supposed to give priority to local residents, it can be difficult for foreigners to get a job, unless they have a specialized skill for which there is not a suitable local candidate. That said, some international companies do readily hire non-Bermudians and if you're knowledgeable about corporate work your odds of finding a job improves dramatically.

Transportation

CONTENTS

GETTING THERE & AWAY

ENTERING THE COUNTRY

Bermuda is straightforward to visit. All tourists landing in Bermuda must be in possession of a return or onward ticket.

Passport

A passport is the preferred document for entry into Bermuda and is required of visitors from all countries that require a passport for re-entry purposes to their home country.

Your passport should remain valid until well after your trip. If it's about to expire, renew it before you go.

Applying for or renewing a passport can take from a few days to several months, so don't leave it till the last minute.

For information on visas, see p150.

FROM THE USA

Visitors from the USA must present one of the following types of identification:
- US passport – it needn't be valid, but if it has expired, the photo should be recent enough that it still resembles the bearer
- An official birth certificate with a raised seal, or a certified copy of it issued by a municipal authority
- US Naturalization Certificate

- US Permanent Resident Card
- US Re-entry Permit

Note that if you're presenting identification that doesn't have a photo, such as a birth certificate, you'll need to also present a driver's license or similar photo ID. (Children 16 and under who are traveling with their parents may present an official birth certificate without a photo ID.)

FROM CANADA

Visitors from Canada need to be able to present one of the following four types of identification:
- Valid Canadian passport
- Official birth certificate or a certified copy, along with a photo ID
- Canadian Certificate of Citizenship
- Canadian Permanent Resident Card

FROM OTHER COUNTRIES

Visitors from other countries, including the UK, Western European nations, Australia and New Zealand, must be able to present a valid passport.

AIR

There are regularly scheduled direct flights to Bermuda from the USA, Canada and the UK. Travelers who arrive from other places need to connect through one of these three nations.

Airports & Airlines

Bermuda International Airport (☎ 293-2470; www.bermudaairport.com; airport code BHA), on the eastern side of the island, is Bermuda's only airport. This small but modern facility has a couple of gift shops, a duty-free shop, a bar and food kiosks. If you have any banking needs, there's a **Bank of Bermuda** (☎ 293-1414; ⏰ 10am-3pm Mon-Fri) at the ground level of the terminal.

Bermuda's arrival and departure formalities and customs are generally straightforward. An unusual quirk is that if you're flying to the USA from Bermuda, you will actually pass through US customs at the Bermuda airport before your departure, and arrive in the USA as if on a domestic flight.

Air Canada (www.aircanada.ca; AC; ☎ 295-4587; hub Pearson International Airport, Toronto) Has a daily flight from Toronto and a once-weekly flight from Halifax.

American Airlines (www.aa.com; AA; ☎ 293-1420; hub Dallas Fort Worth International Airport, Dallas, TX) Has daily nonstop flights from New York City.

British Airways (www.britishairways.com; BA; ☎ 293-1944; hub Heathrow Airport, London) Has five flights weekly from London.

Continental Airlines (www.continental.com; CO; ☎ 293-1420; hub Newark International Airport, New York, NY) Has daily nonstop flights from Newark Airport.

Delta Air Lines (www.delta.com; DL; ☎ 293-1024; hub Atlanta International Airport, Atlanta, GA) Has daily nonstop flights from Boston and Atlanta.

United Airlines (www.ua.com; UA; ☎ 800-241-6522; hub O'Hare International Airport, Chicago, IL) Has a weekly flight from Chicago.

USA3000 (www.usa3000airlines.com; U5; ☎ 877-872-3000; hub Baltimore Washington International Airport, Baltimore, MD) Has twice-weekly flights from Baltimore and New York City.

US Airways (www.usairways.com; US; ☎ 800-622-1015; hub Charlotte-Douglas International Airport, Charlotte, NC) Has daily nonstop flights from Baltimore, Boston, Charlotte, New York City, Philadelphia and Washington DC.

Tickets

Direct flights to Bermuda are available from several major cities on the US east coast, as well as from Canada and London.

It pays to do a bit of research before buying a ticket. A good starting point is with online travel services such as www.orbitz.com or www.travelocity.com in the USA, www.expedia.com or www.travelocity.ca in Canada and www.trailfinders.com in the UK. These are excellent places to get a sense of the range for current fares, but you should also take the time to find

the airline websites to search discounted web fares. These days cash-strapped airlines sometimes offer the very best deals exclusively to travelers who purchase their tickets directly from the airline websites.

Fares vary with the season you travel, the day of the week you fly and the flexibility the ticket provides for flight changes and refunds. Still, nothing determines fares more than business, and when things are slow, regardless of the season, airlines typically drop fares to fill the empty seats.

Fares can fluctuate so wildly, particularly in the US, that it's not uncommon to find prices dropping by half (or doubling!) from one day to the next. With fixed fares a thing of the past it's hard to put a price on air travel, so take any prices that follow as only a general barometer of what you can expect to encounter.

Canada

Air Canada flies daily to Bermuda from Toronto and has a Saturday-only flight from Halifax. Roundtrip excursion fares typically begin around C$500 in winter and C$600 in summer.

UK

British Airways flies from Gatwick Airport in London to Bermuda several days a week, on a schedule that varies with the season. The roundtrip excursion fares typically fluctuate between £500 to £700 depending upon the day of the week and the season of travel.

USA

About 90% of Bermuda's air traffic arrives from the USA. Although the US airlines serving Bermuda operate year-round, the service on some routes gets beefed up in summer. If you have a little flexibility and begin your planning well in advance of your trip, you'll increase the odds of finding a good deal.

Markets that have multiple carriers, such as New York City, typically have the cheapest fares. With the arrival of Bermuda's first discount airline, USA3000, bargain hunters can sometimes find roundtrip fares for as little as $250 to Bermuda from New York and Baltimore.

On direct flights from elsewhere in the USA, roundtrip tickets average around $450, though flights during the busiest summer periods, such as holiday weekends, can cost upward of $600.

SEA
Cruise Ship

Bermuda has made a big splash on the cruise ship map. More than 200,000 passengers sail to the island each year during the cruise ship season, which runs from April to mid-November.

The typical cruise ship holiday is the ultimate package tour. Other than the effort involved in selecting a cruise, such a trip requires minimal planning – just pay and show up – and for many people that is a large part of the appeal. Keep in mind that much of your time will obviously be spent at sea, so you'll have notably less time on the island than someone with a vacation of comparable length who takes a flight. Cruises, which are typically one week in length, spend only about half of that time in Bermuda.

Because cruises cover your rooms, meals, entertainment and transportation in one all-inclusive price, they are sometimes relatively good value. Although cruises cost more than lower-end independent travel, they do not necessarily cost more than conventional package tours that cover airfare and expenses at a resort hotel.

The conventional cruise ship is indeed a floating resort; those sailing to Bermuda hold between 650 and 2000 passengers and have swimming pools, dinner shows, casinos, multiple restaurants and lounges.

In addition to the cruise lines' websites given below, also take a look at **Cruise Lines International Association** (www.cruising.org), an organization of cruise lines that works in affiliation with thousands of travel agencies.

The following four cruise lines all offer regularly scheduled roundtrip cruises to Bermuda throughout the cruise ship season.

Celebrity Cruises (☎ 800-235-3274; www.celebrity cruises.com) Departs from New York City from April to October and from Norfolk, Virginia, from May to October. It docks in Bermuda at both the City of Hamilton and the Town of St George.

Norwegian Cruise Line (☎ 800-327-7030; www.ncl .com) Sails from Boston every Sunday between April and October and from New York City from May to October. It docks at the Town of St George.

Radisson Seven Seas Cruises (☎ 800-393-0031; www.radissonsevenseas.com) Departs from New York City from April to September. It docks at the City of Hamilton and the Town of St George.

Royal Caribbean Cruise Line (☎ 800-327-6700; www.royalcaribbean.com) Departs from New York City from May to October. It docks at both the Town of St George and the City of Hamilton.

Cruises are actually quite equalitarian. Passengers are not divided into class categories, and all are offered the same dining services and amenities – at least when they're outside their cabins. Cruises are offered at a range of rates, however, depending mainly on the size, type and location of the cabin. Price also depends on the dates of the cruise, the number of people in each cabin and your point of departure.

Standard rates for cruises to Bermuda start between $900 and $1600 per person, based on double occupancy. Discounts abound, however, and very few people pay the full rates. These days, the general rule is that the earlier the booking is, the greater the discount – and, of course, the better the cabin selection. Still, cruise lines want to sail full, so if there are seats leftover at the end there will be discounts available close to sailing as well. And always ask about promotions, as there are often deals for travel club members, seniors etc.

Meals, which are typically indulgent affairs, are included in the cruise price, as are most onboard activities. Alcoholic drinks usually are not included and generally are comparable in price to those in bars back home. Also, expect to pay extra for any activities in Bermuda.

Before paying for your cruise, be sure to check the fine print about deposits, cancellation and refund policies, all of which can be very restrictive.

Yacht

Yachting is immensely popular in Bermuda and lots of people sail to the island, some during regattas, others on solo trips. Most yachters who sail to Bermuda depart from the US east coast. Bermuda is approximately 640 nautical miles southeast from the state of Virginia, 670 nautical miles from New York City and 690 nautical miles from Boston. Of course, sailing time will vary with the weather and the boat, but the typical voyage time between Bermuda and the US east coast is five to six days.

TRANSPORTATION

Bermuda's two main boating entrances are at the Town Cut channel and the Narrows channel, both at the eastern side of the island. Because of the vast reefs that lie as far as 10 miles offshore, the approach must be made cautiously, using updated charts. Bermuda has two lighthouses and numerous beacons, buoys and shore lights to aid navigation.

The government's **Bermuda Harbour Radio** (☎ 297-1010; www.rccbermuda.bm), with the call letters ZBM, maintains a continuous listening watch at 2182kHz, VHF Channel 16, and all vessels approaching Bermuda are required to make contact for entry and berthing instructions. A call should be attempted at approximately 30 miles from the island, giving the estimated time of arrival. Weather forecasts and navigational warnings are broadcast 24 hours a day at VHF Weather Channel 2 on frequency 162.4MHz.

All visiting yachts are required to obtain customs, immigration and health clearance in the Port of St George before proceeding elsewhere in Bermuda. The clearance facility is at the east side of Ordnance Island. Instructions on departure formalities should be obtained here as well; there's a $15 passenger tax.

Anchorage for yachts is available in St George Harbour, Hamilton Harbour and the Royal Naval Dockyard, the latter through the full-service **Dockyard Marina** (☎ 234-0300). For information on how to berth in Hamilton Harbour, contact the **Royal Hamilton Amateur Dinghy Club** (☎ 236-2250). Bermuda Harbour Radio can provide information on anchorage options in St George.

Because there are several yacht races between Bermuda and the US east coast in early summer, yachters who are not racing should keep in mind that it can be a difficult time to secure a berth.

RESOURCES & CHARTS

The Bermuda Department of Tourism offers a 24-page pamphlet called *Yachts (Private) Sailing to Bermuda,* an essential resource for anyone planning to sail to Bermuda; download it at www.bermudatour ism.com/pdf /yachts_info.pdf. It includes detailed information on everything from beacon locations to where to pick up ice.

In addition, consider picking up a copy of *The Yachting Guide to Bermuda,* edited by the Bermuda Maritime Museum.

Detailed charts are essential for sailing into Bermudian waters. In Bermuda, yachting books and British Admiralty charts are available at **PW's Marine Centre** (☎ 295-3232; www.pwmarine.bm; 111 Woodlands Rd, City of Hamilton).

In the USA, books and charts can be purchased from the following companies:
Armchair Sailor Worldwide Navigation (☎ 401-847-4252, 800-292-4278; www.bluewaterweb.com; 543 Thames St, Newport, RI)
Landfall Navigation (☎ 203-487-0775; www.landfall navigation.com; 151 Harvard Ave, Stamford, CT)
New York Nautical (☎ 212-962-4522; www.newyork nautical.com; 158 Duane St, New York, NY)

GETTING AROUND

You cannot rent cars in Bermuda. Visitors can ride a public bus or ferry, use a taxi, rent a motor scooter or bicycle – or even hire a horse and carriage.

BICYCLE

Although not nearly as popular as motor scooters, bicycles are another option for getting around. However, Bermuda's roads are narrow, curving and often hilly, so people planning on bicycling need to be cautious of traffic and expect to work up a sweat. When it's going your way, using the Railway Trail, which is open to bicyclists but not motorized vehicles, is a good way to avoid traffic. Bicycles, by the way, are generally referred to in Bermuda as pedal cycles, to differentiate them from scooters.

The following scooter rental shops rent bicycles for around $35 for the first day and $10 more for each additional day.
Elbow Beach Cycles (☎ 236-9237; 60 South Rd, Paget)
Eve's Cycles Paget (☎ 236-6247; 114 Middle Rd); St George (☎ 236-0839; 1 Water St)
Oleander Cycles (☎ 234-0629; Middle Rd, Southampton)

Rental bicycles come in various types but most are mountain bikes. Locks and helmets are provided.

BOAT

Public ferries, which operate daily in the Great Sound and Hamilton Harbour, offer a scenic alternative to the bus. As the distances across water are often shorter than comparable land routes, the ferries can also

TRANSPORTATION

FORGET THE KEYS

Don't expect to get behind the wheel of a car on this island. Bermudians have had such dread of automobiles on their narrow roads that they actually banned them outright for decades. After WWII private automobile ownership was allowed for the first time but not without restrictions that continue to this day.

First off, there's a strict regulation that limits the number of cars to one per household, and no one is allowed to drive another person's car if they don't live in that household. Cars cannot be more than 66 inches wide, so don't expect to see any bloated American cars here – even the Volkswagen Beetle doesn't pass the width restriction.

And there are no car rentals available at all – tourists are simply not allowed to drive cars in Bermuda. Just to make sure you're not tempted, foreign driver's licenses are not even recognized here. If you're itching to hit the road on your own, plan to rent a motor scooter or a bicycle – neither requires a license!

be quicker. The fastest ferry from the City of Hamilton to the Royal Naval Dockyard, for example, takes just 20 minutes, while the bus ride takes a full hour.

There are four different ferry routes, connecting the City of Hamilton with St George and the Dockyard; with Paget and Warwick; with Southampton; and with Sandys Parish. Each route leaves from the Hamilton Ferry Terminal, which is conveniently located on Front St in the City of Hamilton, adjacent to the tourist information office.

Cash is not accepted on the ferries. For details on transportation passes, tickets and tokens, all of which are valid on both public ferries and buses, see Bus below. If you have questions regarding ferries, contact the **Hamilton Ferry Terminal** (☎ 295-4506; www .seaexpress.bm). Information on specific ferry routes can be found in the Getting There & Around sections in the individual parish chapters.

BUS
Bermuda has a good islandwide public bus system that you can use to reach most sights and beaches. The buses are reliable and generally run on time. Pick up a free copy of the bus-and-ferry schedule at one of the tourist offices or at the bus terminal on Washington St in the City of Hamilton.

Buses are quite busy between 3:30pm and 5:30pm on weekdays, when schoolchildren and office workers make the commute home, but at most other times, getting a seat isn't a challenge. Frequency varies with the route and time of travel, but during the day the busier routes generally have a bus operating every 15 to 30 minutes. Sundays

and holidays have substantially reduced schedules.

Although schedules vary by route, most buses begin their service somewhere between 6:30am and 7:30am. Service on some minor routes ends around 6pm. On the two most significant routes – Hamilton to St George and Hamilton to the Royal Naval Dockyard – service continues until around 11pm, with the schedule thinning out as the evening goes on.

Of the 11 bus routes, all, with the exception of the St George–St David's route, leave from the Hamilton bus terminal. Consequently, if you use buses often, you'll find yourself transferring there frequently.

Bus stops are marked with color-coded posts to indicate whether buses serving that stop are inbound or outbound. If the post is pink, buses stopping there are heading into Hamilton; if it's blue, the buses are heading away from Hamilton.

For inquiries regarding bus service, contact the **Public Transportation Board** (☎ 292-3851) between 8:45am and 5pm weekdays.

There is also a private minibus service (p80) that operates solely within St George's Parish.

Bus Passes & Fares
To ride the bus, you must have the exact fare *in coins* or have a token, ticket or transportation pass. Paper money is not accepted and change is not given.

Bermuda is divided into 14 different bus zones. You can pay a fare for three zones (meaning the trip covers one to three zones) or 14 zones (for a journey covering four to 14 zones).

From the City of Hamilton, it's a three-zone fare to the following places:

- the Bermuda Aquarium, Museum & Zoo (bus No 10 or 11)
- the Bermuda Botanical Gardens (bus No 1, 2 or 7)
- Elbow Beach (bus No 7)
- Horseshoe Bay (bus No 7)
- Spittal Pond (bus No 1)

From Hamilton, it's a 14-zone fare to the Royal Naval Dockyard (bus No 7 or 8). It's also a 14-zone fare to the airport, Bailey's Bay or St George's – all of which can be reached by bus No 1, 3, 10 or 11.

The regular adult fare is $3 in coins or $2.50 in tokens for up to three zones and $4.50 in coins or $4 in tokens for more than three zones. Children ages five to 16 ride for $2 in coins for any number of zones, and those under age five ride for free.

Tickets offer a handsome discount compared with the cash fare. The cost for adults is $20 for 15 tickets that are each valid for up to three zones, and $30 for 15 tickets valid for all zones. The cost for children is $7.50 for 15 tickets valid for all zones.

Bus transfers are free as long as they are made with the next scheduled connecting bus. If you need a transfer, request it from the driver when you get on the first bus.

Transportation passes can be handy if you're doing a lot of exploring, as they allow unlimited use of both buses and ferries. Passes valid for a single day cost $12; those valid for three consecutive days cost $28; four days cost $35; and seven consecutive days cost $45. In addition, there's a monthly pass for $55 that is valid for the calendar month in which it is purchased.

Ticket books, tokens and transportation passes are sold at the bus terminal information booth in Hamilton from 7:15am to 5:30pm weekdays, 8:15am to 5:30pm Saturday and 9:15am to 4:45pm Sunday and holidays.

Ticket books and transportation passes are also sold at most post offices, though not the main City of Hamilton post office. The shorter-duration transportation passes are also sold at tourist offices and some hotels.

HITCHHIKING

Hitchhiking is not illegal in Bermuda, but it's rarely done. As one police officer remarked: 'I don't know if people would know what you're doing. They might stick their thumb back up at you, thinking you're just having a good time.'

And of course, as with everywhere else in the world, hitchhiking is never entirely safe and Lonely Planet does not recommend it. Travelers who make the decision to hitchhike should understand that they are taking a potentially serious risk. People who do choose to hitchhike will be safer if they travel in pairs and let someone know where they are planning to go.

HORSE-DRAWN CARRIAGE

Up for a little old-fashioned fun? Then this is the way to go. Although it's more of a romantic ride than a practical means of transportation, horse-and-carriage rides are available in the City of Hamilton. The carriages park on Front St on the east side of the No 1 Cruise Ship Terminal. They typically take a side route west along Pitts Bay Rd or make a circular route north on Bermudiana Rd, west on Richmond Rd and back to Front St via Serpentine and Par-la-Ville Rds.

The cost per carriage (for one to four passengers) is $30 for the first 30 minutes (the minimum charge) and $30 for each additional 30-minute increment. If the carriage is drawn by two horses it is allowed to carry more than four passengers, in which case the cost for the fifth and additional passengers is $5 per person per 30 minutes.

MOTOR SCOOTER

Motor scooters, which are commonly referred to as 'cycles' in Bermuda, are the main mode of transport for touring the island independently. Hopping on one can be a fun way of getting around, but Bermuda's narrow winding roads present challenges for drivers who aren't used to these conditions – or who don't have scooter experience.

In fact, enough visitors spill their scooters that the term 'road rash' is part of the island vernacular. And scrapes aren't the worst that ever happens – serious accidents and fatalities aren't unknown. If you're not used to riding, make sure you're comfortable with the scooter before taking to the road. All rental shops are required to have an instructor show you how to use the scooter and to provide you with an opportunity to practise. If you're not satisfied with your ability to handle the scooter after your instruction, feel free to cancel the contract.

Driver's License

Here's a surprise: you don't need a driver's license to drive a scooter in Bermuda. Just remember when you get out on the road that there may be plenty of shaky novices out there who don't have one! Scooter drivers, however, are required by law to be at least 16 years old.

Rental

Scooter rates are competitive and you may find that you'll do just as well renting from the shop associated with your hotel or guesthouse. Still, if you want to call around and seek out the best price, most cycle liveries will either pick you up and take you to their office or deliver the scooter to you.

When comparing rates, take note of the add-ons that pad up the bill. A mandatory 'repair waiver insurance' of about $25 is the most common one; this is a one-time fee that covers the entire rental period, whether it's one day or one week. The repair waiver insurance covers damages to the scooter, but with some companies there's a deductible (excess), in which case you still could be held responsible for hundreds of dollars in damages. Be sure you understand the policy in advance.

Whichever cycle livery you rent from, and regardless of the insurance offered, you'll likely have either a large deductible for theft or find that it will not be covered at all. Scooter thefts are at such epidemic proportions in Bermuda that it's virtually impossible to insure against theft. Incidentally, it's not just a problem for rentals – most islanders have had theft coverage dropped from their own insurance policies. Inquire carefully about the theft policy before renting; some companies might limit your liability if you can prove you locked the scooter (ie you have the key), but others will hold you responsible under any circumstances.

Rates for a one-person scooter average $45 for a one-day rental, $70 to $90 for two days, $100 to $120 for three days and $190 to $210 for a week – plus the one-time repair waiver charge. For about $10 more a day you can rent a larger double-seat scooter that's capable of carrying a passenger. Carrying a passenger isn't recommended, however, unless you are an experienced motorbike driver.

The scooters come with a full tank of gas and most have a small reserve fuel tank. If you need to refill on the road, there are gas stations throughout the island from St George to Somerset.

Oleander Cycles (☎ 236-5235; www.oleandercycles.bm) and **Wheels Cycles** (☎ 292-2245; www.bermudashorts.bm/wheels) are large reputable operations with numerous branches scattered around Bermuda. Smaller operations include **Eve's Cycles** (☎ 236-6247; www.evecycles.com) and **Smatt's Cycle Livery** (☎ 295-1180; www.smattscyclelivery.com) as well as **Elbow Beach Cycles** (☎ 236-9237; www.elbowbeachcycles.com). Branch offices are listed in each parish chapter.

Road Rules

In Bermuda, as in Britain, driving is on the left. The speed limit throughout Bermuda is 35km/h (22 miles), except in a few municipal areas such as central St George, where it drops to 25km/h.

Bermuda has a handful of roundabouts (also known as rotaries or traffic circles) – you must give way to traffic already on the roundabout, but once you enter you have the right-of-way.

Helmets are required of both drivers and passengers, and are provided by the cycle livery you rent from. Police are not eager to ticket tourists and will generally issue warnings for traffic violations as long as the violator is polite and apologetic.

TAXI

Taxis are readily available from the airport at flight times, and most larger hotels have taxis waiting. In addition, there are taxi stands in heavily touristed areas, such as Front St in Hamilton and King's Square in St George.

All taxis are equipped with meters. The standard rate (for up to four passengers) is $5.75 for the first mile plus $2 for each additional mile. If there are five or six passengers the rate is $7.19 for the first mile plus $2.50 for each additional mile. Prices are 25% higher between midnight and 6am and all day on Sundays and public holidays.

If you need to call for a taxi, **Radio Cabs** (☎ 295-4141), **BIU Taxi Co-op** (☎ 292-4476) and **Sandy's Taxi Co** (☎ 234-2344) are three of the larger dispatchers with a 24-hour service.

TRANSPORTATION

TOURS

If you want to piece together your own private sightseeing tour, taxis can double as tour operators, catering a tour to your interests. The drivers are generally knowledgeable and their commentary can add plenty of local color as you explore. Seek out a taxi with a blue card in the front window, which indicates the driver has been certified as a tourism specialist, meaning that their background on sightseeing is particularly extensive. The cost is $36 per hour for one to four passengers, $50 per hour for five or six passengers.

The St George's Mini-Bus Service (p80) offers one-hour tours of the Town of St George for $20 while the cruise ship season is on. The aforementioned public ferry rides can double as inexpensive harbor cruises. For information on organized sightseeing walks, see Outdoor Activities (p34).

Health

CONTENTS

Because the level of hygiene in Bermuda is generally high, most travelers experience nothing worse than a little diarrhea or a mild respiratory infection. Also, good medical care is available; however, medical care in Bermuda is expensive.

BEFORE YOU GO

Prevention is the key to staying healthy while abroad. A little planning before departure, particularly for pre-existing illnesses, will save trouble later. See your dentist before a long trip, carry a spare pair of contact lenses and glasses, and take your optical prescription with you. Bring medications in their original, clearly labeled, containers. A signed and dated letter from your physician describing your medical conditions and medications, including generic names, is also a good idea. If carrying syringes or needles, be sure to have a physician's letter documenting their medical necessity.

INSURANCE

If your health insurance does not cover you for medical expenses abroad, consider supplemental insurance. The Subwwway section of the Lonely Planet website at www .lonelyplanet.com/subwwway has more information. Find out in advance if your insurance plan will make payments directly to providers or reimburse you later for overseas health expenditures.

MEDICAL CHECKLIST

It is a very good idea to carry a medical and first aid kit with you, to help yourself in the case of minor illness or injury. Following is a list of items you should consider packing.

- Acetaminophen (paracetamol) or aspirin
- Anti-inflammatory drugs (eg ibuprofen)
- Antihistamines (for hayfever and allergic reactions)
- Antibacterial ointment (eg Bactroban) for treating cuts and abrasions (prescription only)
- Steroid cream or hydrocortisone cream (for allergic rashes)
- Bandages, gauze, gauze rolls
- Adhesive or paper tape
- Scissors, safety pins, tweezers
- Thermometer
- Pocket knife
- Sun block

INTERNET RESOURCES

There is a wealth of travel health advice on the Internet. For further information, the **Lonely Planet** (www.lonelyplanet.com) website is a good place to start. A superb book called *International Travel and Health*, revised annually, is available online at no cost; it's published by the **World Health Organization** (www.who.int/ith/). Other websites of general interest are **MD Travel Health** (www.mdtravel health.com), which provides complete travel health recommendations for every country, updated daily, also at no cost; the **Centers for Disease Control and Prevention** (www.cdc .gov); and **Fit for Travel** (www.fitfortravel.scot.nhs .uk), which has up-to-date information about outbreaks and is very user-friendly.

It's also a good idea to consult your government's travel health website before departure, if one is available:
Australia (www.dfat.gov.au/travel/)
Canada (www.hc-sc.gc.ca/english/index.html)
UK (www.doh.gov.uk/traveladvice/index.htm)
USA (www.cdc.gov/travel/)

HEALTH

RECOMMENDED VACCINATIONS

All travelers should be up-to-date on routine immunizations, listed below.

Vaccine	Recommended for	Dosage	Possible side effects
tetanus-diphtheria	all travelers who haven't had a booster within 10 years	1 dose lasts 10 years	soreness at the injection site
measles	travelers born after 1956 who've had only one measles vaccination	1 dose	fever; rash; joint pains; allergic reactions
chickenpox	travelers who've never had chickenpox	2 doses 1 month apart	fever; mild case of chickenpox
influenza	all travelers during flu season (Nov through Mar)	1 dose	soreness at the injection site; fever

FURTHER READING

If you're traveling with kids, Lonely Planet's *Travel with Children* by Cathy Lanigan may be useful. *The ABC of Healthy Travel*, by E Walker et al, is another good resource.

IN TRANSIT

DEEP VEIN THROMBOSIS (DVT)

Blood clots may form in the legs during plane flights, chiefly because of prolonged immobility. The longer the flight, the higher the risk. The chief symptom of DVT is swelling or pain of the foot, ankle, or calf, usually but not always on just one side. When a blood clot travels to the lungs, it may cause chest pain and breathing difficulties. Travelers who have any of these symptoms should immediately seek medical attention.

To prevent the development of DVT on long flights you should walk about the cabin, contract the leg muscles while sitting, drink plenty of fluids and avoid alcohol.

JET LAG & MOTION SICKNESS

To avoid jet lag (common when flying across more than five time zones) try drinking plenty of nonalcoholic fluids and eating light meals. Upon arrival, get exposure to natural sunlight and readjust your schedule (for meals, sleep and so on) as soon as possible.

Eating lightly before and during a trip will reduce the chances of motion sickness. If you are prone to such upsets, try to find a place that minimizes movement – near the wing on aircraft or close to amidships on boats. Fresh air and a steady reference point like the horizon usually help; reading and cigarette smoke don't.

Antihistamines such as dimenhydrinate (Dramamine) and meclizine (Antivert, Bonine) are usually the first choice for treating motion sickness. There are also natural preventatives in the form of ginger (available in capsule form) and peppermint (including mint-flavored candy).

IN BERMUDA

AVAILABILITY & COST OF HEALTH CARE

For an ambulance in Bermuda, call 911.

Bermuda has one general hospital, the **King Edward VII Memorial Hospital** (☎ 236-2345; Point Finger Rd, Paget Parish), which has an emergency room, an obstetric unit, an intensive care unit, a dialysis unit, and a variety of other specialty services. There is also a separate psychiatric hospital. There are no private hospitals. The quality of medical care is generally good, but complex medical problems will usually require evacuation to the USA. For nonurgent medical matters, ask the concierge at your hotel to recommend a local physician.

Medical care in Bermuda is expensive. Though British, Bermuda does not participate in reciprocal health care agreements either inside or outside the European Economic Area. Make sure you're covered for medical costs while in Bermuda.

Most pharmacies are well-supplied and the pharmacists well-trained. The Phoenix stores are a reputable chain of pharmacies.

HEALTH

There are also a number of good independent pharmacies listed in the phone book.

INFECTIOUS DISEASES
HIV/AIDS
As with most parts of the world, HIV is a health problem in Bermuda. You should never assume, on the basis of someone's background or appearance, that they're free of this or any other sexually transmitted disease. Be sure to use a condom for all sexual encounters.

If you have any questions regarding AIDS while in Bermuda, you can call the **Allan Vincent Smith Foundation** (☎ 295-0002).

TRAVELER'S DIARRHEA
If you develop diarrhea, ensure that you drink plenty of fluids, preferably an oral rehydration solution (eg Dioralyte). A few loose stools don't require treatment, but if you start having more than four or five stools a day, you should start taking an antibiotic (usually a quinolone drug) and an antidiarrheal agent (such as Loperamide). If diarrhea is bloody, persists for more than 72 hours or is accompanied by fever, shaking, chills or severe abdominal pain you should seek medical attention.

ENVIRONMENTAL HAZARDS
Bites & Stings
Do not attempt to pet, handle or feed animals, with the exception of domestic animals known to be free of any infectious disease. Most animal injuries are directly related to a person's attempt to touch or feed the animal.

Any bite or scratch by a mammal, including bats, should be promptly and thoroughly cleansed with large amounts of soap and water, followed by application of an antiseptic such as iodine or alcohol. (Bermuda's Department of Agriculture claims that there have been no cases of rabies for more than 40 years.) It may also be advisable to start an antibiotic, since wounds caused by animal bites and scratches frequently become infected. One of the newer quinolones, such as levofloxacin (Levaquin), which many travelers carry in case of diarrhea, would be an appropriate choice.

If you are stung by a jellyfish or a Portuguese man-of-war, quickly remove the tentacles and apply vinegar or a meat tenderizer containing papain (derived from papaya), both of which act to neutralize the toxins – in a pinch, you could use urine as well. For serious reactions, including chest pains or difficulty breathing, seek immediate medical attention.

Heat Stroke
This serious, sometimes fatal, condition can occur if the body's heat-regulating mechanism breaks down and the body temperature rises to dangerous levels. Long, continuous periods of exposure to high temperatures and insufficient fluids can leave you vulnerable to heat stroke. Avoid strenuous activity in open sun when you first arrive.

The symptoms of heat stroke are feeling unwell, not sweating very much or at all and a high body temperature (39° to 41°C or 102° to 106°F). Where sweating has ceased, the skin becomes flushed and red. Severe, throbbing headaches and lack of co-ordination can also occur, and the sufferer may be confused or aggressive. Eventually the victim may become delirious or convulse. Hospitalization is essential, but in the interim get victims out of the sun, remove their clothing, cover them with a wet sheet or towel and continually fan them. Give fluids if they are conscious.

Sun Exposure
Ultraviolet radiation may be a health hazard during the summer. To protect yourself from excessive sun exposure, you should stay out of the midday sun, wear sunglasses and a wide-brimmed sun hat, and apply sunscreen with SPF 15 or higher, with both UVA and UVB protection. Sunscreen should be generously applied to all exposed parts of the body approximately 30 minutes before sun exposure and should be reapplied after swimming or vigorous activity. Travelers should also drink plenty of fluids and avoid strenuous exercise when the temperature is high.

Water
Although several of Bermuda's larger resort hotels have their own desalination plants, the rest of Bermuda depends upon rain for its water supply. Because the rain is caught on rooftops and directed into individual storage tanks, the bacteria count in the water can vary. If you're staying at a smaller

hotel or guesthouse, it's best to inquire with the manager about the water's suitability for drinking.

If in doubt, you can always treat the water first. The simplest way is to boil it vigorously. Chlorine tablets kill many but not all pathogens. Iodine is more effective in purifying water and is available in tablet form. Bottled water is available in Bermudian grocery stores.

CHILDREN & PREGNANT WOMEN

When traveling with children, make sure they're up-to-date on all routine immunizations. It's sometimes appropriate to give children some of their vaccines a little early before departure; you should discuss this with your pediatrician. If pregnant, you should bring along a copy of your medical records in case complications develop while abroad.

HEALTH

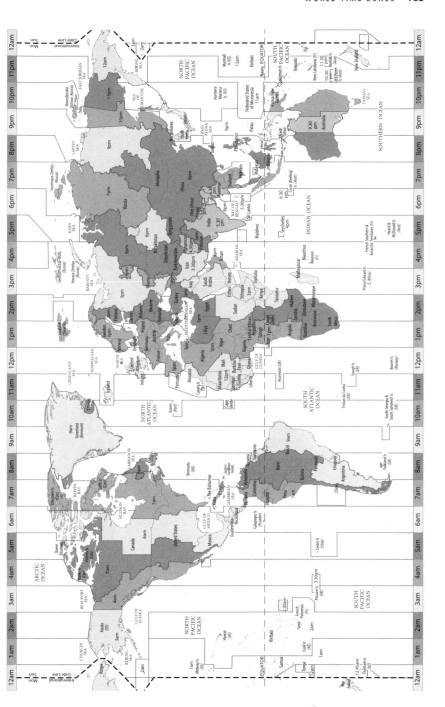

Behind the Scenes

THIS BOOK
This 3rd edition of *Bermuda* was written by Ned Friary and Glenda Bendure. They also wrote the 1st and 2nd editions. The Health chapter was written by Dr David Goldberg.

THANKS from the Authors
We'd like to thank those who aided us with our re-search, especially Mary Ramsay, Joy Sticca and the other helpful people at the Bermuda Department of Tourism, and Maureen Harrison in the Visitors Service Bureau in the Town of St George. Also a special thanks to Tom Butterfield of the Master-works Foundation, who put down his paintbrush and gave us the lowdown on Bermuda's art scene, and Ian Walker, curator of the Bermuda Aquarium, Museum & Zoo, who brought us up to date on en-vironmental issues. Thanks also to Quinton Bean for sharing his insights on island life and to Bill Breisky for turning us on to Bermuda in the first place. Thanks also to all the helpful folks at Lonely Planet, especially to Erin Corrigan for her patience and support as we updated this third edition, to Alex Hershey for providing inspired suggestions and plenty of room to run with new ideas, to our keen-eyed editor Laura Gibb for asking all the right questions and to David Connolly for a bang-up job with the maps.

CREDITS
Bermuda 3 was commissioned and developed in Lonely Planet's Oakland office by Alex Hershey. Cartography for this guide was developed by Alison Lyall. This book was coordinated by Laura Gibb (editorial) and David Connolly (cartography). Editing and proofing assistance was provided by Katrina Webb, Andrea Dobbin, Brooke Lyons and Gina Tsarouhas. Wibowo Rusli laid the book out. Katherine Marsh designed the cover artwork and laid the colour pages out and Candice Jacobus designed the cover. Overseeing production were Glenn van der Knijff (project manager) and Darren O'Connell (acting managing editor). Thanks to Nina Collins, Kate McDonald, Sally Darmody and Yvonne Bischofberger.

THANKS from Lonely Planet
Many thanks to the travelers who used the last edition and wrote to us with helpful hints, use-ful advice and interesting anecdotes. Your names follow:

Mary Abbott, Lin Ang, Kelly Bartlett, Kristina Brown, Catherine Burdon, Barbara Caula, David Cox, Paul Curran, Richelle Davies, Rachel Fearnside, Manuel Joe Flumagger, Marianne Friesen, Sally Guest, Robert Hickey, David Kirkbridge, Juliette Lea, Laura Lee, Cathy Lincoln, Roy Little, David Long, Emma Lozman, Mary E Moore, Leonard J Nyberg Jr, Craig A Orr, Mary Pickles, Merry Rothbard, Jo Samways, Nicola Speakman, Fleur Straessle, Rob Underwood, Joris Van Daele, Mike Walmsley, Jeanne & Frank Wedig, Will Werley, Brian Whittaker, Jean Whittaker, Genga Yo Balan.

ACKNOWLEDGMENTS
Many thanks to the following for the use of their content:

Globe on back cover © Mountain High Maps 1993 Digital Wisdom, Inc.

THE LONELY PLANET STORY
The story begins with a classic travel adventure: Tony and Maureen Wheeler's 1972 journey across Europe and Asia to Australia. There was no useful information about the overland trail then, so Tony and Maureen published the first Lonely Planet guidebook to meet a growing need.

From a kitchen table, Lonely Planet has grown to become the largest independent travel pub-lisher in the world, with offices in Melbourne (Australia), Oakland (USA) and London (UK). Today Lonely Planet guidebooks cover the globe. There is an ever-growing list of books and information in a variety of media. Some things haven't changed. The main aim is still to make it possible for adventurous travelers to get out there – to explore and better understand the world.

At Lonely Planet we believe travelers can make a positive contribution to the countries they visit – if they respect their host communities and spend their money wisely. Every year 5% of company profit is donated to charities around the world.

Index

INDEX

000 Map pages
000 Location of colour photographs

LONELY PLANET OFFICES

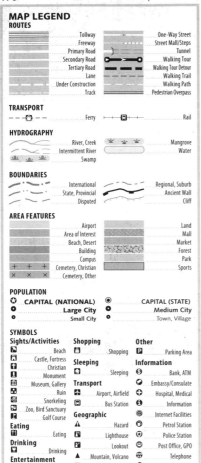

MAP LEGEND

ROUTES

Tollway	One-Way Street
Freeway	Street Mall/Steps
Primary Road	Tunnel
Secondary Road	Walking Tour
Tertiary Road	Walking Tour Detour
Lane	Walking Trail
Under Construction	Walking Path
Track	Pedestrian Overpass

TRANSPORT

Ferry	Rail

HYDROGRAPHY

River, Creek	Mangrove
Intermittent River	Water
Swamp	

BOUNDARIES

International	Regional, Suburb
State, Provincial	Ancient Wall
Disputed	Cliff

AREA FEATURES

Airport	Land
Area of Interest	Mall
Beach, Desert	Market
Building	Forest
Campus	Park
Cemetery, Christian	Sports
Cemetery, Other	

POPULATION

✪ CAPITAL (NATIONAL)	◉ CAPITAL (STATE)
● Large City	● Medium City
○ Small City	○ Town, Village

SYMBOLS

Sights/Activities
- Beach
- Castle, Fortress
- Christian
- Monument
- Museum, Gallery
- Ruin
- Snorkeling
- Zoo, Bird Sanctuary
- Golf Course

Eating
- Eating

Drinking
- Drinking

Entertainment
- Entertainment

Shopping
- Shopping

Sleeping
- Sleeping

Transport
- Airport, Airfield
- Bus Station

Geographic
- Hazard
- Lighthouse
- Lookout
- Mountain, Volcano
- National Park

Other
- Parking Area

Information
- Bank, ATM
- Embassy/Consulate
- Hospital, Medical
- Information
- Internet Facilities
- Petrol Station
- Police Station
- Post Office, GPO
- Telephone
- Toilets

Australia
Head Office
Locked Bag 1, Footscray, Victoria 3011
☎ 03 8379 8000, fax 03 8379 8111
talk2us@lonelyplanet.com.au

USA
150 Linden St, Oakland, CA 94607
☎ 510 893 8555, toll free 800 275 8555
fax 510 893 8572, info@lonelyplanet.com

UK
72–82 Rosebery Ave,
Clerkenwell, London EC1R 4RW
☎ 020 7841 9000, fax 020 7841 9001
go@lonelyplanet.co.uk

Published by Lonely Planet Publications Pty Ltd
ABN 36 005 607 983

© Lonely Planet 2005

© photographers as indicated 2005

Cover photographs: Businessman in Bermuda shorts, Doug Wilson/ Corbis (front); Resort beach in Bermuda, Lee Foster/Lonely Planet Images (back). Many of the images in this guide are available for licensing from Lonely Planet Images: www.lonelyplanetimages.com

Printed through The Bookmaker International Ltd
Printed in China